FIREMANIA:

A Turbulent Saga of a New York City
Firefighter

FIREMANIA:

A Turbulent Saga of a New York City
Firefighter

by
Carl Chiarelli

Kroshka Books

Art Director: Maria Ester Hawrys
Assistant Director: Elenor Kallberg
Graphics: Kerri Pfister and Susan A. Boriotti
Manuscript Coordinator: Phylis Gaynor
Book Production: Tammy Sauter, Gavin Aghamore,
                 Joanne Bennette and Christine Mathosian
Circulation: Irene Kwartiroff and Annette Hellinger

Library of Congress Cataloging–in–Publication Data
available upon request

ISBN 1-56072-312-2

© *Carl Chiarelli 1996*
  Kroshka Books. A division of
  Nova Science Publishers, Inc.
  6080 Jericho Turnpike, Suite 207
  Commack, New York 11725
  Tele. 516-499-3103 Fax 516-499-3146
  E Mail Novasci1@aol.com

Printed in the United States of America

Contents

ACKNOWLEDGMENTS

My thanks to Bob Smith, professional wordsman and volunteer firefighter from New Jersey. Bob's input in editing the more politically and socially incorrect passages from the original script was greatly appreciated. Bob is also active in support of the Burn Unit at New York Hospital.

I also wish to thank John Sineno, retired firefighter and best selling author of the "New Firefighter's Cookbook." John has been active and generous in support of the Burn Unit almost from the time of its inception. His effort in seeking a publisher for my book was typical of John's helpful nature.

To Jim Daly, Bobby Reeb and Jack Paccione, firefighters from Engine Company 44 for their research in locating copies of long-forgotten records, and all members of Engine Company 280, Engine Company 44 and Division of Training personnel for their assistance and forbearance in placing events in the closest possible chronological sequence.

To Paul Hashagen of Rescue Company 1, author of "A Distant Fire," for his help in obtaining old action photos of memorable fires.

I also wish to thank my "Compari" Bruce Branick, Radio Officer and Merchant Seaman since his retirement from the United States Coast Guard. During his travels throughout the world, Bruce authored, "Two if by Sea," a novel that prophesied many of the ills and pitfalls that confront our nation today. Bruce and I were shipmates during World War II and shared many memorable and unbelievable exploits. He was best man at my wedding and is included in a section of the book when we were both assigned to the Coast Guard Cutter *Hibiscus*. At present Bruce is completing a block-buster second book that should be ready for publication in the near future. Good luck, Bruce! To Michelle Lalo for her editing work in ironing out the many wrinkles in the text. Fine job Michelle. Thanks.

To Maria Ester Hawrys, for her skill in assembling, enhancing and designing prints and photos. The book's cover seems to spring to life. Thank you Maria.

To my publishers Frank and Nadya Columbus for their confidence and trust in accepting my script for publication. Also for affording me a wide latitude of expression in the final text.

To Annette Hellinger, receptionist, for her prompt and unerring channeling of messages and information in her pleasant and professional manner and to Maya Columbus for correcting the manuscript.

To Marilyn Mode, former Deputy Commissioner, NYFD, for providing access to the Fire Department Photo Unit files. Special thanks to Richie Smiouskas of the Photo Unit for locating the excellent picture of the actual fire 3-3-1095 which was used as the cover of WNYF. It is also the cover of this book.

To my wife Natalie for sifting through pages of scribblings. Her help in the tedious task of collecting, sorting, and placing events in sequence was greatly appreciated.

To my daughter Valerie for pre-editing some of the early script despite a busy schedule in ministering to my grandchildren, Brian and Jamie, and Bob my favorite Son-In Law. In her spare time she is a full time schoolteacher.

To my #1 son Carl, who, to provide respite from the doldrums of a paper strewn environment, thrust me into a fresh air scenario in pursuit of a tightly wound ridiculous orb. The object was to place this orb into an undersized hole in the ground using instruments of various shapes none of which are adequate for the task. After a day of this distraction I was anxious to return to the tedium of finishing this book.

ABOUT THE AUTHOR

The author was raised in the tough "mean streets" of Harlem and the "Gas House" district on the East Side of Manhattan, the home of many famous professional prize-fighters. He became a promising amateur club fighter, and sparring partner for some top ranked boxers, but abandoned plans for a professional boxing career after the freak death of his best friend, Pete Asaro, in a ring at Queens County, New York.

A combination of hard work and guile helped him overcome poverty and adversity. Mr. Chiarelli broadened his experience by working at several totally unrelated jobs which included two years as a partner of a Seafood Restaurant across the street from where the United Nations Building now stands.

During World War II he served as Quartermaster aboard the Coast Guard Cutter "Hibiscus" which was credited, in part, with the sinking of a German U Boat off the East coast of New England.

Mr. Chiarelli declined offers to join in several lucrative, established enterprises in order to serve as a firefighter in the New York Fire Department. He served as fireman in many engine and ladder companies throughout Brooklyn until promoted to Lieutenant and assigned to Engine Company 44 in Manhattan.

During the last two years "on the job" he served as an instructor at the Probationary Firefighters' Training School which was located on Welfare Island before being established at it's present location on Randall's Island.

After retiring from the fire department, Mr. Chiarelli served as a Fieldman, Engineering Department, for a group of leading fire insurance companies. His duties included investigation of suspicious fires and suspected arson cases. This position put him in close contact with many volunteer companies throughout the country.

INTRODUCTION

The fire departments throughout the United States are composed of men and women from all walks of life.

From the time that the modern fire departments were organized over 200 years ago, the firefighter has enjoyed a position of status in his community. Tradition dictates that the qualities that were required in the past should set the standards for the present and into the future. The career firefighter should be strong (foremost), able, honest and dedicated.

The following is an account of the life and experiences of one man who sought to devote his life to serving his community as a firefighter.

This book provides an insight into the various personalities that go into the formation of an aggressively effective fire fighting force. It relates the experiences, and the unpredictable dangers encountered in the every day performance of the duties of a New York City Firefighter.

Some anecdotes are sad, some amusing, some petty and others are tragic. All are from unexpurgated true-to-life accounts.

THE HISTORY OF ENGINE COMPANY 44

The Fire Company, which was later to be known as Engine Company 44, was originally started as a private Engine Company in August, 1824. This fire company was organized by the master ship builders of the Dry Dock Company for the protection of the shipyards in the vicinity.

It was not until 1828 that they were attached to the New York Fire Department and given the number 44. They had a brick Fire House built for them as their quarters located on Houston Street, between Lewis and Manhattan Streets. It became known as the Live Oak Engine Company 44. The term Live Oak refers to the type of tree used to construct certain parts of the ships in that era.

In keeping with the belligerent attitude of many of the firefighters of the time, they were often referred to as the "Terrible Turks" because of their street fighting prowess, a trait, which I must confess, carried over to the present.

How the company eventually migrated to their present location on East 75th Street is not very clear. What is clear, however, is that the spirit of the men from the past is matched by the present firefighters. There has been no diminution in the commitment, honor and devotion to duty.

The New York Fire Department of today remains the last bastion against the constant forays of each succeeding administration in their efforts to emasculate the Department, and make it a "Job Bank" at their disposal, with no regard for morality and excellence of performance.

CLOSE ENCOUNTERS

CAINES WAREHOUSE
KAMIKAZI BUS

On reporting for duty on the morning of February 4th, 1960, I had a very uneasy feeling. We did not have a real working fire, "all hands" or worse, for the past several days. This was not unusual, however, since "workers" sometimes ran in cycles. But for some reason the feeling was pervasive and shared by others in the working group. No, none of us had ESP or prophetic powers, nonetheless, it was a feeling that I'm sure all people experience at one time or another, and sometimes becomes a self fulfilling prophesy. At 3:53pm the alarm bells started ringing. Before the box number, 1095, was completely transmitted we were by the rig, its engine revved up, and ready to go. In quick succession, after we left, the alarms for this fire went from "all hands" to multiple alarms 2-2-1095 and 3-3-1095 within a time span of fourteen minutes. It turned out to be an alarm that almost wiped out the entire working group.

The fire was in a furniture warehouse only six blocks away from our fire station so we arrived in about a minute. We didn't have to look for an address as we were met by the smoke from the location as soon as we turned onto Third Avenue. The fire was in a very advanced state with heavy smoke pouring from the third, fourth and fifth floors of this five-story building. We were the first company to arrive on the scene due to the speed of our response and proximity to the fire building. We immediately stretched a 2-1/2 inch hoseline to the third floor of the building. To make matters worse, the only access to the third floor from the second floor landing was via a huge wooden trap door in the ceiling. The door was a full two inches thick, five feet wide by ten feet long and about two hundred pounds in weight. It was balanced from the third floor by a rope and pulley attached to a heavy iron counterweight. As soon as the hoseline was charged, two of my men, Joe Harty and Larry Rooney, cracked open the trap door. We almost got our ears burned off by the blast of heat. We quickly closed the trap door. On the next attempt we directed the stream from our nozzles against the trap door before, and while the door was being opened, until we gained access to the third floor. The fire was so intense that it sounded like the roar of a jet engine accompanied by the crackles and pops of exploding flying embers some of which were the size of golf balls. I allowed only two firemen at a time on the third floor landing with me, and platooned them so we wouldn't all be "burned out" together. We directed the full flow from our hose directly into an adjoining room that appeared to be the origin of the fire on this floor. It had practically no effect. In fact, it seemed to intensify the blast of heat coming from the room and we could see fire racing across the floor toward us. That could only mean that there were sizeable amounts of flammable liquids involved. By this time the second due engine company, Engine Co. 22, had advanced a hoseline to our position. With two hose streams now pouring about 480 gallons of water a minute into the room, we still weren't making much headway. While Engine 22 continued to pour water into the room, I instructed my men to direct the hose stream between this storage room and the hall, as a water curtain, while I searched for another angle of attack on this stubborn blaze. I didn't get too far down the hall before a wall of fire, enveloped in dense black smoke, was racing towards me from the far end of the building. I ran as fast as I could to the position we had taken close to the trap door. I yelled for Larry and Joe, who were on the nozzle at the time, to direct the hose stream behind me as I was losing the race with the oncoming Red Devil. They did so but in shooting the stream over my head they knocked off my helmet. The fire brands were now burning divots off the top of my head. Luckily, in a few minutes I was able to recover my helmet, but I was still getting burns on my hands from the flying embers. Under my breath I was cursing my good friend, from the previous night tour, who had borrowed my gloves but then neglected to return them to the pocket of my turnout coat. Engine Company 22 had withdrawn to the floor below but we still had a man from Ladder 13 holding the trap door open since it was our only means of escape.

Meanwhile, the Chiefs directing operations from the street had ordered deck pipe streams into the floors above us. The building at this time was fully involved. From our position I could hear strange creaking, crunching and groaning sounds coming from everywhere within the building as if it was dying. There was no training or procedure to follow. How do you know for sure when a building is ready to collapse? You don't. I had never been involved in such a situation so I had no experience to fall back on.

One thing I did know - just as I had the feeling of apprehension on reporting for duty that morning - this building was going to collapse, and very soon. By now most of my platoon was already on the fire floor, and I screamed at them to get the hell out, and fast. They weren't moving quickly enough, so I started to throw anyone not going fast enough down the stairs. As we had shut down the hose line to back out, the heat again intensified. The man from Ladder 13 was still holding the trap door open. The heat had burned away the restraining and balancing rope from the pulley, and the door had to be kept open manually to prevent us from being trapped on the fire floor. As I was about a bit more than halfway down the stairs, he could no longer hold on and the trap door came crashing down on my head. Fortunately, I had recovered my helmet and was wearing it. However, I was knocked down the stairs and had blood running down my coat and onto my hands. Of course, I didn't know that at the time. We then ran, jumped and tumbled down the next flight of stairs and out onto the street followed by a dense cloud of smoke, soot and dust as the interior of the building collapsed. It was so close, in fact, that some of the cloud of dust preceded us out the front entrance.

The chief in charge in the street had sent his aide to tell us to evacuate, but he was met on the second floor by falling bodies. If we had waited to be summoned and retreated in an orderly manner, that would have been "all she wrote." We never would have made it out in time! We were approached on the street by Battalion Chief Wedick. He noted the blood on my coat, face and hands, and thought that I had been wounded. He ordered us to the department ambulance with a department doctor in attendance. On the way to the ambulance I washed away the blood. I couldn't see any cuts so I figured that the blow to the head by the trap door had caused a nose bleed. We proceeded to the department ambulance. Doctor Post treated Fireman Rooney for burns on his ears, Fireman Dodd for burns on his ears and for fatigue. I was treated for burns on my hands and for a sprained knee. This was the same knee that I had severely banged up my first year on the job when I had to leap to safety from a fire escape in Brooklyn.

Standing in the middle of the street was Fire Department Chaplain, Father Leo Farley. Father Farley was a wonderful and understanding man. The first thing he said to me was, "Carl, I married you to your wife, Natalie. I baptized both of your children, and when I saw that cloud come out the front of the building before you and your men appeared, I thought I was going to have to give you your last rites."

I was never lucky in gambling. I always missed opportunities. The only stocks I bought went off the sheets. I never won at the racetrack. In fact, one day at Aqueduct, my horse was six lengths in front and pulling away at the stretch with a sixteenth of a mile to go. I turned to my brother Slim, and jokingly said: "The only way I could lose this race is for the horse to break his leg and be shot before reaching the finish line." You guessed it: that's exactly what happened. For good luck we had bet $44.00 on the race. I felt so bad for the horse as if I had jinxed him by saying what I did. There were other cases where luck played a part. However, my company and I were sure lucky at box 3-3-1095.

My good fortune in averting death and disaster followed me throughout my career in the Fire Department. For that I was always thankful. Although I was never a devout Catholic, on this occasion I thanked God many times for sparing me and my men. I am really not superstitious, but I wonder if Father Farley, who offered a prayer for us, had anything to do with my feeling of urgency on the fire floor and the narrow escape we had in beating the collapse to the street. Gives one something to think about! After all, why throw men down the stairs? Why not beat an orderly retreat? What made me so sure of a collapse when I had never been involved in one? We would have looked awfully foolish if the building had not failed and the fire got away because of my actions. We would have been the laughing stock of the division!

Ironically, preliminary work had begun in installing an automatic sprinkler system in this furniture warehouse. In a few days the system would have been in operation and any fire would either have been held in check, or extinguished in its incipient stage. The real tragedy would have been if the delay in the installation had resulted in the multiple loss of life.

I was still occupied with these musings as we lingered by the Field Wagon. According to the Medical Officer, we were to consider ourselves on Medical Leave, and to report to the Medical Officer on the next day for a more thorough examination. Our next move was to be decided by Battalion Chief Wedick who had ordered us to the ambulance. Instead of waiting, we decided to go in the direction of our pumper, which was operating a deck pipe stream at the front of the building. I was approached by a Deputy Chief that had responded on the third alarm. Of course he did not know that we had been ordered to the ambulance. He asked me if my company could assist in stretching another hose line to the roof of an adjacent building.

To prove that the blow to my head must have impaired my reasoning, instead of explaining our situation, I checked with my men to see if they were in accord to being unofficially reactivated. As expected they all agreed and we stretched a 2-1/2 inch hose line to the roof of an exposure building. In the interim, Battalion Chief Wedick had gone to the ambulance to see if any of us had sustained an injury that was serious enough to require hospitalization. When the Medical Officer told the Chief that he had recommended that we "stand fast," Battalion Chief Wedick became understandably upset at our disappearance. He was livid by the time he tracked us down on the adjacent roof. He then gave me a dressing down that I richly deserved. Why did I reactivate my company on my own when there was an over abundance of fresh, eager troops available? He then specifically ordered us to the Field Wagon and had an incoming engine company man the hose line we had stretched from our own pumper. This time there was no complaint. We were actually near exhaustion. I had yet to deal with the one blot on our operation. A problem member had failed to take his turn at the nozzle. He became hysterical at the sight of the billowing flames and searing heat. The roar of the fire and flying brands attested to the fact that this was not a routine operation. However, when one of the team refuses to do his part, the burden is transferred to his "brothers." I do not ask anyone under my command to face any danger that I myself am not exposed to. The MSA masks we started with at the fire were expended in short order and removed, making our position even more punishing. Yet none of us complained of smoke inhalation because you are almost automatically placed on "Sick Leave."

Before the fire was declared under control, eleven Engine Companies responded and operated thirty-one hose streams. In addition, four Hook & Ladder Companies and some special units, including Rescue 1, also operated at the scene. Six firefighters and one civilian were injured. The good news: no fatalities. Engine Company 44 members refused medical leave on the spot, which we all later regretted!

That morning I had Probationary Fireman McCormack, detailed to Engine Company 44, fresh from Fire College. It is a date that I am sure he will remember as his introduction to the Fire Department's operation at a major alarm. I allowed him to assist in stretching hose to the second floor. After we were exposed to the initial blast of heat and smoke on opening the trap door to the third floor, however, I ordered him back to the street to assist the Motor Pump Operator (MPO). To his credit, in contrast to our "Phantom Fireman" he wanted to be part of the attack to the third floor.

Remembering how I had been kicked down into a cellar fire as a Probie when I strayed into a strange engine company operation in Brooklyn, I decided to keep Fireman McCormack in a safer area until he had some seasoning! The bottom line on this operation, which admittedly was one of the hottest we encountered in some time, is that because one of the team faltered, the remaining men had to endure longer periods on the nozzle, resulting in burns and fatigue. The white front piece on my helmet had been scorched beyond recognition, and had to be replaced. I certainly could have used another man, if only to hold open the trap door. Who knows? I may have been spared the blow to my head that later was to be one of the reasons for forcing me out of full duty with my company, and into limited service as an instructor. As noted elsewhere, "they're not all heroes." Some misfits worm their way into the Department. They enjoy strutting their stuff in their neighborhoods, capitalizing on the reputation and sacrifices of the vast majority of firemen, but when it comes time to "put out" they are exposed. Unfortunately, the line officers and training school personnel do not have full power to weed out the misfits. Like the pseudo-soldiers in the Armed Services who enjoy all the perks during peacetime, when hostilities break out they suddenly become conscientious objectors, overnight reverends, or beat a hasty path to a foreign country.

The hazards of the job are not limited to fighting fires, or to operations at emergencies where life and property are threatened. At times there are some near disasters on the busy streets of New York, when responding to or returning from an alarm. There was always the danger of collision en route. We have had some close calls occasioned by either drunken drivers, drivers under the influence of illegal drugs, and even of some prescription drugs, that diminished their capacity to operate a vehicle safely.

We narrowly avoided a serious collision near the Grand Army Plaza in Brooklyn when an auto driven by a young fellow drove directly into the path of Engine Company 280 as we were responding to an alarm for fire. It was a cold winter's night. All his windows were tightly closed and the car radio was on full blast. He never heard the bells, siren or horn blasts. We were a two-piece company, and the first piece had already passed the corner when he shot across the street while looking at the departing rig. He never saw the second piece, which was the hose wagon. I was on the back step at the time and Briscoe Payne was driving. It was too late to try braking. As Briscoe swerved to avoid hitting the car, the hose wagon spun completely around, and the rear of the rig was on a collision course with the errant car. Fearing that I was going to be crushed between the two vehicles, I jumped off the back step at the last moment. I seemed to be running while still in midair and I was lucky to land on my feet. I ran about 100 feet before I could come to a stop. By some miracle the collision was avoided. The car sped off and we proceeded to the fire. I think this incident justifies the agility requirements of the physical examination given to all fire department applicants.

On another occasion, I was detailed to Ladder 120 along with a full complement of men and a spare rig. En route to an alarm, the ladder truck was struck broadside by a Police Emergency Wagon. The Tillerman was thrown against the first floor of the corner building. Within minutes, the Police evacuated all their members from the Emergency Wagon, while City and Fire Department ambulances removed the injured firemen. The word was, though not proven, that the driver of the Police Emergency Wagon was DWI. There have been other instances where firemen have been thrown off the back step and killed, sometimes in response to an MFA (Malicious False Alarm). At least that danger has been reduced, with the newer apparatus which eliminate riding in the open, either on the back step or on the running board.

The most serious close call that I was personally involved in happened while I was the MPO assigned to Engine Company 280. It was a clear, bright afternoon when we were responding to an alarm. We were traveling at a fair rate of speed as we approached Empire Boulevard, which is a wide main street. Well before we reached the corner of the intersection, a policeman was in the middle of the street stopping all traffic and signaling vigorously for us to proceed past the intersection. Normally, with a policeman holding up traffic on a clear day and a dry roadway, we would go by without slowing down. I made it a habit, however, and later stressed the procedure when I instructed chauffeurs, never to step on the accelerator going into intersections. Since this was an unusually busy street, I had gone even further and as a precaution actually had my foot on the brake pedal before reaching the corner.

There was a city bus stopped at the corner on Empire Boulevard. I could see the driver, hunched over the steering wheel, looking at us approaching. Without warning, and paying no attention to the patrolman in the middle of the roadway, he stepped on the gas and raced us to the intersection. If I hadn't started to press the brake pedal down the engine would have struck the bus about five feet to the rear of the driver's position. This would have resulted in a major accident with many fatalities.

It is impossible to conjecture on what motivated the bus driver. It almost appeared to be a planned execution of the passengers aboard the bus with the Fire Department as the executioners! We had to brake really hard, and still only missed hitting the rear of the bus by mere inches as it sped away. The patrolman stood dumbfounded in the street. I wonder if, in the state of shock that this incident left him, he had noted the identity of the bus driver, or if punitive action was taken later, probably not. Another very fortunate circumstance was that in this case we were not followed by our hose wagon which was then at the repair shop in Queens. Had the hose wagon been following the engine as usual, I doubt if they could have avoided rear-ending us. In that case all the casualties would have been firemen.

DEPORTMENT AND
CHARACTER OF FIREMEN

After World War II I applied for the position of Fireman. I was told that if your personal record was not "as clean as the driven snow," it was futile to even take the test. Boy, has that changed!

Time was when one saw that the firemen had arrived on the scene there was a sense of trust and relief no matter what the emergency was. Remember when there is a fire or other emergency, most people are running away from the scene, while the firemen are running towards the cause of the emergency, whether it is a fire, gas leak, building collapse, or in danger of collapse, a serious accident or other pending disaster. In many cases a fireman may be left alone in your apartment or home. That is why in the past it was so important to thoroughly examine the character of any person seeking appointment to the Department.

Before the Department became a target for "Social Engineering" since World War II, that practice had been strictly adhered to. If an applicant was found to have lied on an application or to have behaved in an unacceptable manner, he would immediately be dismissed - especially during the six months probation period. It may appear to be "far fetched," but even to have committed a minor traffic violation at that time would have disqualified one for the position. A fireman had to be scrupulously honest as well as strong, loyal and devoted to the job.

Unfortunately, if today's practices of "social engineering" continue, there is a good chance that instead of being rescued, you may be raped, robbed, ripped off or roasted. Those are the "four R's" that may tarnish a proud and honorable profession. Honesty and other vitally important character qualifications no longer seem to be as important as they once were. Answers to the test for the position of firefighter have been passed out in some areas. The tests themselves have been made so ridiculously simple that it is next to impossible to fail. There was a case where a few women had been passed over and not hired because they couldn't manage to carry or drag a 120 pound weight the required distance.

Not to be swayed by this logical decision by the Fire Department, the decision was litigated. The case came before a Federal Judge, Sifton, who rendered a decision that must have caused Solomon to spin in his grave. He decided he knows better than seasoned fire department training personnel and that these women had been "discriminated against", and get this - he reasoned that **physical strength is not important for the position of firefighter.** He immediately had these women reinstated with back pay from the time they would have been appointed, totaling about $80,000 each. This bonanza exceeded all that I had earned in gross income for my first 12 years on the job. But what good would any of these women have been if someone had to be pulled out of a burning building? Should each one carry a scale to see if the victim is less than 120 pounds? What about the heat and smoke? What if they were wearing a mask in which case one's capabilities are reduced by 20%? How about a routine fire where a charged length of hose weighs over 170 pounds for each 50 foot length? Sounds ridiculous, doesn't it? Then how does an edict by an ultra-liberal federal judge, who has probably led a sheltered life, supersede or obviate requirements for the position that have proven to be essential from empirical knowledge? Whatever happened to common sense? Sometime later, after much criticism, this judge did concede that strength is, indeed, important. Now isn't that a momentous judicial example of extraordinary wisdom. None of his past decisions, however, were negated, and today instead of applicants for the position of firefighter training to meet the requirements, the requirements have been dangerously lowered to accommodate the least qualified applicant. All these tinkerings with established tenets are for the sole purpose of meeting the objectives of the social engineers.

Abraham Lincoln once said: "*Any society that takes away from those most capable and gives to the least will perish.*"

Regarding the subjects of strength and character as requisites for the position of fireman, it reminds me of some glaring examples that I encountered as a Training Officer. The first has to do with strength. At the time I was assigned to the Welfare Island Training Center as an instructor training probationary firefighters. We had just completed a drill which required the stretching of two and one half inch hose. After the hose had been disconnected into individual lengths of fifty feet each, I ordered one of the probies to roll up a length and place it on the pumper. Well he rolled up the length properly and tied it to specifications okay. Then to my amazement he attempted to roll the hose up the side of the pumper to reach the hose bed. This proved to be quite a problem. I then took the probationary fireman aside. This is the gist of the conversation:

Lieutenant Chiarelli: "Why are you trying to roll the hose up the side of the rig? Weren't you shown the proper way to load a hose?"

Probie: "Yes sir. I was shown how to load the hose, but I cannot lift it onto the pumper as it is too heavy."

Lieutenant Chiarelli: "The hose, including the brass fittings, only weighs from seventy to a maximum seventy-five pounds."

To demonstrate, I took the rolled up length and threw it onto the upper hose bed of the pumper. Then:

Lieutenant Chiarelli: "Weren't you required to lift weights as part of the physical test for the job?"

Probie: "The lifting of heavy weights is no longer required."

Here is a case of a young man, twenty-three years of age, who cannot lift seventy pounds, thrust into a job where he may be required to carry a person to safety. Does anyone wonder what this has done to the morale of the real men on the job? What about the reputation of the New York City Fire Department, which was once held up as probably the best Fire Department in the country - if not the world?

Another glaring example had to do with character. It took place in 1963 while I was interviewing probationary firefighters and going over their records. There have been other bad examples, but this one really stood out. I was seated across the table from this young man with a shaved head, a Fu Manchu mustache and a Be Bop. I couldn't believe what I was reading in his "dossier". This guy had been in and out of jail. Forget about the minor stuff, but these three serious ones stood out:

1. ARMED ROBBERY
2. RAPE
3. ASSAULT WITH A DEADLY WEAPON.

Remembering the strict character qualifications of the past, after the initial shock, I asked him the following questions:

Lieutenant Chiarelli: "How did you ever get to the point that you are seated at this table, across from me, with this record?"

Probie: "I passed the test." (Which is doubtful given the revelations of cheating at the time.)

Lieutenant Chiarelli: "What about the arrests for rape, robbery and assault with a deadly weapon?"

Probie: "Well, man, I was only twenty years old at the time."

Lieutenant Chiarelli: "How did this get past the examiners, before you even got this far?"

Probie: "Well, man..." (in a defiant, arrogant manner, showing resentment that I should be questioning him.)

Lieutenant Chiarelli: "Don't you 'well man' me you SOB. You address me as Lieutenant or Sir."

Probie: (Another surly sounding) "Man..."

With that I scooped up the entire folder and went over to the officer in charge at the time. I put the folder in front of him and said:

Lieutenant Chiarelli: "What is this bullshit? Haven't you seen what's in this dossier?"

Chief: "Take it easy. We are supposed to..." (I heard enough.)

Lieutenant Chiarelli: "Not me. I want no part of this. I want out of the desk detail."

Well, I transferred out of the detail immediately. I could not stand what special interests were doing to this most noble of professions.

Don't get the impression that this is an isolated incident peculiar to New York City. This practice of "social engineering" is being extended into practically all of the big city police and fire departments.

Now, affirmative action may or may not have a place in our society. There are differing opinions on this subject. Not only from the "establishment", but also from some responsible minority groups. The unfortunate result is that instead of individual applicants striving for excellence, the departments are tailoring the tests to bring in the least qualified applicants. This is a disgrace and an affront to every person who trained and studied hard in order to qualify for a position. Following is an article taken from the *Queens Chronicle* by Ernie Naspretto on this subject.

N.Y.C. FIREFIGHTERS EXAM NOTICE: ALL DEAD PEOPLE NEED NOT APPLY.

At a time when this "gorgeous mosaic" called New York City is going through financial disaster, it's nice to know that the brains that spend our tax dollars will pay $400,000 for a Fire Department exam that can be passed by anyone who isn't currently deceased. The standard multiple choice Civil Service Exam is being revamped in an apparent effort to get more women and minorities into the Fire Department. Isn't that special? Now of course the New York City Department of Personnel doesn't care if these women or minorities can read a rest room sign. The idea is to get more women and minorities, PERIOD!

"There is absolutely nothing wrong with the City trying to recruit women and minorities onto the payrolls, especially since they are representative of the City population. However, when the geniuses that run this "gorgeous mosaic" make a mockery of Civil Service Exams, they also make fools of Civil Servants. Applicants taking next month's Fire Fighters exam will be asked to pick, are you ready for this, three(3) answers out of four (4) choices. An applicant picking the right answer as a first choice will score a full point. An applicant picking the right answer as his second choice will score half a point."

"And, the genius that picks the right answer as a third choice would still receive a quarter of a point. If the correct answer doesn't appear anywhere within the applicant's three answers that applicant will be beaten and tortured (only kidding on this one)."

I took the Fire Department Fire Fighters written exam in 1982. I didn't even bother to take the physical test. I just read the description of it and sprained my shoulder. However, I scored a ninety-nine (99) on the written part. At first I was impressed with myself until I found out that about 14 million other geniuses scored a 99. If I remember correctly, the test went something like this:

PICK OUT THE PICTURE WHICH MOSTLY RESEMBLES A
FIRE HYDRANT.
(a) Picture 1a - a shotgun,
(b) Picture 2a - a wheelchair,
(c) Picture 3a - a fire hydrant,
(d) Picture 4a - a photograph of Ringo Starr.

The point is the exam never made it to the scholastic level of the Bar exam. If the City wants to hire more women and minorities, then simply have the interested persons fill out the required forms, then feed all the Social Security numbers into a lottery system. To administer a ridiculous exam takes credibility away from a city that has very little credibility left."

Think the above is "far fetched" in describing what is happening in the nation's cities? The politicians have been trying for years to bring the position of firefighter under the complete control of the patronage system, supervised exclusively by the Mayors and their flunkies. They have succeeded in part in the Police Department where qualifying by Civil Service exam is only up to the position of Captain. In the Fire Department, all positions, including Chief of Department are filled by members that have successfully passed the Civil Service Exam for the position. Some latitude is provided in choosing the Chief of Department whereby the top three on the promotional list are required to "qualify orally". A lot of credit must be given to the rank and file and to their unions, to have resisted this rape of the Department up to this time.

LIFE IN NEW YORK CITY

MATTRESS FIRE
SPEAKEASY, LOTTERY,
ON WELFARE,
HARLEM, HUSTLING POOL

Without realizing it, it seems that I had been training to be a fireman even before I reached my teens. My first baptism in fire happened when I was about nine years old when we were living in Manhattan, New York. I was looking under my mother's bed for a coin that I had dropped the previous evening while I was fighting with my older brother Angelo, which was a daily occurrence. We had no flashlight, so I lit a candle and slid under the bed to conduct my search while my brother was in the kitchen doing his homework.

As you may have guessed, the flame from the candle ignited the bottom of the mattress. I yelled for my brother to bring in some water quickly as the mattress was on fire. He came in with a drinking glass full of water. That started fight number two between us. Meanwhile, the fire was spreading rapidly. I took all the cooking pots out of the closet and had my brother continue filling them, while I kept throwing water onto the fire from below - which is quite a neat trick - try it! Soon the fire broke through the top of the bed, blazing merrily while I was keeping it in check. Soon the room became heavily involved in smoke. As the flames subsided, we thought we had the fire in check, and we both took to the fire escape for a breath of fresh air. By now the smoke was pouring out the windows which alerted our next door neighbor, a nosey old crone. When she inquired about the smoke, I told her that we were frying a couple of eggs and the pan had burned. She shut her window and went back inside, never even considering calling the Fire Department. Meanwhile, the mattress had re-ignited. We now attacked the fire with renewed vigor until we were convinced the fire was completely extinguished. We dried the pots and replaced them lest someone suspect there was something awry!

As a further cover up, we took out a fresh blanket and neatly made the bed, thereby hiding the burned out hole in the mattress which was now the size of a sixteen inch long playing record. After opening the windows to clear out most of the smoke, we stepped back to survey the situation and concurred that we adopt option number two which was to make a run for it before our parents came home. Never dreaming that the damn thing would re-ignite again later, I took off and was prepared to leave the city, if not the country. My brother decided to go home and face my father's wrath. After all, he didn't start the fire, he only assisted in extinguishing it.

When the fire re-ignited after we left the house it spread to the standing wooden closet and the cedar trunk at the foot of the bed. Most of the clothing and bedding were ruined. The remaining fire had been put out by my parents with the help of neighbors. No one ever thought of calling the Fire Department. The search for me began. I vowed never to return home. When my father dispensed a beating, he was unrelenting. By today's standards the beatings would qualify us as "brutally abused" children. From my vantage point on a nearby roof, I spotted my brother alone when my parents were leaving to search in a different direction. I came down and he convinced me that all would be forgiven if I returned home with him. After all, after seeing the extent of the fire my parents feared that I may have been badly burned. At the time I couldn't understand how they could be so happy to see me.

This experience introduced me to the suffering that must be endured in inhaling the acrid and noxious fumes given off by a hair mattress fire. In my years with the Fire Department, it was generally agreed that this type of fire was the most punishing to fight without a face mask. Ask any firefighter that has had to fight his way up a few flights of stairs, lugging a water charged hose line though a maze of rooms before reaching the seat of the fire. If anyone had asked me as a nine-year old, after I had sucked in all those fumes, if I aspired to become a fireman, the answer would have been an unqualified, "NO, NADA, NO WAY JOSE!"

In thinking back to that time, after my experience as a Fireman, on how a nine year old could survive the thick black smoke and searing heat for so long, I had to wonder what the motivating driving force was. The answer had to be one of the most compelling motivators of all - FEAR. All I could think of at the time was my father swinging the 3 6 ounce "Chuck Klein" baseball bat that we kept in the apartment for protection.

Up to the time of my early teens we were considered very well off. My father, who had come to this country from Sicily, was a real "Greenhorn", but he really had an enterprising spirit. By the time I was nine years old, my father already operated a local grocery store, a pet shop specializing in bird feed (as a front), and he was also a partner in a "Speakeasy" located in a bogus store front on Second Avenue and Fortieth Street in Manhattan. The grocery was a success on its own merits, but it was also a front for a bootlegging operation and a satellite location for the Italian lottery in which Pop was also involved. With all of these illegal enterprises my Dad was involved in, paradoxically, he was also the most honest and ethical man that I ever knew. In addition, he was also the most generous, which turned out to be his eventual downfall.

During these days of Prohibition, every Saturday Pop would give me a twenty dollar bill. With this money I would take many of the kids on our block, and often from adjoining blocks, to the movies, including all the extras. Generous though this was, it was also good business as most of their parents shopped at our grocery.

I still remember the day I saw a policeman stationed outside the grocery with a clipboard and logging on a sheet, as alcohol in one and five gallon cans were being unloaded from a truck and into the basement of the store. He was actually keeping count of how many gallons were being delivered. I didn't think much of the incident at the time. At that age who knew that it was against the law? It was later that I learned the distinction. My father was breaking the law, stupid and ineffectual though it was. The cop on the other hand was breaking a trust. He was derelict in his duty, and openly and brazenly engaging in graft. I later knew that I never wanted to be a policeman. Every so often there would be a "crackdown" on speakeasies and on the Italian Lottery. This charade was performed to show that diligence was being exercised to offset corruption. Some poor miscreant from the neighborhood would be jailed and later released but the graft continued until the repeal of Prohibition.

Most affected by the "crackdown" was the Numbers Operation. Two of the main drops for the policy slips were under surveillance. One was a barber shop in midtown Manhattan, and the other, a barber shop in Harlem. I was enlisted on one occasion to deliver the policy slips to these locations when I was about ten years old. Who would suspect a ten year old kid going for his Saturday haircut? This was to be a one-time deal as I recall. I don't believe I was aware of doing something wrong since then I would be nervous and might betray my mission and the policy slips hidden under my shirt. I started by taking the trolley on Second Avenue up to Harlem. I would stay at the location a reasonable length of time and get a trim just in case the location was being watched. The barber would take his share of the policy slips and my hair, as the exchange was made under the wrap. I thought this was great fun! After this exchange I would then take the trolley to the second drop, which was my regular barber shop located on Second Avenue and Forty-Third Street. The Barber, Angelo, never accepted money from me as he had an arrangement with my father. I had started with a full head of hair. After the second drop and trim I was left with a crop of hair that was somewhere between a baldy and a crew cut. After the drops were made successfully, and the return slips safely ensconced under my shirt, I went to a tenement building on East 40th Street, where I was met by my Godfather, yes, actually my Godfather Salvatori. The ensuing scene could have been snatched from an old Godfather or Mafia movie.

In the dining room there was a large and heavy round oak table with a mound of dollar bills of many denominations stacked neatly around the surface. After the men had a good laugh at the new hair style I was now sporting, they stood me up on the table amongst the stacked bills. Having a flair for the dramatic myself, I grabbed fistfuls of the bills and threw them over my head, much to the delight and laughter from the other "number's men". I was then taken off the table and each man gave me either a five or ten dollar bill, plus hugs and handshakes. When

I got home and showed Mom the bundle of money, she let me keep a five spot and put the rest away for me.

Somehow, in later years, I suspected that this whole exercise in deception had been in collusion with the local police, so that a minimal amount of lottery action could be conducted surreptitiously. When I brought this up with my father and godfather, they would just smile and not commit one way or another.

That was the extent of my participation in "organized crime". Soon the "good life" that my Pop thought would go on forever began to unravel. First went the Speakeasies. Then, of course, the end of Prohibition took its toll. Shortly after, the grocery store was closed as it was a financial disaster. Most of Pop's business was based on credit and trust given to people who were unable to pay their debts. With the ensuing hard times none of the debt was ever repaid. My father was too proud to ask for any repayment. Besides, he never kept any formal records.

With the money that my Mother had squirreled away, Pop opened a couple of classy Italian restaurants in the best sections of the Bronx. In keeping with the posh decor the place settings were Sterling Silver. Before long business was declining in direct proportion to the disappearance of the place settings. By 1933 the restaurants were closed. Gone were the three automobiles which were now replaced by a more functional used 1931 Ford pick-up. Pop tried some various other legitimate ventures and we moved to Harlem to a less expensive apartment.

I fell in with a bunch of older boys who engaged in some stunts that made daredevils look like sedentary wimps. One of their favorites at the time was jumping from roof to roof, or from rooftop to a fire escape, just for kicks. The last stunt came into play one Sunday when I was supposed to be in church but instead was shooting craps on a nearby roof of a two story building. Our lookout gave me the signal that my Dad was approaching. Rather than face him I chose to leap from the knee wall of the roof to the bottom section of the fire escape of the adjacent building. From there I ran to church in time to make it for the collection basket. Dad never knew that the twenty-five cents almost didn't make it to the church. Sounds like a pittance, but it was a lot more than the dime I got for my school lunch. There was no such thing as hot and free lunches then.

I was about to be introduced to the realities of attending Junior High School in Harlem. The school was the Nathan Hale Junior High School on 105th Street. I was at my gym locker when I was approached by an older black kid with the greeting, "Hey man, you got to give me ten cents for the locker." My reply was that I only had ten cents which was for my lunch, whereupon I was threatened with bodily harm until I paid up. One of the traits that I had inherited from my father's Sicilian heritage is: "we don't take no shit from anybody". Bully boy then invited me out to the school yard to set an example of what awaited a non-payer of the "DUES". The school yard was quickly ringed by onlookers and coat-holders.

Much to everyone's surprise, I beat the crap out of the smart-ass to the point where he quit. The next day as I was coming to school I was hit in the back by what felt like a Mack Truck. One of the kids had rammed his knee into my back after a running leap. I was then surrounded by the same "enforcer" I had beaten and five of his cronies. I was punched by him as the others held me down. Two held knives on me in the event I broke loose. I was left lying in the street and told that the ante was now up to twenty-five cents. I missed school that day and I told my brother Angelo what happened. At no time did we ever consider submitting to the extortion.

At that time a pistol that fired blanks could be bought for twenty-five cents. However, the blank cartridge readily accepted a "BB", the kind used in an ordinary air rifle. I gently tapped the BB into the blank and lay in wait for the bully at the school. When he arrived I grabbed him from behind, showed him the pistol and stuck it under his neck. I then made him some offers that he couldn't refuse. In the event that my offers were refused, I demonstrated what would befall him. There was a Chinese laundry next to the school which exhibited a hanging metal sign at the front of the store. I took dead aim with the pistol, shot and hit the sign. The BB left a hole the size of a twenty-five cent piece as it tore through the metal sign. I then advised him that my brother knew who he was, and if "by accident" any harm came to me, my brother would come after him and blow his MF brains out. He didn't know my brother, nor did he know this was a one-shot pistol. What he did know was that I wasn't bluffing. From that day on he became my in-house protector. Never again did anyone come after my lunch money!

My father was a very well respected man, and through the many contacts he made during the "good years", he was made an organizer for a couple of trade unions in the construction industry. We had moved back to lower Manhattan, to 25th Street on the East Side. Things were going good again for a while until my father was stricken by a potentially fatal sickness similar to Lou Gehrig's disease. He was given some radical, experimental treatment at Bellevue Hospital by a Dr. Thompson, who was pioneering the procedure which in itself was very dangerous with less than a fifty percent survival rate. He survived but was no longer the strong, tough and decisive person he had been. He could no longer hack the organizational duties of the unions and had to resign.

Meanwhile, I had taken the entrance examination for entry into Stuyvesant High School and had been accepted. I was in my last year before graduation when our whole comfortable world disintegrated. There was no income. It was then that what the old Italian bootblack had said rang true: "There is no free lunch". We applied for temporary relief at the Welfare Office that was so engrossed by the fact that my father owned three expensive automobiles only a few years earlier and we were now applying for assistance. But how can one designate bootlegger as a job description? Meanwhile, there was no food on the table. Mom and Pop were enduring the humiliation of borrowing from friends and family. We had been served an eviction notice and still the idiotic Social Worker assigned to us was still searching for where we stashed our former wealth. He was on this "witch hunt" even as the City Marshall and moving crew showed up and dumped all our belongings at the curb in front of our tenement building. My Mom was seated on a chair with an infant in her lap and a six year old daughter at her feet.

In the interim between the social worker's investigation and the eviction I had graduated high school with scholastic honors and was getting a freebie education at City College. I was into my third week at the University and had made the boxing team. Some poor souls were paying for the pent-up anger I was experiencing because of the situation at home.

That's when I took off for the Welfare Office. When I spotted the asshole that led us on for months I had to be restrained by police and security. It took five of them to restrain me until I was told that something would be done to at least take my mother and the children off the street until shelter could be found for them. Although we were finally taken off the street I had to quit college and was given a job with the WPA (Works Progress Administration) at 62 dollars a month, which was the largest part of the rehabilitation deal with the Welfare Office. All of us were deeply ashamed to be on welfare, although it was only for a short while. Soon my brother found some part time work in construction and I had applied for a job opening at a local fish market which paid 11 dollars for a six day week, working twelve hours a day. When I reported for work the kicker was that they also owned the adjacent pet shop, separated from the fish market by a plain glass partitioned wall. In effect, I was working two totally unrelated jobs for the price of one measly salary of 11 dollars a week. At least it kept us in food as I brought home fish every night as part of the deal. Never any expensive fish, only the stuff we sold at retail for ten to fifteen cents a pound. Work started at seven a.m. in the pet shop where I cleaned thirty canary cages and two parrot cages. Then I went to the show window where the puppy dogs were kept.

We couldn't get rid of the last polly because of the price and partly because she refused to talk whenever a prospective customer showed some interest. Otherwise she did plenty of talking. Polly and I became good friends. We had one thing in common: we didn't like the conditions in the shop. Had I not worked there I believe she would have talked up a storm to escape the pet shop. She actually hated the boss. If he so much as put a finger in the cage she invariably bit it, and pollys can give a nasty bite. As for me, I could playfully pull on her tongue and all she would do was squawk. This palsy situation between myself and Polly further infuriated the boss. He kept dropping the price but she kept up her conspiracy of silence for customers, meanwhile hurling invectives at the boss in private.

The only reason that I remained at this job for two years was that it provided a source of food and mainly because I was able to supplement that income by shooting pool for money at night. I gave Mom the full 11 dollars salary, and more, from winnings at the pool tables. At age seventeen, instead of being in my second year at college, I was the house hustler at the Rainbow Billiard Academy. The owner, John DeLucy, was a "Popeye the Sailor" look-alike even down to the big chaw of tobacco. We had a symbiotic relationship. When I won we would split the take. If I lost, which was seldom, it cost me nothing. On occasion it was the hustlers that were hustled.

One night a stranger sauntered in, or was it staggered in, and announced he would play anyone in the house for ten dollars. You could almost smell the whiskey through the door before he entered. DeLucy said, "Okay, play the kid," as he gave me a wink. We played straight pool, fifty points to game. When Spinach, as Delucy was nicknamed, came by the table for the third time, which was getting on my nerves, I was leading 42 to 18 and ready to run out when he signaled me to miss.

He had already told me to take it easy so the mark would demand a rematch if he didn't lose by much. Well, I did as Spinach suggested, though not too conspicuously. The mark then proceeded to run off the full rack, broke and run the next and again until he ran off 32 balls and the win. Well, Spinach damn near choked on the omnipresent chew of tobacco. He coughed up the ten dollars and demanded a rematch after he recovered from the shock. The mark looked at his watch and said he had to run. DeLucy knew we had been had. The way this miraculously recovered drunk ran off the last 32 balls I'm not sure that my best game would have beaten him. Do that scam twice and you had twenty dollars which was more than most people made in a week at the time.

One day while cleaning soft shell crabs at the Fish Market, I pricked a finger on my left hand. After I got home my arm ached all night and I awoke the next morning with lumps under my armpits and saw that all the blood vessels of my left arm had turned a bright red. I went to work as usual at 7 a.m. but by late morning my arm was so painful that I decided to visit a clinic on 59th Street after I made a delivery of fish to the Kungsholm Restaurant on 55th Street. I made a sad sight in the waiting area with a blood stained apron and a delivery basket all reeking of fish odors. When I got to an intern, he took one look as I rolled up my sleeve, told me it was bad and ran off to fetch the head doctor, who immediately ordered me to take the next bus from the clinic directly to the hospital on Welfare Island (ironically, I would again be on Welfare Island 24 years later as an instructor in the NYFD). As I waited in the lobby I decided it was ludicrous for me to go to a hospital smelling like Moby Dick, so I left intending to return the next morning. I would rid myself of the basket and smelly clothes, take a bath and go to the hospital in style.

When I got to the street in front of the clinic, the same doctor that had examined me yelled out from the third floor window, "Hey, you in the apron, where are you going? I said to be on the next bus to the hospital." I explained that I was going back to work, would inform my boss and parents and be back tomorrow in the morning, to which the Doc replied: "You won't be alive tomorrow!" Talk about serendipity. If he had not looked outside at that precise moment I would have gone home. I had not registered with the dispatcher at the clinic who had alerted the hospital that I required emergency treatment. No one knew where I was from. All I had left them with as a reminder of my presence was a rotten fish odor! The same doctor then came down to the lobby and made certain that I registered. We had no phone at home so he arranged to notify the fish market, have them pick up the basket and apron and notify my parents. Compare his concern with the quick-buck doctors of today. He made Dr. Kildare look like the Butcher of Buchenwald.

While I was recuperating from what was a severe case of blood poisoning, I got a thorough examination. The next thing I knew there were three doctors standing over my bed informing me that my family should come in to sign a surgical consent form. Two of the doctors determined that I had a hernia which would get progressively worse if it was not taken care of immediately. Since I was already in the hospital it was wise to do it then. They operated and the result was negative. No hernia! So much for second opinions! But I did later require two operations to undo the damage done by those doctors who were probably undergoing on-the-job training. I left the hospital as soon as I was able to walk. This hiatus put a new wrinkle on life for me as I never returned to the fish market. I only felt bad on leaving because poor Polly the Parrot would now be left alone with the cruel boss that she hated.

Charlie Fleisher, a partner with his brother at a very famous seafood restaurant, The King Of The Sea, located on 53rd Street and Third Avenue in Manhattan, had been engaged to lay out plans for a new seafood restaurant. The new location was presently a successful tavern operation and one side of the premises were to be converted to a restaurant and clam bar. When Charlie was asked who he could recommend to operate the establishment, he immediately told them I would fit the bill. The hang-up at the time was that I was still in the hospital, itching to get out. Charlie and the tavern owners came to the hospital and made me an offer that couldn't be refused. I was to be a full partner in the restaurant operation of the business with the tavern owner's son Benny. To pay off the price of refurbishing I was to pay back $875 for my end. I would work fourteen to sixteen hours a day, seven days a week and take home twenty-eight dollars a week until the "nut" for the renovation was paid off. Then I would share equally in the profits with Benny. I would be responsible for all decisions concerning the seafood business and was to operate the clam bar, which included preparing oysters and clams on the half shell. We put an ad in the paper for a chef (not a cook), and wound up with a gem. He was a Norwegian who performed wonders with fish. He made a clam chowder so good that I never went a day without at least a cup of it. He asked for forty dollars a week for five days and against the wishes of the owners I hired him. His dishes became the franchise. We even started taking business away from the most famous seafood houses in the area, including The King Of the Sea. I then hired a waitress to work the dining room. The place was a booming success and I eventually had to hire another waitress to handle the lunch trade which was growing larger each day.

Besides serving the counter trade and clam bar, I also had to be the cashier during the hectic lunch hour. My lazy partner wouldn't show up until after the rush was over. Within three weeks the lunch business was so good we couldn't handle it all. People lined up halfway around the block waiting to get in. Some were so anxious to dine here that they would order drinks at the tavern bar and ask if they could order lunch. We were now serving lunch to the barstool customers. Business was exceeding our wildest expectations. I now had Charlie Fleisher on the payroll for $25 dollars a week, just to do the marketing and prepare the menus, which we changed weekly. The bar business itself more than doubled. Night time business wasn't nearly as good so I decided to institute take-out orders. There were plenty of teenagers in the neighborhood ready to make a buck as delivery boys. We then ordered sectioned paper plates to accept fish, chips and coleslaw and flooded the area with flyers. I handled all the nighttime take-out orders, including preparation and cooking. Still no help from my partner. All he did was tend bar from after dinner to closing. I also pitched in when the bar trade called for it. We had hit the proverbial Mother Lode. For once I no longer regretted having missed out on college. People were now coming from well outside our area because of the quality of the food. I could see a bright future in the restaurant business ahead.

That is when greed reared it's ugly head. With the expanding and unexpected volume of business, the renovations must have been paid off in the first two months. I was still taking home only twenty eight dollars. I decided to wait six months to see what transpired. At that point the tell-tale signs did not escape me. First, I never got to count the take from the lunch trade. Between Benny and his father, they kept emptying the cash register on a regular basis. At first, I took them at their word, as I had no reason to distrust them.

The next move they made was to get rid of the chef as they begrudged the $40 salary we had agreed on. I couldn't convince these dense greedy people that the chef made our reputation. That's when we had our first real brouhaha. They replaced the chef with a $20 a week cook. The clam chowder was now a poor vegetable soup spiked with tough bits of chowder clams. Never was any mention made that the "nut" was met and I was to share in the profits. By their actions and demeanor it was obvious they were ready to renege on the verbal pact we had made. They became evasive and annoyed that I should question them. I saw the hand writing on the wall and decided to leave. They were already ruining the business. I didn't want to renegotiate our agreement. Instead, I told them that their greed had blown the business and predicted they would be out of business in two months. I would stay on for two weeks until they found a replacement - if they made it worth my while. What a bummer! It was now 1940, and I had to consider taking a few bouts, after resuming training, unless I got a call from the Civil Service Commission on the "Superman's"[1] Test I had taken. Besides, it looked like we would soon have to go to war with the Axis powers.

---

[1] Superman's Test: So called because it was the most physically demanding test ever given for a municipal position by the New York Civil Service Commission. There were 110,000 applicants competing to fill 1,500 vacancies.

RESTAURANT BUSINESS
MAFIA ENCOUNTER

It was a hot muggy night in the summer of 1940. I had left the hospital and I was still suffering from the botched hernia operation that had not healed properly. I was busy behind the clam bar cleaning up after a very hectic day and evening. My partner, Benny, was behind the opposite bar which was the tavern section of the restaurant. It was about two a.m. on this Friday night, and there was only one customer seated on a stool at the bar talking to Benny.

Meanwhile there was a big Grand Opening party in progress on Second Avenue between 48th and 49th Streets, where a couple of well-known Mafia Dons where launching a new bar and grill. They evidently ran out of liquor and sent this guy Barney, a well-known Kook and Gofer, to our bar to pick up two quarts of rye and two quarts of scotch whiskey to keep the party going. As Benny placed the bottles on the bar for Barney to pick up, Barney turned to the lone customer, who happened to be cross-eyed and wore eyeglasses, and without provocation blurted out, "I see you looking at me through the mirror from behind those glasses."

From my vantage point behind the clam bar, watching this comedy unfold, I found it amusing. It appeared to be a play written by Mark Hellinger. Little did I realize what was to happen next. It started harmlessly enough.

Cross-eyed Customer: "I really wasn't looking at you. I was just looking into the mirror at the bar."

Barney: "I can tell you were looking right at me. Are you looking for trouble?"

Customer: "I'm sorry, you..."

(At this moment, Benny, from behind the bar, sensing trouble, gets into the conversation.)

Benny: "Come on, Barney, let's not have any trouble. Take the liquor and go back to the party."

At this point, Barney, obviously under the influence, unleashed a volley of invectives at both Benny and the innocent customer, whereupon Benny, from behind the bar, grabbed Barney by the shirt collar and attempted to throw him out of the bar. I could see that things were getting ugly, and I came out from behind my counter and attempted to calm things down. Barney grabbed one of the liquor bottles on the counter and swung it towards my partner Benny's head. I got there just in time to deflect the bottle, which went crashing down to the floor. Benny now wrestled Barney onto the floor and unleashed a few punches to his face. I broke that fracas up, and together with Benny, we unceremoniously dumped Barney out the front door.

With all of this uncalled-for action, the stitches from my operation broke open, and I could feel the warm ooze of blood coursing down my leg. We were about to rejoice that the incident was over without serious consequences when Barney came charging into the tavern through the open side door, grabbed a ten inch carving knife from the kitchen tray, and charged at Benny. I tackled him before he got to Benny, and again we wrestled him to the ground. Now comes a new player! The customer, realizing this whole commotion started because of his cock-eyed gaze that was reflected in the mirror, decided to get into the act - as if we didn't have problems enough. He grabbed the heavy metal bar, which was used to block off the side door after closing, and started a swing that would have split Barney's head open down the middle. I managed to grab that off him, and told him to leave immediately, and not get involved. I could only guess at the consequences when the Dons at the party saw that their envoy had his face mashed in and was returning without the requested good will liquor. We then threw Barney out again and closed and locked the doors. I still had on my apron with Barney's blood on it, and blood from my open stitches, running down my leg, when Benny decides that I run after Barney before he gives his side of the story to the Dons.

The Dons, of course, would take this incident as an act of disrespect and may come back to us shooting. This is not a far fetched scenario. This mentality was well demonstrated in the movie about the Mafia, called Goodfellas. I have learned of lesser incidents than what transpired here that ended in tragedy.

I didn't even think of taking off my apron as I started hobbling after Barney, hoping to get in our side of the story. Too late! Barney, and now an angry mob, were already out in the street. As I approached the mob, looking to get to the kingpin (let's call him Manny), Barney yells out, "That's one of them!" I was immediately surrounded by a horde of half drunk and violent men bent on mayhem and murder. As they formed a circle around me, four or five rows deep, one of the mob pulled out a knife and started towards me. I was desperately trying to tell them our side of the story, and what I had done to avert disaster, but it fell on deaf ears. With that, the hit man lunged at me with a six-inch blade. As I backed off, he misses, but the knife caught and ripped part of my blood-spattered apron. I'm still trying to explain before he makes another attempt when to my relief I see a patrolman approaching from across 48th Street. Instead of coming to see what the disturbance was about, this heroic cop made a ninety degree turn into 48th Street and disappeared so as not to get involved!

Now the circle tightened around me and this time there was to be no escape. I vowed I would not be sacrificed without a fight. Ironically, I was the only one who didn't lay a hand on Barney, except to heave him out of the bar to avert disaster. I was in a hopeless situation as the circle closed about me to a diameter of about eight feet. I was prepared to kick, punch, bite, scratch, or anything in an effort to escape the inevitable. The knifer started at me again, when a miracle happened. One of the men at the outer perimeter of the circle yells out, "Stop! That's Matteo's son!", whereupon the head honcho steps forward and asks if Matteo was, indeed, my father.

As I have previously noted, my father was a very well respected man by all groups which saved me for the time being. But that is not the end. There is vengeance to be exacted. After all, an envoy was viciously attacked for no apparent reason according to Barney. Now, after this reprieve, Barney admitted he wasn't sure if I had participated in the attack. God only knows what he had said about the cross-eyed customer but they now wanted to question him too. It was now agreed that a representative contingent, headed up by the head honcho Manny, would go to our bar and question Benny to clear up the question of any willful disrespect. Well, a group of twelve descend upon the scene of the crime. It started off peaceful enough, with Benny behind the bar being questioned by Manny. The honcho apparently didn't like one of the replies and as he is facing Benny from across the bar he snatched up the ceramic potato chip dish and hurled it towards Benny's face. I was standing right next to Manny and I hit his hand, deflecting the dish, which went smashing to pieces on the mahogany bar. I was advised that this act alone would not go unpunished. Being Matteo's son, it was to be overlooked for the moment. It was now agreed, by cooler heads, that a meeting be scheduled. The head honcho and two of his cohorts plus my father, Matteo, and Benny's father, Domenick were to attend. The meeting was to take place the next night in the dining room of our bar for that purpose only and closed to business for the duration of the gathering. The meeting went on as scheduled. It was to start with humble apologies by Benny and myself. When my father found out about the almost tragic end of his son by the angry mob, although Pop was no longer the rough and tough man to be feared, some angry words were exchanged, with regrets proffered to quell my father's anger.

They made the point that when it was discovered that I was Matteo's son, all hostilities against me stopped. Besides, wasn't I forgiven for laying a hand on Manny when I deflected the plate aimed at Benny's face?

After that, drinks were ordered with apologies all around. Would you believe that they still wanted to know the identity of the cock-eyed customer? Of course Benny and I knew him but we claimed he was a stranger that had dropped in for a night cap.

It was very difficult to convince these people. It seemed that they wanted someone to offer up, innocent or guilty, in retribution for what they still considered an affront. They didn't seem to mind who was offered up - even if it had to be the conductor of the Third Avenue El.

SUPERMAN'S LIST
BOXING TEAM

The next year, the call finally came as a result of my having taken the "Superman's Test". They started hiring from that list to fill positions in other municipal departments. I took the first job offered at 62 and a half cents an hour, and was assigned as a porter in the New York Subway system, stationed at Coney Island in Brooklyn. In the summer that was undoubtedly the dirtiest station in the entire public transportation system. The other porter assigned was Stanley Graham, a tough kid from Harlem. He had been the National AAU Boxing Champ, a fact that he constantly reminded me of.

One of the nastiest duties as porters, was the cleaning of toilets. Stanley was assigned to the Women's and I the Men's. During the season, Coney Island was a favorite spot for all bathers in the five boroughs. It was impossible to maintain cleanliness after the assaults from arriving and departing trainloads of passengers. Stanley complained that as soon as he finished cleaning he would be followed by a trail of urine before he got fifty feet away. There would be tissues, paper towels, and unmentionables everywhere, along with stopped up toilets. We had to find a solution. That's when we arrived at the only plausible remedy.

After the next cleaning, we liberally splashed concentrated ammonia from our cleaning supply, over the tile walls of the toilets before the arrival of the next train. We positioned ourselves a safe distance away, hidden from view to observe the efficacy of our experiment. The first one to barge in before feeling the initial effect (she must have had a stuffed nose) quickly came out choking and gasping for breath. Most of the others just got one whiff, which was enough to snap their heads back, and hurriedly left. One leather lunged individual, to our amazement, withstood about twenty seconds in that environment. About two hours later we got an unannounced visit by a supervisor and were fired on the spot!

Before long the Sanitation Department began hiring from the Superman's List. I was ordered to report to their headquarters for processing prior to being appointed. There was a group of thirty people waiting to be interviewed. I was singled out and ordered to report to Deputy Commissioner Gabarini's office. Now what? I had no idea why I was being summoned. At the time, applicants for city jobs were thoroughly investigated. Any unfavorable revelations, be it character, residence, or even minor infractions of the law would be grounds for denial of appointment. I wondered, as I sat waiting for the Deputy Commissioner to arrive: Did they discover that my father once operated a speakeasy over twelve years ago? I was running lots of other doubts over in my mind, when I was called into the Commissioner's office.

Commissioner Gabrini: "Sit down. I've a few questions to ask you. I see by your draft status that you are the sole supporter of a family of five. Is that to change soon?"

Carl Chiarelli: "In my last call before the Draft Board, I had asked to have them arrange for an allotment for my family so that I may volunteer for a service of my choosing."

Commissioner Gabrini: "I see from your file that you were on the High School Track Team, and also did some boxing in the amateurs. Would you be interested in trying out for the Sanitation Department Track or Boxing Team - or both?"

Carl Chiarelli: "I would be more interested in the Boxing Team."

Commissioner Gabrini: "Okay Chiarelli. I will arrange for your tryout. In the meanwhile you will be assigned to the Chain Gang until we get the results of the tryout."

I had no idea what the Chain Gang was. I felt like I was about to be condemned for all my past sins!

When I got to the location, which was a pier at 23rd Street extending into the East River, I was met by Superintendent Fitzgerald. This was the repair headquarters for most of the snow removal equipment. It was the only location for the repair of skid chains used by all department vehicles. Thus the name, Chain Gang.

After just two rounds of a scheduled three rounds of sparring with one of the regulars on the boxing team, the team manager called a halt, saying he had seen enough. I was guaranteed a place on the team in the welterweight class. He said he would inform the Commissioner and I would be permanently assigned to the Chain Gang. I couldn't have been more pleased. I was to be paid for what I was already doing for nothing. I was looking forward to locking horns with boxers from the other departments: Police, Fire, Corrections, etc., especially the Police. Many a beating I had absorbed, in growing up, just for being on a corner with friends or playing cards on a bench outside in the summer. Or the time I was hauled into jail when I just happened to step into the Billiard Parlor when a card game was in progress in a rear room. As for convenience, the 23rd Street Pier was only three blocks from my home on 25th Street, between 1st and 2nd Avenues.

I got plenty of ribbing from the Chain Gang members when they observed my daily regimen. I would arrive at 7 a.m. every morning from Monday to Friday, with a fresh orange in hand. Then came the road work from the pier along 1st Avenue, past the slaughter house in the mid-forties (the present location of the U.N. Building), to 86th Street and return; An average of about seven miles. On my return, to cool down, I would lay on the large tool storage box at the rear of the room to the taunts and jeers of my co-workers. The tool box had a heavy canvas cover, so I was given the moniker, Canvas Back. After limbering up, by 9 a.m. I would join in the repair work to the accompaniment of loud cheers and jeers from all the Chain Gang members.

I continued training while anxiously waiting for the inter-departmental matches to begin. It appeared that the program might possibly be suspended due to the war. That would be a shame as the proceeds of the gate went to charitable organizations.

During the summer, the sanitation department would detail workers that had a background in construction trades (carpenters, electricians, plumbers, and skilled mechanics) to Sanita Hills, a small town in Holmes, located in upstate New York. I was sent because of my background in construction but also to resume training. I was to assist in every phase of the project, as needed. My first duties were as a part of the Dynamite Crew. I was to transport dynamite and blasting caps, assist in the preparation of the charges and then clear debris and level the blast site. In addition, I would chop down trees designated for removal. The logs then would be trimmed and loaded on a pick-up truck to be transported to each blasting site. The logs would then be stacked over the dynamite charge and bound together by steel cable to contain the resultant fallout.

All of these activities, although necessary for the project, had the effect of hardening and conditioning the members of the boxing team. It was no accident that Commissioner Gabarini had sent me to Sanita Hills. The workload was arduous and demanding. No coffee breaks! It was clear he wanted me in shape for the expected boxing matches. My experience at this work camp, plus the heavy manual labor performed in the construction line pushing a wheelbarrow, carrying hods full of brick or mortar, toughened me to a point that I didn't have an ounce of fat left on me. I enthusiastically tackled the roughest and toughest jobs, especially since they were all outdoors, were interesting and challenging. After work was finished for the day, members of the team would engage in a few rounds of sparring.

The Sanita Hills project was the creation of the then Commissioner Carey. He purchased the elevated railroad cars from the Second and Third Avenue Els which were being torn down. He paid a nominal purchase price of one dollar each for the cars (otherwise they would have been scrapped), and had them shipped upstate to his acreage in Holmes, New York. The interior of the cars were gutted and then made into one and two bedroom cottage cars. All furniture was built in, and included all the amenities: hot and cold running water, bathrooms, showers, and even included built-in refrigerators.

After the project was completed, Sanita Hills served as a vacation resort for members of the Sanitation Department and their families. There was excellent fishing in the adjacent Big Whaley and Little Whaley Lakes. Cribs were floated for children to swim in safely, and of course there was canoeing. There were weekly square dances and barbecues. The family vacation packages were reasonably priced so as to be affordable for members of the Department.

It was a very successful venture, and practically all of the work and planning was done by members of the Sanitation department. Sometime after World War II, Sanita Hills was turned over to the Girl Scouts of America.

In the Summer of 1943, I finally convinced the draft board to approve an allotment for my family of four. The paltry allotment was so miserly that I had them withhold the maximum from my military pay, leaving me with a big twenty-six dollars a month. The alternative was to again have the family apply for Welfare once more. We all had already vowed, "never again".

In August of 1943 I was chosen to lead a contingent of Draftees marching in formation from the Draft Board on 23rd Street to the Induction Center on 42nd Street in Manhattan. "Farewell civilian life."

Chapter 6

MILITARY SERVICE

BOOT CAMP, QUARTERMASTER SCHOOL, MATRIMONIAL LEAVE, THREE SHIP COLLISION, CAPTAIN'S MAST, MAN OVERBOARD, A LIBERTY TO REMEMBER

From the beginning I had a foreboding that Military training was destined to spell trouble for me. Not the rigors of Boot Camp, but the bull and chickenshit designed to break one's individual spirit. I had visited the U. S. Marine Post in Alexandria, Virginia, the previous year and spent a few days with my friend Bill Puzo who was stationed there. I had every intention at the time to "Join the Marines". After first-hand observation of their bullshit training techniques, I scratched them from my list.

I made up my mind that Sea Duty in the Navy was the branch of the Service for me. From reports of friends in the Army, who wrote about the filth, mud, and exposure to vermin and disease, I opted for service at sea. I was accepted for service in the Navy and directed to report the next day for processing. On reporting the next day, I learned that I was assigned to the Coast Guard, which during time of war was a branch of the Navy. I was surprised to see that a cousin of mine, Pete LoBrutto, was also assigned to the Coast Guard. I was pleased to learn that Boot Camp would be in Manhattan Beach in Brooklyn.

I had recently become engaged to my future wife, Natalie, and I imagined that being close to home would give me some time with my family and fiancee, before being shipped out. It might as well have been the Aleutians. Leaves were scarce, far between, and of short duration. Now began my personal battle with the dispensers of chickenshit.

We were marching around the cinder path at the perimeter of the base when sweat ran into my eye. Instinctively, without breaking stride I wiped it with one quick swipe. In that fraction of a second the boatswain's mate caught this act and barked out, "Chiarelli." Just by the intonation of his voice, I sensed I was to be in this guy's pocket for the duration of Boot Camp.

It started by my having to run around the parade field, as the platoon kept marching, until I caught up to them, while holding my rifle over my head. As I approached the platoon, the Boatswain's Mate would yell out, "Again!", It was over 90°F and dust was being kicked up but I was going to take the punishment without a whimper. After approaching the platoon, having lapped the field for the third time, he yelled out, "Again!" like he was whipping me with his tongue! I didn't mind the running as punishment. I ran a lot more in training back home. In fact, I was gaining weight in Boot Camp while everyone else was losing. So when I approached after lapping the field for the fourth time, I had to open my wise-ass mouth, and this time I asked him, "Again?"

He saw his punishment was not having the desired effect and told me to get back in formation. That was the beginning of my ongoing relationship with this boatswain's mate that almost landed me in federal prison. Every evening after chow, the platoons would be in formation by the quarterdeck (salty name for stoop) as the boatswain's mate would call out the extra duty list. Punishment would be meted out for all the bad guys that had screwed up. We would be assigned every imaginable unpleasant duty, and at times be kept working to 1 a.m. the next morning, and then be ready for formation at 5 a.m. This became a permanent activity for me and Boatswain's Mate K always started calling off the extra duty list with a loud "CHIARELLI" for emphasis with a big grin. I was losing sleep but was determined not to get deeper in trouble so I endured without complaint.

At the end of the week's punishment period, I was anxiously waiting to finally be off the extra duty list so that I could catch up on some sleep. I was relieved when he didn't start the list with my name, as he did for every day of the punishment period. When he finished the list without my name being included, he walked off the quarterdeck. However, when he was about a dozen steps away, he spun around and hurried back, pointed his finger at me and at the top of his voice yelled out, "AND CHIARELLI!"

In the condition of near exhaustion that I was in from lack of sleep, I became a madman. I knocked down anyone in my path as I ran to the quarterdeck. In one leap I hurdled the railing and sprang upon my tormentor. By the time we hit the ground I had already landed a couple of wild punches. It took six combined Boatswain's Mates and SPs to subdue me. I was then escorted by the base security and SPs to the Base Commander's quarters for a hearing. The consensus was that I would be sent to the stockade and then to federal prison. Striking an officer, even a 1st Class Non-Com, during time of war, was, and still is, a very serious offense. I believe that SOB purposely led me on until I cracked.

When I was led to the Commander's office he was seated at his desk, in the company of two other officers. I stood at attention as he was perusing my file. After what seemed like an eternity, he dismissed the other officers and we were left alone. As luck would have it, he was a regular career officer, not a ninety day wonder as the newly recruited wartime officers were often referred to. After we were face to face a while, the Commander had me stand at ease. Then the questioning:

Commander: "Seaman Chiarelli, do you realize the seriousness of your action?"

Me: "Yes Sir."

Commander: "Do you understand that you could be sent to prison for the duration of the war and for a long time after? You have committed one of the most serious crimes in the military during wartime."

Me: "I understand Sir. At the time I believe I went crazy and lost control. If I wasn't stopped I think I could have killed the boatswain's mate for what he did."

Commander: "I'm going to forget what you just said so don't repeat it. I've gone over your file and performance record and this incident is inconsistent with what can be expected of you. From the beginning, give me your honest account of what led up to the attack on Boatswain's Mate K..."

I related how it all started by my wiping sweat from my eye, then how the boatswain's mate had delighted putting me on report for far more periods than he had others who had committed more serious infractions. I attributed my loss of control to having lost so much sleep while at the same time being driven to exhaustion. I then recounted the incident that had pushed me over the brink after the boatswain's mate had concluded the extra duty list only to return to enthusiastically add my name again.

The Commander listened without interruption, then:

Commander: "Chiarelli, from what you have told me, but more from what I have read in your file, I'm going to give you one last chance. You will rejoin your platoon and do extra duty every day for the next two weeks, starting immediately after chow until dismissed. You will, however, be released in time to get sufficient sleep. This is the only chance you will get, so don't blow it. After the two weeks, I want you to come back to see if any further action is warranted."

Me: "Thank you Sir. I'm very grateful. You will never have another problem with me again as long as I'm no longer in Boatswain's Mate K's platoon."

Commander (visibly angry): "You WILL be in the same platoon. No matter what happens I don't want to hear the slightest rumble. Don't let me regret giving you this chance."

Me: "Commander, you will never regret what you have done for me."

Although no one said as much, I got the impression that this officer was aware of the sadistic nature of my platoon leader. I promised myself that I would not let the Commander (and myself) down. Also, I'm sure that he had discussed this case, in private, with Boatswain's Mate K. As one of the Commander's conditions I humbly apologized to the boatswain's mate when I returned to the platoon. He watched me like a hawk but I never strayed, that is, until two days before the probation period was to expire.

We were marching in formation at the far end of the field. There was a light drizzle and fog, so we all wore rubbers over our work shoes. The platoon was in three sections. I was in the rearmost section, as the boatswain's mate was leading at the front of the column. Directly behind me, was a seaman with a bizarre sense of humor. Knowing I was on my best behavior, he was testing how far he could go before I unraveled (as he later put it). He would switch step as we marched and his toe would catch the heel of my shoes. He succeeded in disengaging my rubber shoe. I was doing a slow burn and gestured for him to stop as I kept marching. However, he persisted and on the next switch pulled my shoe off my foot. I saw red! I turned and caught him with a punch on his temple. He fell in a heap and the whole third section of the formation was in disarray. In a few steps the platoon was stopped and Boatswain's Mate K came to the rear to investigate. The seaman (Raul) is on the wet ground semi-conscious, as I and others tried to get him up. He had a knob at the side of his forehead the size of a walnut.

"Okay," said the boatswain's mate, "what happened?", looking mostly at me. I said I had no idea and no one gave me away. Seaman Raul finally got up and explained that he suddenly felt faint and could only remember falling. This story was corroborated by all and he was sent to Sick Bay for observation. At least he enjoyed a few days of light duty to recover from his fainting spell.

Well, I passed that last hurdle and finished the two weeks probation doing extra duty every night without further incident. I was then summoned by Commander Coleman who expressed relief that I had passed the test. Of course, he was aware of the fainting incident and wondered aloud how peculiar it was that the victim was sporting a king-sized lump by his forehead when everyone testified that he had fallen on his back. I detected a suppressed smile, but he went no further.

He then advised me that my test scores were excellent and I could qualify for any school of my choosing. I asked to be considered for the upcoming test for quartermaster, as that held the most promise for being assigned to sea duty. I passed the quartermaster test and was assigned to Quartermaster School. I was glad to be free of the clutch of that sadistic SOB, Boatswain's Mate K. I vowed that if ever I met him in the future after the war I would even the score with him. I took all the BS he dumped on me, but when he went on a personal vendetta that was unforgivable. He was hiding behind the machinery of the military to protect himself.

I enjoyed the relaxed environment of the Quartermaster School in comparison to the Boot Camp. I liked the subject matter: Seamanship, Navigation, Signaling, Wheelwatch, Ship's Security, Fire Control at Sea, and other pertinent subjects. Much of the experience actually helped when I later joined the New York Fire Department. We were instructed in the purpose and use of every type of portable fire extinguisher that would be provided aboard ship. We then got some practical experience in fighting fires in flammable liquids, at first in the open, and then in confined spaces. We got some valuable experience in the proper application of chemical and mechanical foam extinguishers. We were introduced to the benefits and limitations of the use of long extension fog nozzles in fighting fires below decks of a ship.

CONFLICT AT SEA
MATRIMONIAL LEAVE

It was nearing the end of the Quartermaster School. I couldn't wait to get off the base and be assigned to a ship. After all the test results were in, the top two percent of the class was immediately promoted to the rank of Quartermaster 3rd Class and given a patch with that designation to be sewn onto the right sleeve of the uniform. I was fortunate to have finished in that group and had the rank sewn onto my "dress blues." Also, as was the custom then, the top two percent were forthwith assigned to a ship. Things were going so well that it seemed too good to be true. Well, it was too good! To begin with, tradition was broken and our quartermaster 3rd Class rank was to be withheld until we were assigned to a ship and served six months as a Quartermaster Striker. And then, only at the discretion of the Commanding Officer, would we get our quartermaster 3rd Class rank. We were told this was only a formality and that reinstatement of the rank was automatic.

Little did I dream at the time that I was destined to be assigned to a ship commanded by an officer appropriately named "Captain Cook" (his real name). From experience I sensed that nothing would go well from there on, especially after being stripped from the rank that we had enjoyed for only a day.

Things looked brighter when assignments to our new units were announced. I was elated to learn that I was to report immediately to South Boston Harbor, Massachusetts, for duty aboard the Coast Guard cutter designated simply as W218. The graduating class had been promised a few days leave before reporting to our assigned units. Those leaves, too, were canceled. That was a big disappointment shared by all, especially for those that had family members travel from all over the country to be with a loved one before being "shipped out."

The trip to Boston was uneventful. We were met at the station by a bus which was to transport us to our assigned units. I was left off at the pier by the driver. My spirit was lifted when I saw the beautiful ship docked at the far end of the pier. All the other seamen on the bus were saying how lucky I was to draw that ship. You should have heard all the "oohs and aahs" as I gathered my seabag and made my way to the end of the pier and up the gangplank.

I was met on the deck by the Duty Officer and "requested permission to come aboard, Sir." Permission was granted and I presented my assignment papers. The Duty Officer took one look at my papers and said, "Sailor, you're on the wrong ship. This is the Coast Guard training ship, *Sea Cloud.*" He then pointed out across the dock to the opposite pier. "That's the ship you are looking for. It is called the *Hibiscus.*" I looked in the direction he pointed and my heart sank. It was a scroungy looking tub by comparison. It was undergoing extensive repairs and looked a mess. This "buoy tender" was being outfitted with a five pound cannon, port and starboard anti-aircraft guns and "ash cans" for combating submarines.

When I got to the gangplank, before I could request permission, I was flatly told by the Duty Officer, "Jump aboard. We've been expecting you." I had a feeling of doom and gloom as my feet hit the deck, with a foreboding of events to follow aboard this ship. I wasn't to meet the Captain for a few days and I wasn't exactly given a warm welcome. The first thing that was made evident was that the entire crew was hostile to Italians. There were two other seamen of Italian heritage aboard.

They seemed to tolerate the verbal ethnic abuse. It was "Dumb Dago," "Stupid Wop," and any other slur that they could muster up at the time. I guessed that they had it in for Mussolini and took their anger out on anyone with an Italian-sounding name. Funny, no one had problems with crewmen of any other heritage, just Italians!

I was introduced to the non-commissioned officers, both quartermaster 1st Class, who made a point of reminding me that they were my immediate superiors, as were all other rated personnel in the "Bridge Gang." This included the radar men, signal men, radio operators, etc. My duties were spelled out and included all the unpleasant assignments, as I expected. I was then taken below and assigned a bunk in the cramped sleeping quarters at the top of a triple stacked affair. Forty bunks were crammed in a space scarcely suitable to accommodate half that amount. Just when I thought I had reached the nadir, I was greeted with another bombshell. Although as a quartermaster striker signaling was my secondary responsibility, I was to do all of the signaling by blinker light. I soon found out why. No one, from the Communications Officer, a Lieutenant, to the rated Quartermasters and others in the Bridge Gang, could read or transmit messages by blinker light. Before my arrival the 1st Class Signalman had been transferred off the ship. How did all these guys earn their commissions? Proficiency in signaling was a requirement for earning a rank or commission. Wasn't anything on the level any more? So be it! A request was in for a 1st Class Signalman. Before long I put in for a transfer, requesting overseas duty aboard the troop ship, *Wakefield*.

In the meantime, my duties included making all the entries in the ship's log, which were to be neatly printed by hand, on the daily activities. This was in addition to around-the-clock quartermaster watches and wheel watches. I then had to print out the monthly reports on operations (normally the responsibility of the Executive Officer) in addition to the routine duties on the bridge. There wasn't much time left for myself. Whenever we were tied up in port I would get off the ship and run a few miles in an effort to stay in shape physically. Meanwhile my attitude on fitness and completing my overload of duties proficiently and without complaint seemed to rankle the quartermaster 1st Class (my immediate superior), and his staunchest supporter, Mr. Tollefson, the Executive Officer, who went along with every decision by quartermaster 1st Class Robertson (Robby).

I didn't have a friend on the bridge until a fine Irish gentleman, Ensign O'Brien transferred aboard after having made several crossings escorting supply ships to Russia along the very dangerous "Murmansk Route." He quickly sized up the situation and tried to intervene with the Captain to effect my transfer to the *Wakefield* or another ship doing overseas duty. Meanwhile, I had put all hands on notice, especially quartermaster 1st Class Robby, the most abusive one, who was constantly displaying his brute strength by taking on all comers and wrestling them to the ground. I had just dispatched one of his cronies at a local pub during our last "liberty" ashore when the schmuck, referring to me, proclaimed loudly, "Hey fellas, look at the dumb black Guinea drinking gingerale at the bar." That did it!

First I threw the half remaining drink in his face (it was rye and gingerale). I then grasped both ends of his dress blues kerchief from around his neck. While tightening the kerchief I threw this pile of crap to the floor and warned him that this was only a sample of what was to come if he repeated any of his uncomplimentary remarks. He refused my offer to discuss the matter outside. Like all other big blowhards, he declined. When this incident got back to the ship, some were glad to see that someone had stood up to that big jerk. Not so his pal, Robby, who now began piling on some subtle abuse to anger me into making a stupid move. He succeeded!

We were underway from Portland, Maine to Boston, and I was at the helm when quartermaster Robby burst into the bridge to inform the Executive Officer that I was guilty of some imagined violation. They were discussing what punishment should be meted out when I blew my cool and actually let go of the wheel as I turned to face my lying accuser. The Captain immediately cautioned me to "mind the wheel" in no uncertain terms. As much as a martinet that the Captain surely was, he saw that I was being needlessly provoked and informed all concerned that complaints be made only after we were docked. After we were tied up I was busy making the entries in the ship's log before leaving the bridge when I heard quartermaster Robby chanting out --Chiaarrellli -- in a drawn out, mocking manner from the wing of the bridge. He was waving a pair of boxing gloves that he had procured from our sports locker. I was then informed that instead of "putting me on report," he had decided to teach me an unforgettable lesson. When I looked down at the dock from the bridge I could see that practically all of the crew was arranged to form a clear space of about 20 foot square, much like a boxing ring.

I knew this was to be retribution for the incident at the bar with one of his cronies during liberty. Robby figured he was bigger, stronger and surely tougher than I, and he was itching to beat up on me. By this time Ensign O'Brien had entered the bridge as the Duty Officer. I could see he was feeling sorry for me as I tried in vain not to get into this fight. It was a no-win situation. If I beat him I had an enemy for the duration of my time aboard this ship. The dialogue went something like this:

Quartermaster Robby: "OK, Chiarelli, instead of putting you on report, I'll give you a chance to fight it out. Let's see how tough you are."

Me: "Look, Robby, I don't know what phony story you cooked up on the bridge. You know it's not true."

Quartermaster Robby: "True or not, the Executive Officer left the punishment up to me."

Me: "Whatever you're up to, I don't see that we have something that we have to fight about."

At this point I could see that the little Irish Ensign was commiserating with me, thinking that I was afraid of this big Limey bully and that I would be "creamed" if I fought him.

Quartermaster Robby: "Everybody is out there waiting for us to come down. You aren't going to chicken out and show them how scared you are, are you?"

Me: "Robby, you may as well put the gloves away. I'm not going to fight you."

Quartermaster Robby:"Well, like I always said, I knew that all you "bleeping" Guineas were yellow."

Me: "Robby you just said the magic words. OK, let's get down to the dock. Just remember, I didn't ask for this fight, you did."

Such was my innate confidence. I thought that I could beat anyone when I was angered and in the right. On the way down to the dock we passed by the radio shack. My friend, Hal Lawner, the radio man at the time, looked at me as if I was going to the guillotine. He knew everyone on the ship feared this guy. Ensign O'Brien remained on the wing of the bridge overlooking the makeshift ring formed on the pier. Even I was asking myself, "How do I keep getting into these situations?" For me it was deja vu, a la Yogi, all over again as when I had been forced into a fight with my restaurant partner years earlier.

When we got to the pier there was already a self-appointed referee who was really enjoying the proceedings. He designated a timekeeper and asked if we preferred two- or three-minute rounds. I left that to Robby who chose three-minute rounds. "OK," says the referee (who was also the Gunnersmate in charge of the sports locker). "No dirty tactics. Keep it clean. Let's go!"

Robby came out like a raging bull, thinking I would fold with his first punch. I either blocked or slipped every punch he threw. All I countered with as a flicking jab to his face. After two minutes he decided that we should change to two-minute rounds. After a minute's rest, he again came out swinging with the same result. I blocked, slipped and countered with a few jabs. As we clinched, I looked up to the wing of the bridge and saw Ensign O'Brien jumping up and down at this unexpected spectacle. When we got to the third round I figured it was time for **him** to be taught a lesson. As we clinched with one minute to go, I told Robby it was time for him to go. I caught him with a three-punch combination. When he fell forward I caught him in a clinch and asked if he had had enough. He answered in the affirmative.

Me to Robby: "If you're OK, we'll break the clinch and then spar around a bit until the time is up and the fight is over."

Robby: "OK, thanks."

He knew I was letting him off the hook. If the roles were reversed, he would have beat me into the ground mercilessly. He later said as much and again thanked me for the manner in which we ended the encounter. No one was fooled by the ending, however. For the next month, with the blessing of the Gunnersmate, the crew and even Robby himself, I was teaching the finer points of boxing to many of the seamen that volunteered. I really didn't mind it. In fact, I welcomed the action as it helped keep me in shape for the Sanitation Boxing Team after the war was over. And if the inter-departmental boxing program was resumed, I would fit right in. After all, in early 1994 who knew when the war would end.

The thought was also on the mind of my fiancée, Natalie. We decided to get married in October of 1944 if I could arrange a leave. With the help of Ensign O'Brien I was able to get the only leave of my entire time in the service. We had seven days. Two of the days were spent traveling to Maine and back -- part hitchhiking, part train and part bus. The Captain, true to his sadistic nature didn't approve my leave until dark, after the last train and bus had left Portland, Maine, thus wasting my first day of leave. I left the ship with Yeoman 1st Class Safko who was also on leave. We hitched on every conceivable conveyance. The last was a truck loaded with lobsters and fish bound for Massachusetts. I think the odor remained with me until the next day when I finally made it to New York after I was able to take a train from Boston.

I got only one concession from our Captain Cook. He granted my good friend, Bruce Branick, a three-day leave so that he could stand in as my best man. Did I say "stand in?" Actually, he was so "crocked" during the ceremony that if he wasn't leaning against me, he would have crashed to the floor of the church!

After the ceremony the reception was held at the George Washington Hotel on Lexington Avenue and 23rd Street in New York City. It was to be the only "football wedding" I was every involved in. A football wedding, for those unfamiliar with the term, has nothing to do with Dan Marino or the New York Jets. It was so called, I imagine, because instead of the customary buffets and ubiquitous formal dinners, small Italian loaves of bread, stuffed with every imaginable combination of Italian cold cuts were the main fare. These heroes were then tightly wrapped and labeled. The final product resembled a football though not quite as bloated. It may also have been named a football wedding because of the practice of hurling a hero, on request, to a recipient up to twenty feet away. With all the prim and proper affairs of today, with each generation attempting to outdo the previous, the fun and informality of a football wedding is, unfortunately, a thing of the past.

The night before the reception the family and close relatives were busy preparing the heroes, and they were also responsible for their distribution. There was always more than enough and plenty of take home "doggy bags" afterwards.

After the ceremony and reception, all that was left of my leave was scarcely two full days for our honeymoon. Since my originally scheduled ten-day leave had been canceled by the Captain, I felt it was only fair that I request a few days' extension. After all, I expected to be married only one time, and by the Captain's own admission I was doing more than what was called for on the reports of the ship's monthly activities, normally the duty of the Executive Officer. Besides, the ship was still in dry dock. With all that rationalization in mind, I sent the following telegram addressed to the Captain: "Planned erroneously. Stop. Confronted Baker.[2] Stop. Request five (5) days extension. Stop. Sea (QM) Chiarelli."

However, when the telegram arrived in South Boston, the ship had left port and couldn't be reached by radio as my best man, Bruce, who

---

[2] Baker is a navy term for a red pennant used for signalling.

had returned after the wedding, had the radio apart trying to correct a malfunction. (Radios aboard ship were not very dependable then). The Base Commander, thinking that it might be an important coded message since it was directed to the Captain himself, decided to send out a launch to intercept the ship and deliver the message by hand. The telegram was handed directly to the Captain who handed it to the Communications Officer to be read to him. When he read out the "planned erroneously, confronted **Baker**" part, the other officers on the bridge broke out in laughter. Not so the Captain. He did not get the gist of the message and was annoyed that the base had sent out a launch after him. He had expected that it would be an important message.

The other officers agreed that on the strength of the comical nature of the telegram I be granted the leave extension. The Captain, however, had the final say, which was conveyed in his response. The telegram read: "*USS Hibiscus* to Sea (QM) Chiarelli. Lower baker, bloodhound, return on time. Signed, Captain Cook." I could see the fine hand of the Yeoman in the response.

The Captain had no sense of humor whatsoever or he might have granted the leave extension.

When I returned from matrimonial leave, I was greeted with the good news that we had been assigned a 1st Class Signalman, Norman Schweers. He hailed from the same neighborhood in New York as I and we had some friends in common, and thus we hit it off pretty good. I thought I finally would be relieved from the total responsibility of signaling which was becoming more frequent in our operations. This exhilaration was short lived, however, when Schweers confided to me that he could scarcely read a full sentence in blinker unless sent so pitifully slow as to be of no practical use. This came as a shock. I still had the same problem, and in addition, in my spare time I gave the Signalman 1st Class private signaling lessons so as not to give away his embarrassing secret that would cause him to lose his 1st Class rating.

The plot further thickened when our Executive Officer, Mr. Tollefson, reasoned that since we now had a full fledged and ranked Signalman, I had become a "Supernumerary Afloat." Honest, that was the label he pinned on me. We were soon scheduled to undergo some repairs in drydock in Boston Harbor and he decided this was in retribution for the "spanking" I had administered to his protégé, Robby. He approached the Captain with his "Supernumery Afloat" designation and his solution was to temporarily assign me as Captain of the Head once we were in dry dock.

What irony! Now not only was I teaching signaling to the Signalman, but I was also being removed from the bridge gang at a time when we would be enjoying extra liberties ashore to compensate for the many extra hours we stood watches during normal operations.

In the event that "Captain of the Head" is misconstrued as a promotion, any sea going gob knows that it is the person responsible for the daily cleaning, stocking and operation of the toilet. What a kick in the ass! Talk about just desserts!

Well, I reasoned, there was still a war going on. Some of my graduating class perished, along with 33 seamen aboard the Cross Rip Lightship when it capsized and sank during a hurricane that year. Others from my class also hadn't survived. So what's the big deal? So, I would be deprived of the extra liberties that I had earned which would now be enjoyed by Schweers. I decided to make the best of a lousy situation.

It wasn't long before complaints on the operation of the head reached the bridge. To cut down on cleaning time, I used the old "raw ammonia on the walls trick" that was so successful in Coney Island. After that was resolved, I was ordered to take down the signs I had posted on the door to the head and on the interior wall facing the occupants of the "johns." The signs read, "During the current shortage of toilet paper, all Seamen are instructed to take only one sheet from the roll and to use both sides of the sheet." It was then signed, "By order of the Captain." Attesting to the brainwashing by the services, I was informed that some boneheads actually attempted to comply with the order. The officers were concerned that I had neglected to indicate that the sign was endorsed by the Captain of the Head, not by the ship's Captain as it implied.

Being denied these two major tools in administering the duties of Captain of the Head, the job became quite tedious. After dry dock I did not return to the bridge until an incident took place that almost had us "blown out of the water" by friendly fire.

The *Hibiscus* was underway at night when out of the inky blackness, seemingly out of nowhere, we were challenged for a recognition signal by blinker light. (A month earlier in Nova Scotia waters when one of our ships had failed to respond correctly she was fired on and severely damaged. That incident, at least, bought us a few seconds.

When that blinker challenge hit the *Hibiscus*, pandemonium broke loose. The whole communications crew on the bridge froze with indecision with the initial flash. Then came the frantic scramble as the Communications Officer was called upon. He in turn called out to the 1st Class Quartermaster who was at the helm. The quartermaster in turn told Schweers, the 1st Class Signalman, to give the response. The Captain, assessing the immediate danger, yelled out, "Get Chiarelli up here." I knew the routine and, in fact, had instructed members of the bridge gang on the action to take in the event of such a challenge. Since this had never happened in our area, the crew became mentally paralyzed.

Fortunately, I raced up to the wing adjacent to the bridge with the first flash to see how Schweers reacted to the unanticipated challenge. There was not time to get cute, so I burst in as the Captain yelled out. I checked the response signal for our sector and time of day and ran to the blinker light to give the proper response signal. The response was a fraction late, but it worked out this time.

After this dangerous episode, the Captain ordered me reassigned to the bridge immediately. I told the Captain that I preferred to remain at my present post. Although it was the crappiest (no pun intended) job on the ship, I had lots more free time to myself. I was also angry for having been deprived of liberty time that I had earned.

The Captain responded to my suggestion with just three words, which, in the service is the equivalent of the "Voice from the Mount." He simply said, "That's an order." I had no choice but to return.

The tide of the war in Europe turned in our favor. I was on the flying bridge when I heard wild shouts of rejoicing from below. The radio man announced he had just received news of Italy's surrender. Most of the enlisted men began referring to their "points" earned during time spent in service. The feeling was that this was one step closer to the end of the conflict and that much sooner to when we could return home. I went down to the main deck to join in the jubilation. Everyone was cheering except our Radar Man.

I couldn't believe what he was yelling out. At first I thought he was fooling around, but the rhetoric was getting louder and nastier: "Them lousy yellow, back stabbing Guinea bleeping #%$$@#s." It kept getting worse. I was surprised that no one had taken him to task; they just let him rave on. Given the attitude of many on the ship towards Italians in general, I wasn't completely surprised. This German-American, a stereotypical Nazi wannabe, was bad mouthing all Italians. He then included the entire population of Italian Americans. He continued this tirade into supper time and got nastier as each of the other two seamen of Italian parentage took their places at the chow tables.

That was the atmosphere at mess (chow) when I came down from my bridge watch and took my place on the bench at the table next to the foul-mouthed Radar Man.

We were seated back to back to each other, separated by a two-foot aisle space. It was quiet for awhile as we dug into an unusually good supper of roast fresh loin of pork, sauerkraut and mashed potatoes smothered in brown gravy. I had scarcely taken a second bite when this Nazi-wannabe piped off again. "I think I smell another yellow bleeping Guinea #%$@%." Suddenly, I think that everyone seated at the three long chow tables stopped chewing at once. I did too! He then began another volley when I decided that I had tolerated enough abuse. He never got to finish the next sentence. I got up and turned to face his table. I tapped him on his shoulder. As he turned towards me, still seated, I picked up my dish with all it's juicy contents. I then said, "Well, Kam (nickname), here's one Guinea that's not yellow." With that I grabbed him behind the head and smashed my wonderful meal into his face. After this force feeding I became almost uncontrollable.

"OK," I said, "Now what are you going to do about it?" He did not answer. I then tried to pull him out of the mess room and onto the buoy deck. I had endured his crap all afternoon and wanted to show him up for the hypocritical ass hole that he was. It took a bunch of the crew to get me away from him. I didn't speak to that Nazi wannabe again, except to exchange bridge watch.

I couldn't eat at all after that scene and went up to the flying deck to cool off until it was time for my next bridge watch. Nick Jeannette, who was the cook at the time, saved some of the pork roast. After he had secured the kitchen, he made a thick sandwich and brought it up to me on the bridge. (Twenty years later I was to join Nick in the insurance business on Long Island, New York.)

Late one night we were steaming 15 miles offshore en route to Norfolk, Virginia, with a vessel in tow. I had just come off wheelwatch and was taking a break in the chart room. I looked at the repeater screen of our radar and noticed a "blip" about three miles towards shore of our position. At first it appeared to be a "ghost" so I erased the screen and repeated the scan but the "blip" didn't disappear. I checked the chart but there was nothing in that direction that would register on the radar screen. I then called in the Bridge Officer on duty.

Me to Lieut. T: "I have an unidentified target bearing three miles to starboard that appears to be a clear blip."

Lieut. T: "It's probably a ghost."

Me: "I checked that out. It's definitely not a ghost."

Lieut. T: "It must be a small island."

Me: "I checked the chart. There is no island. Besides, this island is moving in a parallel course to us." (I couldn't pass up that sarcastic quip.)

Lieut. T: "It's probably a fishing trawler."

Me: "If so, it should have a splash light on deck."

Lieut. T: "Well, what do you suggest? What do you think it is?"

Me: "I don't know. It's a distinct blip. I could give a blinker light challenge for this sector and see if we get a response." (This was stupid reasoning on my part as you will see below.)

Lieut. T: "Never mind that for now. Keep it under surveillance. I'll check it again later."

With that he went back to the bridge. Nothing could be seen by binoculars. The blip on the radar became more distant until it disappeared from the radar screen.

We gave this incident no further thought, that is until we reached Norfolk, Virginia. there we were greeted by a front page news story of how nine German spies had been apprehended on the shore of Frenchman's Bay. The story then described how they had been dropped off the night before by a German submarine.

I am certain that was the blip we had on our radar screen. Had the mature and seasoned Lieutenant Thompson gone along with my suggested blinker challenge, we might never have made it to our destination. Not only were we grossly outgunned, we probably were targeted for a while. We could have been recipients of a "fish" (torpedo). If their main objective was to deliver the spies, they would have just submerged until the area was clear. On the other hand, if the blip had been one of our patrol ships, we weren't challenged simply because a spy ship wouldn't be traveling along the coast with a ship in tow.

It wasn't until the end of the war that the *Hibiscus* participated in the sinking of a German submarine not too far from Bar Harbor, Maine. The submarine had already torpedoed a merchant ship off shore called the *Silver Star*. Ironically, this action took place the day after Germany surrendered.

The explosions from the "ash cans" that we contributed to the attack damn near split open our deck plates. That's how slow our beloved *Hibiscus* was. The ship was more suited to tending buoys than attacking enemy shipping.

As a gesture of triumph, Navy divers retrieved the cap of the sub's Commander and presented it to the Captain of the *Silver Star*. Small consolation!

BUZZARD BAY, MASSACHUSETTS

The biggest, most destructive, and horror-filled fire that I ever experienced was not during my years of service in the Fire Department but while in service during World War II.

Our ship, the "Hibiscus," was tied up at Wood's Hole, Massachusetts, on a day that the fog was so dense that visibility was scarcely twenty feet in any direction. The air was very still, and all that could be heard was the omnipresent racket of the chipping hammers on the deck paint, the distant sounding of the fog horn from the lightship, and passing vessels in the harbor. I had just concluded logging the usual quartermaster recordings on the readings of the meteorological instruments, when I could hear the signals from the radio room.

Instead of the usual Code Groups, periodically copied by the radio man, the signals were spelling out an ongoing disaster at sea. The location was at the harbor approach to Buzzard's Bay, an aptly named treacherous body of water. There were three ships involved. One was an oil tanker, the second a gasoline tanker, and the other an ammunition ship. You couldn't imagine a more dangerous scenario. The three had collided, and all were involved in a fire aboard. There were no rescue ships in the vicinity, and due to the heavy fog, there was no ship responding from the surrounding bases due to the danger of running aground, or further collisions. Getting in and out of these ports during clear weather was risky enough and visiting ships required a "Captain of the Port" escort to guide them through the narrow ships lanes.

That is when our Captain Cook took command of the situation and volunteered to respond to the scene of the disaster. He earned the admiration of "all hands" with the mastery by which he guided the Hibiscus through the narrow ships lanes. We were in danger of running aground ourselves in which case there would be no aid at the site of the collisions. The Captain positioned seamen well forward at the port and starboard side of the ship's bow. The radar man was posted at his screen, calibrated to the closest scale, and Seamen at both sides of the ship heaving lead lines (which give accurate distance to the bottom of the channel), each in turn reporting measurements as the ship slowly made its way past all the obstacles. A 225-foot ship does not change direction quickly. It was slow, laborious going but we finally made it out of the channels and sped toward the scene.

While we were underway we could hear sounds of loud explosions. Even at a distance, the fog took on a pinkish hue indicating an extensive area was involved in the fire. As we got closer, our worst fears were realized. The entire surface around the ships was on fire, fed by a floating mixture of oil and gasoline. The fire enveloped the two remaining ships afloat; the ammunition ship and the oil tanker. The gasoline tanker had already sunk. The heat given off by the large body of fire was so intense that it had partially lifted the fog from the immediate vicinity which helped in our rescue efforts. We approached as far as the flames allowed and sounded bells and whistles to announce our presence and direction from the accident scene. The captain ordered to me keep directing an intermittent light from our blinker to guide any survivors to the ship. (During a fog it is difficult to determine the direction that a fog horn or bell is originating from.) The horror scenes that were to unfold for the ensuing three days still plague me half a century later!

Some seamen, very few, had managed to make it through the flames in small boats. One sight I cannot forget. In what appeared to be a common rowboat, a sailor, his face blackened with soot, was propelling the boat with a single oar. At the bow was the only other occupant. His arm was draped over the side of the rowboat and he was very badly burned and appeared to be dead. His buddy at the oar was yelling, "We made it, Mate!", all the while as we took him aboard. He was cautioning us to be careful, as his mate's arm, dangling over the side, was being smashed between the boat and our ship with the rise and fall of the waves. When we got him aboard, he was indeed dead, but his buddy kept repeating, "We made it, Mate." The poor fellow was in shock from the experience.

The surface fire continued to burn throughout the night and into the next day. Just when it appeared that the ammo ship would no longer explode it would start another round. The grisly task of picking the oil-soaked and hardly recognizable bodies from the sea continued. The next day, as the fog partially lifted a high ranking naval officer came aboard and assumed control of the rescue and salvage operations. Several other ships had joined in the rescue operations. The "Hibiscus" became the center of communications and radio channels became so overloaded that all communications between ships was to be by blinker light only. Being the only member on the bridge that could read blinker accurately, the captain ordered me to remain on the flying bridge without relief until the operations were concluded. I took my mattress from the bunkroom and placed it on the deck, next to the blinker light to get whatever shut-eye I could manage between signals.

I was assigned a seaman as a recorder that would also stand watch at night while I attempted to sleep. I would be awakened by a kick in the ribs with the first sign of a blinker light. Actually, I didn't mind this arrangement as it shielded me from the scenes of horror developing on deck. At last count, the deck was stacked with twenty-eight bodies most of which were burned beyond recognition.

It wasn't until the third day that the ammunition ship ceased exploding. It was later towed to a nearby port. Meanwhile, the Hibiscus made way for a hospital in New Bedford, Massachusetts, which was to receive the few survivors that we managed to rescue, and the dead we had stacked on our deck.

While underway, our executive officer assumed control on the bridge, as I logged my activities for the last three days. He then suggested I take one of the seamen to the buoy deck with me and log the dog tags from each of the dead for identification. It was all I could do to keep awake after the three-day vigil at the blinker light. I was ready to explode at the suggestion, as there were many well-rested members available from the bridge force. In addition, I doubt that I could have carried out the request given the condition of the bodies on the deck.

Fortunately, Boatswain's Mate Neil, the 1st Class Non-Com Officer was on the bridge. He sensed there was going to be a problem with that request from my reaction. He also had been one of the many recorders during my three-day stint at the light without relief. Before it went any further, Boatswain's Mate Neil told the executive officer that he and one of his crew had already obtained preliminary information on the identifications and volunteered to complete the job. From that day forward, I was deeply indebted to Boatswain's Mate 1st Class Neil!

CAPTAIN'S MAST

Shortly after the Buzzard's Bay disaster, the executive officer was replaced by a Lieutenant Seavey, a career officer. In contrast to the ninety-day wonder officers, he was a welcome replacement. We got along fine, especially when he learned that the captain had entrusted me with preparing "The Monthly Report of Operations", which was normally the duty of the executive officer. All he had to do was review the report before submitting it to the captain. He appeared to be a good, stable, reliable officer, and indeed he was, that is, while he was sober - under the influence of liquor was another story.

We were tied up in South Portland, Maine. It was a bitterly cold night, and I was stationed on the bridge as I had the midnight to 4 a.m. quartermaster watch. One of the duties was to distribute liberty cards to the off going platoon. On return from liberty, the seaman's cards were again placed in a file box kept on the bridge. The quartermaster was responsible for the ship's security, and carried the only firearm, a fully loaded Colt 45. There was also a fire watch performed by a seaman, who made half-hourly rounds of the ship, and reported the results to the quartermaster, which would be entered in the log. Except for the nasty weather outside the night had been uneventful.

At 0100 (1 a.m.), Mr. Seavey staggered aboard, drunk as a skunk, and barely made it up the gang plank. He dispensed with the formality, customary on reporting aboard ship, and just stormed onto the Bridge and demanded to see the file of the liberty cards.

I presented the file to him, thinking he wanted to act out some supervisory acumen. As calming overtures, I bade him a pleasant good evening and welcomed him aboard. I almost sensed what was coming next. Lieutenant Seavey let out a volley of invectives, and suddenly flung the liberty cards across the deck of the bridge, scattering them all over. I didn't say a word and proceeded to pick up the cards from the floor. While I was bent over, Mr. Seavey, with the toe of his shoe, planted a kick that caught me in a most sensitive area between my butt and the jewelry. The pain was excruciating and the kick sent me pitching forward. I quickly got up and decided to call the fire watch, Maybe together we could calm him. He was acting like a maniac! However, as I got up, he lunged at me with a punch which I just managed to evade. With the forward impetus of the punch, and my instinctive reaction to ward off the blow, **somehow** my elbow managed to crash forcefully against his temple. The combination of his drunken state and the **accidental** blow to the head rendered Mr. Seavey unconscious and sprawled out on the deck floor.

Again that dark cloud! How did I get into this situation? What was going to be his reaction when he came to and sobered up? By now the fire watch had come to the bridge. He had heard the commotion as Mr. Seavey boarded the ship. The liberty cards were still strewn over the deck and I couldn't revive the Lieutenant. I then related to the fire watch what had transpired on the bridge, exactly as he would respond when questioned. I only left out one detail of the actual occurrence. With that part resolved, I again attempted to revive Mr. Seavey but was unsuccessful.

Finally, with the fire watch's help, we carried Mr. Seavey to his cabin in "officers country" the only real habitable part of this type vessel. He still hadn't come to, so I removed his socks and shoes, and the shirt that he had slobbered over. We then laid him snugly in his bunk and covered him with a blanket. Before leaving I checked and saw that he was breathing evenly but heavily and moaning occasionally. I took off his wrist watch, a multi-function type with many protruding stems, lest he might scratch his face while sleeping and placed it in a compartment of one of his upright desk drawers.

We then left to resume our duties. Later, I had the fire watch relieve me temporarily and I rechecked Mr. Seavey's condition. He appeared to be okay. My watch was over at 0400 and I was relieved by

Quartermaster Cleveland, and recounted, as I told the fire watch, that Mr. Seavey had struck his head on the navigator's balls. There is no pun intended here. The navigator's balls are two solid metal balls almost the size of bowling balls, set on either side of the magnetic compass. They are used to compensate for local magnetic attraction which may affect the reading. The pain from the kick I had received was so intense that sleeping was out of the question. I tried some cold applications and finally made it to the bunkroom. I was still awake at 0700, when Boatswain's Mate 1st Class Neil came to the bunk room to inform me that I was to report to captain's quarters, in full dress blue uniform at 0800 sharp. I was to stand captain's mast, which is the Navy version of an Army court martial. During wartime it is a very serious business.

Upon conviction it could mean life imprisonment! Looks like I finally did it! Quoting Yogi, "It's déjà vu all over again." I may as well go out clean, so I shaved and showered, and at 0800 sharp reported to the captain's quarters.

All the ship's officers were seated in a semi-circle, in full dress. The 1st Class Yeoman was there with pad and tape to record the hearing. I felt this was the end of the war for me. When others would be going home, I would be rotting in a federal prison. By this time I'm sure the captain was aware of the condition Mr. Seavey was in when he arrived at the base. He had kicked over the pot-belly coal-fired stove at the security shack manned by the Marines. The Marines on duty not only had to contend with putting the fire out but they lost their source of heat. To recount Mr. Seavey's actions would be redundant and probably work against me. The atmosphere was one of hostility and suspicion. I had no choice but to give the account that I had gone over with the fire watch. Finally the Captain spoke:

Captain: "Before we begin the formal proceedings, I'm going to give you the opportunity to give us your version on what happened on the bridge with Mr. Seavey."

Chiarelli: "Mr. Seavey arrived aboard during my watch at 0100. When he came to the bridge to check the liberty cards, I could see he wasn't feeling too well as he was a bit unsteady. When I approached to assist Mr. Seavey, he apparently stumbled near the ship's compass, and I believe he struck his head on one of the navigator's balls. I helped Mr. Seavey up and asked if I could assist him to his cabin which I did with the help of the fire watch on duty."

Captain: "All right, Chiarelli, we know Mr. Seavey wasn't feeling well. Just continue and don't leave out anything."

Chiarelli: "We assisted Mr. Seavey to his cabin and helped him into his bunk. To make him more comfortable, I removed his shoes and socks." (I didn't mention the slobbered shirt.)

Captain: "Okay, then what happened? What did you do after?"

Chiarelli: "Seeing Mr. Seavey was comfortable, I sent the fire watch to resume his duties, and I returned to the bridge."

Captain: "Is that all you have to say?"

Chiarelli: "Yes Sir."

Captain: "Think carefully before you answer now, as this is a very serious matter." (long pause, then...) "What became of Mr. Seavey's watch?"

Chiarelli: (Stopping to think, since what I did was a reflex action, as I always removed my watch on retiring) "Oh, that, I removed the watch and placed it in his desk compartment."

Captain: "In that case it should still be there, shouldn't it?"

Chiarelli: "Yes Sir, it should." (It was now evident that the main charge here was suspected thievery, as it was a very expensive watch. There was also a recent rash of lockers broken into and personal belongings missing.)

Captain: "Okay, we will go to the cabin together, and you will show where you put the watch."

As we were going to the cabin I began to think - what if the watch is no longer there? What if the fire watch had returned and *he* had taken it? Suppose Mr. Seavey only claimed the watch missing to exact revenge for the bump at his temple from the *accidental* contact with my elbow?

They evidently thought I stole the watch. Maybe they thought I was also involved with the rash of valuables missing. As a quartermaster, I had full run of the ship when all were asleep. What do I do now if the watch is no longer there?

Everyone except Mr. Seavey filed into the cabin.

Captain: "Okay Chiarelli, show me where Mr. Seavey's watch is."

Whereupon I opened one of the 4 inch by 4 inch drawers, and my heart sank when it was empty. I quickly opened the next two drawers on the same side, and thank the Lord, the watch was exactly where I had put it. I can't explain how the whole atmosphere changed. I could see all the officers were relieved, none more, it seemed, than Mr. Seavey himself. The others were almost apologetic and all charges were immediately dropped. Apparently, Mr. Seavey was vaguely aware of his actions on the bridge at the time of his *accident*. They were more concerned that one of the bridge force might be a thief. Had that been the case they were all prepared to make me an example by exacting swift and harsh punishment.

I firmly believe that had the watch not appeared "assault on an officer" would have been added to the charges. They never did apprehend whoever was ransacking lockers. Another interesting aside, my locker was never broken into, although never locked, while other nearby lockers were forcefully broken into and robbed. I was beginning to suspect myself!

What a relief that this dangerous and unpleasant episode was over. Enlisted men had been sent to prison during the war for far less serious infractions. Some were imprisoned for the duration and beyond. By his actions after this incident it was clear that Mr. Seavey regretted his actions of that night.

MAN OVERBOARD

My first bona fide rescue came about unexpectedly while I was on quartermaster watch as the Hibiscus was tied-up (docked) in Portland, Maine. I had the midnight to 8:00 a.m. watch and was on the bridge, in the wheelhouse, when I heard a loud "crack" as one of the seamen coming aboard from liberty was midway on the gangplank between the dock and the ship's deck. I saw him disappear as he fell into the void between the ship and the dock. At about the same time the deck watch, alerted by the loud cracking sound of the breaking plank yelled "MAN OVERBOARD!" I ran out to the outboard wing and looked down the side, expecting the worst, as the ship was gently heaving against the dock. It was separated only by the "camel" (a 12-inch diameter log). Somehow the seaman had managed to escape being crushed by the action of the ships pitching and rolling. I could see he was precariously perched just above the "camel" on a heavy timber cross member of the pier.

Visibility was poor in the dim light of approaching dawn but there was enough to see he was slipping on the cross member. He kept screaming in his half drunken stupor and I was afraid that he may already have had his dangling leg crushed. I told the deck watch to go below for help. I then took the life preserver located on the wing and made a quick "clove hitch" on the bridge railing and lowered myself down the side as he ran for assistance. As I got below, all I could do was balance myself with the rope of the preserver and ride with one foot on the slimy "camel" and the other stretched out against the cross member of the dock. It was an untenable position, but it was enough to keep the seaman from falling and being crushed between the ship and the dock. It must have been a matter of minutes but it felt like hours before additional help arrived. In fact the loud crack of the gangplank snapping in two had already alerted a few seamen as the simultaneous cry of man overboard was called out. I kept doing a dance on the rolling "camel" and was only kept aloft by my straining on the thin lifeline rope which was not designed to sustain weight. After what seemed like an eternity, a rope, looped at the end, was finally lowered. One of the seamen, on another more secure rope, lowered himself down to place the rope around the half-conscious victim. I couldn't help secure him into the lowered rope for it was all I could do to maintain my balance on the two slimy surfaces of the camel and crossbeam. I was counter balanced only by a thin rope hastily, and not too steadily, secured by a half hitch clove on the ship's rail.

They finally lifted him out from the hellish abyss. Instead of being grateful for my part in retrieving him from a possibly fatal, and certain injurious situation, he was abusive and blamed me for his having fallen in the first place. I attributed this outburst to his inebriated bruised condition and to shock. He was of course partly correct in stating it was my fault "in the first place." I had the quartermaster watch and was responsible for anything that took place during my tour of duty. As is common knowledge among seamen, the rise and fall of the tides between highs and lows is quite a large spread at the latitude we were located. In fact more northerly, at the Bay of Fundy, there is a difference of more than fifty feet between high and low tide. For that reason, our fire and deck watch crewmen, during their half hourly rounds, would check the lashings securing the gangplank for adequate slack. The slack would be adjusted, as required, with the rise and fall of the tide. In this case the slack had either not been adjusted properly, or not at all for periods of time. That, together with a surge of waves occasioned by a passing tanker, had caused a pitch and roll creating a strain that caused the gangplank to snap in half. According to the deck watch the slack had been checked an hour earlier and reported to me as sufficient. It may very well have been so. However, the responsibility eventually rests with the quartermaster on duty. After an investigation by the bridge officer and carpenters mate, the exact cause was inconclusive.

The officers had initially decided to let me off with a reprimand as I hadn't actually checked the slack. However, after reviewing the action taken in putting myself at personal risk to keep the seaman from being crushed until additional help was summoned, that too was dropped.

A LIBERTY TO REMEMBER

One evening we were docked at East Boston, Massachusetts. I was given a liberty pass good from 6 pm to 6 am the next day. Together with others of the bridge gang, we hailed a taxi and decided to spend the time in the big city known as "The Hub." It was a treat for us as most liberties were in sparsely populated areas close to a docking base.

All the guys decided to take in a move which was not to my liking so I was left on my own. I had a few dollars and a monthly government check for a big $26. Seeking to kill some time while I decided how to spend the liberty and to have the check cashed, I stepped into a classy looking tavern on Main Street. I sat on a stool at the bar and ordered a drink of rye and gingerale. I figured on having a couple of drinks. I would pay the tab by check. The bartender, however, would not accept payment. He declared that "No serviceman's money was good at his bar." So I decided the one drink was enough and would try another place to have the big check cashed.

With that, a patron at the end of the bar, who evidently had one too many, came over to me and ordered the bartender to "Give the sailor a drink on me." To demonstrate his affection for men in the Services, he graced me with a playful hug around the neck. In his drunken state he staggered as I attempted to get untangled from this unwelcome embrace. This grappling resulted in my being knocked off the stool and we both went tumbling to the bar room floor with the fall cushioned by my head. I got up, dazed, and quickly departed before I was maimed by the loving attention.

It was nearly dark when I spotted Boston's most famous billiard parlor located on Main Street. I went in, hoping the place would provide some action and that maybe I could get my check cashed. The place was busy and all the tables were fully occupied except for the corner of the parlor where a tournament-sized three-cushion billiard table was located. A gentleman was at the table practicing three cushion billiard shots. He appeared to be a good shot as I watched him while sitting at one of the stools provided for spectators. After a while he gave me a "Hi, Sailor," and asked if I played three-cushion billiards. He was glad to hear that I did and asked if I would be interested in playing a fifteen point match, with the loser to pay for the time on the play clock. I though that was great, since even if I lost I could have the $26 check cashed. I won two of the three games we played and I never saw a guy so happy at losing. He then asked if I played pocket pool. I told him that was really my game, not three-cushion billiards. We became very friendly and exchanged names.

He then suggested we play a round of straight pool on a table that had become available. He seemed to be a likable chap and I wondered if he could afford to pay the bill for the time that was running on the clock, as his suit sorely needed pressing and appeared to have been slept in for a week. I made him a proposition that we would continue playing but only on the condition that we split paying for the time on the clock. He gave me a quizzical look, but agreed. I now felt that I could play my normal game without feeling guilty that I was hustling the poor guy. I won the three games we played. He was again delighted. I later found out why.

Before I knew what was going on, an attendant brought him a damp and a dry towel. I got no such VIP attention. When I tried to pay my share on the time clock, the manager declared all was taken care of. I told Murray that since he had paid the tab, I was going to take him to the delicatessen across the street and treat him to a beer and a pastrami sandwich. At first he looked at his watch and declined, but changed his mind when we got to the street.

To my surprise he hailed a cab and told the driver to take us to the Mayflower Hotel, which was the most famous, classiest, and most expensive hotel in all of Boston. When I heard his instruction to the cab driver I regretted the offer I made him. I told Murray I was not going to back out of our deal, but we would have to get my $26 check cashed. He said there would be no problem.

When we got to the hotel he received quite a reception from the doorman and the Maitre'd. It was obvious that this guy was toying with me and that he was a very influential guy in town. The place was packed to the rafters and there was a floor show in progress. Murray was provided with a necktie by the host -- as I said, it was a classy joint. Next a spot was cleared by the floor show and a table for two inserted. A bottle of the best Scotch whiskey and set ups were brought automatically. I told Murray I didn't drink Scotch and that just one glass of rye and gingerale would be OK with me. However, they brought a quart of Canadian Club with the set-ups.

During intermission I got to know more about my newly found companion. His name was Murray Rosenthal. He owned five shoe factories, one of which was the famous Mary Jane Shoes. He was a very rich bachelor and he loved to gamble, especially on pocket billiards.

It wasn't uncommon for him to win or lose up to $10,000 in one session of playing cards in a sociable game with some of his business associates and competitors. He made me promise that I would contact him when I got to spend another liberty in Boston. He wanted to arrange a match with some of his pool playing associates. This explained his uncommon jubilation as I was running off rack after rack in our pocket pool match earlier that evening. As the night wore on we became quite friendly and he made me an offer that was difficult to refuse.

He offered me a public relations position in his corporation. I would answer only to him. The salary he mentioned was overly generous and several times more than I was earning in the Sanitation Department. He was anxious to have me play pool against one of his associates that he claimed was "into him for a bundle." I thanked him for his interest and promised I would give his offer serious consideration. I then told him I was to be married the following month on the 22nd of October and wasn't sure if my future wife would be willing to relocate to Massachusetts. I did, however, promise to look him up after the war was over.

I soon discovered that this hotel became the meeting place for all the musicians, stand-up comedians and show people after all the other night clubs closed down at 1 am with Boston's Blue Laws. There it became a private party where they would all unwind. It seemed that everyone knew Murray and came to his table. I was introduced to Benny Goodman, many top comedians from other clubs and Johnny Johnson who was a big band singer at the time. Also present was the cast from the play "Marinka," which had gotten rave reviews. The way I was received by all his friends you would think I was a famous general instead of a lowly sailor.

By 3:30 am the party ended and the whole gang congregated outside where a fleet of taxicabs was lined up. When I got into the back seat one of the girls from the "Marinka" troupe landed on my lap declaring, "I got here first, he's mine." I didn't realize I was up for grabs. The cab took us to a famous Chinese restaurant called Ruby Foo's which had been closed to business for hours. The cleaning crew was mopping up. When the manager was summoned to the door and notified that Murray and his entourage had arrived, the restaurant was reopened for yet another private party. The kitchen served out delicacies in abundance. This continued till almost 5 am. Being a worldly guy, and thinking in terms of the reputation attributed to sailors in general, Murray told me that to cap of the liberty I could have any of the chorus line girls from the club. When I reminded him that I was to be married the following month he respected my decision to decline the invitation. He said he wasn't surprised that I turned down the offer and was gratified to see that I had a sense of loyalty.

I thanked Murray for showing me a heck of a good time. He laughed when I recounted how my liberty had started by getting my head bashed on the bar room floor while I was only trying to get my check cashed.

"By the way, Murray," I told him, "I'm still stuck with this $26 check." He made me promise to contact him when I was in town again. I told him I felt like Freddie the Freeloader since I never got to buy him that pastrami sandwich. He then asked if I had enough cash for a taxicab back to my base. I said I did. "OK," Murray said, "Drop me off at my hotel and you have enough time to get back to the ship."

That's how it ended. I dropped him off and left with a hearty handshake. I had just barely enough to pay the cab fare. The cabby wasn't interested in taking the cab fare from my $26 check, so I had him wait while I went aboard for some extra cash to give him a respectable tip.

Until the day of my discharge I never contacted Murray. I did not feel comfortable in situations where someone else is picking up all the tabs. I did call him as I promised after I returned to civilian life. He reminded me of the generous offer we had discussed. I told him my wife was reluctant to relocate to another state. Without being overbearing, he said the offer would remain open. With all the perks and the expense account it would have been about ten times what I was earning. I was still considering making the move until the time that I was called for the position of Fireman in the NYFD. The money situation didn't change much, but at least it was what I wanted to do. The decision also kept peace in the family.

Many years later, on returning from a vacation trip in Canada, I drove into Boston and decided to surprise Murray and take him to dinner. This was my small way of repaying him for the unforgettable day in September of 1944. I was never able to locate him. The shoe factories were gone and he wasn't in the phone book. The phone number I had was no longer in service. Almost twelve years had passed from our meeting and many changes had been made. If he was still in Boston I was never able to find him in three days of searching.

In 1962 I met Johnny Johnson whom I had originally been introduced to by Murray at the Mayflower Hotel. Johnny was to play Willie Mosconi in an exhibition match at the Golden Cue in Mineola. He never got to the table as the unbeatable Mosconi ran off 150 points. Johnny had been a state billiards champion. He was reputed to have played the comedian Jackie Gleason (himself a good player) by giving Jackie a big 100:30 handicap.

After his match with Mosconi, Johnny watched as I played a match with the house champ. I won easily. Mr. Johnson then invited me to play him in a televised exhibition match being sponsored by AMF to be held at the Pepsi-Cola building in Manhattan. He was taking on all comers to the delight of a packed audience. At the time I was stationed at Welfare Island as an instructor in the Fire Department Training School and was nearing retirement. AMF manufactured billiard tables and other sporting equipment and was currently promoting pool matches utilizing celebrities and professional billiard players in televised exhibitions. I was advised before the match with Johnny that a good showing might result in my being offered a position by AMF in their promotional campaign. I never expected the fanfare on this publicized event when I arrived at the Pepsi-Cola building.

The lobby, which was bedecked in luxurious red carpeting, was filled with hundreds of spectators. The pool table was located in the center with the playing area roped off by red satin dividers. Two scantily-clad models were the score keepers. I was asked my name which was to be printed on a large blackboard. Instead of giving my own name, Carmelo Guiseppe Chiarelli, I gave the name of my nephew, Ralph Tilelli, for brevity. Ralph had left a construction job that he was supervising so that he could witness the match and provide moral support.

Johnny Johnson was in good form as he displayed some fancy trick shots. He then played the first of the 75 point straight pool matches. He won handily. I must admit that I was nervous as I stepped up to the table for my match.

I had never played before TV cameras or such a large audience. Another distraction was the scantily-dressed models calling out my shots to the audience and marking the score on the blackboard. This resulted in my having to wait about 15 seconds between shots. I got off to a very slow start and felt that I would be an embarrassment to the crowd and to my nephew.

Determined to shake the nervousness and fully concentrate on the game, I looked at Ralph who gave me an encouraging sign. On my next trip to the table I ran a couple of racks that put me back into the game. I was then faced with a very difficult break shot to keep the consecutive run going. The smart play here was to play a safety. Instead, I gave my nephew a wink and called the shot to break open the balls. Confident that the shot would be missed, my opponent approached the table ready to shoot. From the very fine cut shot, the called ball slowly went towards the called pocket while the balls from the rack that had been broken open, were dangerously rolling over the path at many times the speed of the ball crawling towards the pocket.

When that ball dropped into the pocket there was a roar of appreciation from the crowd. Even the scoring models, originally and understandably rooting for the host, came over and extended a handshake and a hug. That almost unbelievable shot unnerved Johnny. I went on to win the match.

An official game is not 75 points -- 150 points is. However, I had the distinction of beating Johnny Johnson, who, in five years of playing matches with professionals, had lost only to the legendary Willie Mosconi. Johnny was so good that if we continued playing I probably would have lost the next five games!

CALL TO FIRE DEPARTMENT

ENGINE COMPANY 280

In March, 1948 I finally got the call from the Fire Department. I was directed to report to the Probationary Fireman's Training School, which at the time was located on the east side of Manhattan, on 68th Street. The head of the school was a rough, tough, burly Irishman with thick bushy eyebrows by the name of Captain McGinty. He was a strict disciplinarian and barked out orders with authority.

The Fire Department is a semi-military organization, at least it was, and the training included marching, close order drills, and many other activities common to the military services. Also, as was the practice in the service, probationary firemen were whipped into shape with daily exercise routines. These included marching, running laps within the compound, pushups and other activities to promote and maintain strength and agility.

Trainees were introduced to tools of the job and performed hose stretches up stairs, fire escapes and into cellars, with settings made as realistically as possible. We were exposed to smoke in a "smoke room" with and without the benefit of masks. We climbed ladders, raised ladders, and were introduced to burst hoselines during operations and how to quickly snap on a hose jacket as an emergency repair without interrupting the flow of water. Many of these operations became more realistic when the training school was relocated to Welfare Island in 1960. At the latter location, building contents were actually set on fire and attacked with charged hose lines under the close supervision of the training officers.

As was then the custom, while still assigned to the training school, near the end of the training period we were also assigned to an operating engine or hook and ladder company for on the job training.

We responded to fires and all other emergencies. When possible, the probie was put in a group working with a captain or a senior lieutenant, who would keep the probie close and not allow him to venture into a fire situation alone. As expected, the probie was given all the tedious and unpleasant duties. The officer would also assign a senior experienced fire fighter to teach the probie the finer points of the job. You got to know the exact location of all the tools on the rig because it was your job to keep them spotless, and replace them to their designated locations. Two of the fire fighters assigned to me were Ben Stern and Victor Vitale. Two distinct and opposite personalities, Ben was very serious and proper while Vic had more of a "devil may care" attitude. Both, however, were excellent fire fighters.

By some coincidence, every time that I reported for duty at the fire house, no sooner did I step into the building and sometimes just into the block, when the alarm bells banged out a signal for a fire that we were first due at. It got to the point that as soon as I was spotted coming in to work, even from the corner of the street, the company got ready to roll. It became the joke of the company. I learned some very important lessons that were later a factor in survival during various types of fire and emergency operations.

On one occasion, while responding to a fire in a cellar at a location where our company was the third due, I happened to stray away from Lieutenant Mulligan. He had gone to report to the battalion chief in charge of the operation for orders and momentarily left me by the engine. I was fascinated by the large amount of heavy black smoke coming out of the cellar at the front of the building. I decided to get a realistic whiff of this stuff during actual fire conditions, as opposed to the man made stuff at the training school.

There was a hose line stretched, but not yet charged with water. The men of the first due engine company were on the line but no one was in the stairwell where all the smoke emanated from. After all, why should they be? We were taught not to advance into a fire without a charged hose line. However, I stepped down into the well until I became completely enveloped in smoke. Meanwhile, the hose line became charged, and a couple of firemen of the first due company advanced down to my level. The chief was at the top of the well barking orders for them to advance further, but that was as far as they went. Before I knew what happened, the hose line was thrust into my hands and in the next instant I could hear the thick Irish brogue of the battalion chief as he yelled, "Get down in there!" He accompanied that with a kick on my back at the shoulders that sent me and the hose line tumbling down the stairs to the floor of the basement. At least I had learned enough to keep the hose line open. It had plenty of back kick, but I held on and shot the stream wildly all over. I was partially in shock to find myself in this unanticipated situation with a hose line that was difficult for one man to control.

Meanwhile, the officer of the first due company, whose line I was now operating, noted that his men were all accounted for at the top of the well and in the street while water was being splashed all over the basement. No one at this time had a gas mask. They were not provided to everyone in 1948. I got more of a feed of smoke than I had bargained for and my impulse was to drop the line and run. I wasn't supposed to be there in the first place. Before I had to make that decision I was relieved of the hose line, unceremoniously at that, by two firemen of the first due company. Meanwhile, up the street Lieutenant Mulligan was going bananas wondering at what happened to the probie who was his responsibility.

He was both relieved and angry when he saw me emerging from the column of smoke. I was a sorry sight with a soot blackened face and smoke columns at my nostrils. I won't repeat what Lieutenant Mulligan bombarded me with, but that was the last time I made the same mistake. Even the chief who kicked me down the stairwell and the members of the first due company didn't know who the mystery fireman in the smoke filled stair was. To allow for the lesson from this experience to sink in, Lieutenant Mulligan assigned some extra duty tasks for me, none of them pleasant.

Until the training schedule was completed, my time was shared between the school and Engine Company 280 in Brooklyn. On one occasion, we were being schooled on the use of the life net and its limitations. To demonstrate, the training officer had one of the probies jump off the second floor landing of the fire escape. Then, stressing that any jump over three stories was dangerous, he asked for a volunteer to make the jump. Without waiting for a response he called, "You Chiarelli, would you like to make the jump?" You don't refuse such invitations so I climbed to the third floor landing prepared to leap. Even from that height the net looks pretty small. Captain McGinty stood by the net to check that the men were properly positioned before he gave the signal for me to go ahead with the jump. When he asked if I was ready I replied that it looked too easy and that I would execute a one and one half gainer into the net. He replied, "You do anything like that and you better not land." Of course I had no intention. I was unsure as it was that I would land in the proper position in the net. The jump was captured on film. After that year, the net jumps were limited, as some serious injuries had resulted. Even from a second floor level, if one does not land properly, injury to the neck and back can be expected.

The next day, as we were breaking for lunch, the chief's driver told me to report to Captain McGinty's office. As I was on my way to the office I wondered if I was to pay for the one and one half gainer wisecrack at the life net operation. When I got to the office, Captain McGinty had my file on his desk. He noted that I had worked as an auto mechanic for the city and asked if I still had my tools. I said that I did. He then asked if I thought I could bring back to life the old hook and ladder truck at the school that had been idle for years. It had only been used for training, as the ladder itself was operated manually. I agreed to give it a try. Resurrecting an engine that had been dead for many years (no one knew how many) wouldn't be easy but I accepted the challenge. The next day I came in with my tools and worked on that engine for the next two days. When the time came to test if the resurrection was successful, the chief had his driver at the controls in the driver's seat, Captain McGinty and the probies took a position a safe distance away to witness the event. I then positioned myself, laying on the running board with the hood open, to check the operation of the controls. I then gave the signal for the driver to start the engine. As the engine was cranked, there was a tremendous explosion accompanied by a cloud of smoke that completely enveloped the hook and ladder and me on the running board. I was so embarrassed that I hoped the cloud would never lift. When it finally lifted, I jumped into the cab and saw that the driver had not retarded the spark lever. We tried again with the spark retarded and the engine sprang to life, much to my relief, and was accompanied by the cheers and applause of the entire class.

At the end of the training period all the graduates were assigned to permanent companies. This was a small class of forty-five, and all didn't survive the training. One in particular that I remember, was a probie who froze completely midway up the thirty five foot ladder. He had a death grip on the rungs and wouldn't let go as two of the training officers tried to help him down. It took some doing to get him down. Ladders were raised adjacent to the one he was on for both moral and physical support. When they finally got him down he decided to quit right on the spot. He was obliged on his request, as he would have been a danger to himself and to others with his phobia. Another resignation was tendered on the spot, after exposure to the smoke room. A few were held over for additional training. The lucky ones were assigned to active companies.

I was pleased to learn that I had been assigned to Engine Company 280, where I had served my on the job training. I soon learned that about a year earlier, the company had been involved in a scandal and except for the Company Building Inspector, Fireman Ritzo, the entire company personnel was replaced. The roof of the fire house was on a level with buildings extending towards a hospital on Washington Avenue. One of these buildings housed the nurses who were assigned to Prospect Hospital. Since the fire fighters had been trained to be aggressive and opportunistic it wasn't long before there was some co-mingling taking place on the roofs, and who knows, possibly in quarters in the dead of night. Seems that every move I made had been subject to controversy so it was only fitting that I drew Engine Company 280. It wasn't the busiest company, but we got our share of workers, especially in the Bedford Stuyvesant section. Now that I was working regular tours I got to know all the members of the company. That's when it became apparent that the fire service attracted people from all walks of life and every conceivable trade before joining the department.

We had lawyers who had given up their practices, with some still doing part-time work, Frank Ricciardi, a cracker jack radio and TV man, insurance men, carpenters, electricians, butchers, and yes, bakers. We even had a milk company representative, Jim Hussey. Bill Kamerling was an ace salesman for a home improvement company. He was also very superstitious and would not change his undershirt while he was on a roll in sales. So when he stunk up the kitchen, you knew business was good. Surprisingly enough, many of these men with outside interests made good, aggressive firemen, and could be counted on in a crisis situation. Sid Rosen, our moonlighting kosher butcher, always came to work on his night tours armed with enough flank steak to feed two working shifts. The only catch was that he was a lousy cook and either myself, Marty Seery, our MPO, or Lou Vaio would have to prepare exotic marinades and cook Sid's charitable offerings.

We had some good cooks in our company. Many had specialties. My speciality was Pasta Fagioli, a power packed Italian bean dish. It provided a rib sticking hot meal, especially good on cold winter days. It was also popular because it cost each man only about sixty cents for a king-sized portion. Like any other good thing, this meal had a significant side effect which manifested in the bunkroom during the night as stacatto passages which punctuated the sounding of the alarm bells. We had a temperamental Argentinean, Charlie Deza, who specialized in chef salads. He was infamous for the alien, exotic ingredients that he introduced into his concoctions. On one occasion, when his salad was broken down, in cost, at five times the rest of the meal, he was summarily dismissed from performing any further culinary miracles.

We covered the gamut of every nationality, ethnicity, and religion. We had single, married, divorced, and whatever in the company. One hybrid, Bill Keane, I believe was part English but was a devout practicing Catholic. He already had eleven children and his wife was pregnant with the twelfth. I was raised a Catholic, as were others in the company, and we chided him on this as being unfair to his wife. We also reminded him of the availability of condoms. This line of conversation got Bill a bit testy and he remarked that the church does not approve of condoms. When I jokingly suggested that he have the condoms blessed, although I said that in jest, Bill didn't speak to me for weeks and only after repeated apologies. With the paltry salaries we made at the time he was eligible for family assistance but was too proud to apply. Here was a devoted couple who were into practicing rhythm, neither of which could carry a simple tune. Another Fireman, single at the time, rode around with the sorriest pile of junk for a car. A week didn't pass that I didn't have to do some repair work just to keep it running.

One day, Lou Vaio came to me and confided that he had a serious personal dilemma. He was engaged to this fine Irish girl for some time and she presented him with an ultimatum, "Either we get married soon or we part our ways." He then told me he needed a new car as another fender had fallen off his twenty-two year old Buick. Remembering that car meant full-time, pro-bono employment for me, without hesitation, I urged him to get a new car first. Of course he didn't heed my advice and I had a great time at their wedding. To this day, they remain very good friends except that his wife wishes he had heeded my advice. He never did get a new car.

Lest one gets the impression that I am portraying all fire fighters as heroes, let's set the record straight. ALL FIREMEN ARE NOT HEROES. As in every case involving large groups, despite all the safeguards and tests, some undesirables slip through the cracks.

Fortunately, due to the testing and the screening, very few make it into the department mainstream. A few examples come to mind.

THE ACTOR. We had one in Engine Company 280, who had a cute act until the brothers put him on notice. While some members were occupied fighting a fire in an apartment he would actually smear some soot on his face and step out into the hall, or stoop and appear to be an over stressed hero, while in fact he was taking a breather at the expense of the brothers operating at the fire. To protect the guilty, let's call him Fireman Oscar, as he was deserving of the award. I was exposed to this act twice and that's where it ended.

My first year on the job we had a good working fire in a restaurant on Eastern Parkway in Brooklyn. In responding to the blaze I was driving the hose wagon. (We were a two-piece engine company.) After I made the run for the hose to be stretched by the two fire fighters on the back step, I proceeded to park the rig so as not to impede our operation and other incoming apparatus. The smoke from the fire filled an entire street as I started to run to the restaurant after parking the hose wagon. As I ran into the block I passed Fireman Oscar who was running in the opposite direction. Without stopping, he told me our Captain McConnell was alone on the nozzle. That is a cardinal sin in the department. No one should ever be left alone on the nozzle, let alone the captain. As I ran into the building to relieve the captain, I wondered where in hell Fireman Oscar was headed and why the officer was left alone. It was a really hot fire. At one point I had to get down on one knee. The floor was so hot that the momentary contact resulted in a blister the size of a baseball. When we returned to quarters the actor gave a weak excuse (which was no excuse at all). Except for the action by Fireman Oscar, it was a neat operation as Joe Doyle rushed in to join me at the nozzle.

The only casualty was the twenty pound turkey left boiling in the huge covered pot on the stove. The proprietor, thankful for the minimum damage incurred by our operation, begged our captain to take the turkey back to quarters. He claimed he wouldn't be permitted to serve it by the Health Department. The captain finally consented. After all, aren't we "smoke eaters"? Turkey sandwiches were served for the next two tours of incoming and outgoing platoons. After this and another incident by the actor, I put him on notice that his act would no longer be tolerated. I'm sure Joe Doyle and the captain also had a word with him. He was later promoted and left the company. As an officer, I wondered how he would ever find an audience for his act. Unlike other departments, officers in the fire department are usually the first into a fire to make sure that conditions are safe for his crew. It is no secret that good fire officers lead by example!

Chapter 8

FIRE OPERATIONS

MATTRESS FACTORY, BABY IN THERE, LEAP TO SAFETY, ANGEL OF DEATH, FAT LADY HOLIDAY FIRES

1ST YEAR ON THE JOB

It was 2 am. We had returned from a routine fire. After the hose was removed from the pumper, washed and hung in the hose tower, I went up to the bunk room to rest as I had the 3 am to 6 am housewatch. As I laid on the bunk it was difficult to understand my feelings. From the age of 16 on, I had always worked very hard for a living and here I was, laying on my back and being paid for it. It was almost a feeling of guilt.

As a bricklayer's helper I was once laid off on a job when there were more than 10 or 15 minute intervals between trucks. To fill in an 8 hour day it usually required being on the job over 10 hours,but only being paid for the eight. And here I was being paid full time for resting! I was soon to find out what I was being paid for. All my reminiscing came to a halt with the clanging of the alarm bells. It was a location where my company was the 1st due engine. This was a gung-ho outfit and if you weren't on the rig within fifteen seconds you would be left behind in which case you would have to make it to the fire on your own or face the wrath of the fire officer and the "brothers." On rare occasions that has happened. By the time the secondary round of bells were sounding we were out of quarters. The men on the back step hanging onto the straps and alternating grips while putting on their turnout coats.

We had only gone a few blocks when it became obvious that we had a real "worker" on our hands. As we approached, the smoke was so thick we could barely see ten feet ahead. One of the men had to walk ahead of the rig to guide us to a hydrant as we entered the block. As we got to the building involved you could hear the roar of the flames as they were leaping out of all four floors. We stretched a two and one half inch hoseline and attacked the blaze from the first floor on up. The smoke was brutal and seared our lungs. Even before we went into the building, as we waited for the line to be charged, the heat was so intense that smoke was rising from our rubber turnout coats. At the time we didn't have any air masks and all we could do to keep our lungs from bursting was to put our face inside our turnout coat until the line had become charged. I had flashbacks of the mattress fire I had started as a child; the one my brother and I had tried and failed to extinguish. And I remembered my decision at the time, that firefighting was not for me."No way, Jose "is how it was put after that experience. Now this was my first big fire and I remember saying to myself, "What the hell am I doing here". Well, I was here and it was time to "put out" and earn my keep. We inched our way up the stair while other companies stretched additional hoselines to back us up.

The hose wagon outside was using a deckpipe stream to the upper floors. As the superheated water from the deckpipe streams rolled down the stairs to meet us, it felt like we were bucking the hot springs of Yellowstone Park. The fire was so wide spread that there was a real danger of the upper floors collapsing. falling plaster ceilings bombarded our heads and shoulders as we progressed. Only then could I really appreciate the design of the helmets which protected us from having hot plaster fragments and burning paint make their way past the collar and down our necks.

After what seemed like forever, the blaze was finally under control and did not endanger adjacent buildings. Now it was time to "overhaul" and the hook and ladder men were busy pulling down remaining ceilings so that we could douse the remaining fire between the "bays" and other concealed spaces in the walls. After the fire was officially extinguished it was time to take up our hoselines. These were drained in the street and laid onto the rig. Our work was not done, however, as the hose would then have to be washed and hung in the hose tower on return to quarters and then replaced with fresh dry hose. Only one hoseline was kept in operation for "overhauling" the mattresses which were being tossed down into the street from the fourth floor on down. That chore was normally the responsibility of the ladder companies. As the engine company we had taken the punishment, choking, coughing and vomiting as we fought the fire floor after floor. We were now completely spent. We still had the cleaning and replacing of hose ahead of us as we got to our rig ready to return to quarters. It was now 6:30 am and our work was still not finished. The chief in charge had prematurely sent the second due ladder company back and there was lots more overhauling to be done. So we were again pressed into action at the request of the chief. Although most of us could scarcely breathe we spent the next two hours removing mattresses remaining from all the floors involved and throwing them into the street to be overhauled. It was after 9:30 am when we were relieved at the fire by the incoming platoon. It was after 10 am when we were finally able to leave for home. Of course there was no overtime in the "good old days". Being treated for smoke inhalation wasn't even considered. That came with the job. As for the over taxing physical stress, it now became apparent why the physical and medical requirements were so demanding.

Also gone were the feelings of guilt that I had experienced eight hours earlier. That brief hiatus was repaid in spades. Except for the MPO, not one of us had the stomach for any breakfast. I wondered how many more nights like this were in store before the winter was over. I was due back in for the next 6 pm-9 am tour that very night. I got my answer soon enough!

THEATER COAL FIRE

I didn't bother to go home. Instead I visited my mother and later my sister. Both lived in Manhattan. In between I resurrected my lungs breathing some fresh air. Got a couple of hours nap at Mom's and was back at the firehouse by 5 pm. I was still feeling the effects of the previous night so I changed into my turnout gear and got a bit of rest before roll call at 6 pm. The guys had a nice dinner prepared at 7 pm but I couldn't finish it. After watching the news I decided to go up to the bunkroom and beat the city for another couple of hours.

At 11 pm we received a telephone alarm followed by a class 3 box for a theater in our district. We were on our way even as the alarm bells were sounding for the location. As we rolled up the theater was being evacuated. The smoke from the basement was so thick that it was pushing up through the coal supply manhole on the sidewalk. It was difficult going down to the basement (we did not have masks) especially after the night before at the mattress factory. It was hot and smoky but not as cutting as with the hair mattresses. The fire here was confined to the coal bin. Evidently the coal had ignited spontaneously which is not unusual. The fire was deep into the pile and now the real hard part of the job had begun. There was at least one hundred tons of coal that had to be shoveled from one end of the theater basement to the other. Each shovel full had to be washed down by a hose stream to prevent rekindling. I thought I had done all the shoveling in this lifetime when I was in the construction industry and, later, in the sanitation department. Well, I sure was able to demonstrate my aptitude with a shovel. I now discovered another facet of the job that I had unknowingly been preparing for. We kept on working in shifts, until the entire pile was wet down. It took us almost four hours before we were reasonably sure there would be no rekindling, a common occurrence with coal fires.

People think firefighting is all glamour when they see us racing through the streets, sirens shrieking and horns blasting. What is hidden from the public is the torment and physical abuse that often must be endured. It is no accident that an inordinate number of firefighters suffer severe heart attacks. A fireman, Conte, in the company before I was assigned, was a model of physical fitness. He was, in fact, also a male model for a famous garment company. One night the company responded to a fire in the projection booth of a theater. It wasn't a very tough fire but old burning film is very toxic. On returning to quarters, Conte complained of a headache and nausea. The officer asked if he wanted to go on sick leave but Conte declined and claimed he'd be ok if allowed to lay down for a while. Well, Fireman Conte laid down. A short time later a fireman went to check on him and Conte appeared to be dead. The doctor was called but attempts to revive him were futile. The doctor pronounced Conte D.O.A. He was 39 years old and in the prime of life.

MY BABY IS IN THERE

Nothing has a greater effect of producing almost frantic action than the cry, "My baby is in there". We were working the day tour in Engine Co. 280. Marty Seery was the MPO, Joe Doyle and Briscoe Payne, who was one of the two blacks in our company and well respected, were busy stretching a hoseline to the building entrance. Meanwhile, Lou Vaio and I were met at the stoop by a screaming, middle aged woman and a young man. Both screamed that the baby was trapped on the fourth floor. There was not too much fire evident but there was plenty of acrid black smoke, such as given off by an ordinary hair mattress.

It seems this type of emergency never occurs on the first or second floor. As the others were laying out the hose, Lou and I raced up to the fourth floor. Luckily there wasn't any fire in the apartment but the smoke made visibility impossible. Lou and I crawled on our hands and knees searching under beds and sinks and looking for a crib where a baby would normally be. We were choking and throwing up and yelling for the hook and ladder men hoping they had arrived. No baby was found. Maybe in the interim, before we arrived, some neighbor had taken the baby out. At any rate the fire itself was no big deal and Joe and Briscoe had it under control as Lou Vaio and I came down to help.

Joe and Briscoe were laughing at us and the mess we looked like after crawling over the floors in search of the baby. When Lou asked, "What the hell are you guys laughing at", the answer was not so funny. It turned out that the "baby" the woman and her son were screaming about was actually a thirty-two year old man, her other son. He had been one of the first to leave the building and was admiring our operation from the corner tavern. You can imagine our reaction when we heard this. When they had been reunited in the street they should have notified the chief to have us discontinue our search. Instead they all rejoiced and just plain "forgot" about the firefighters searching for their "baby".

While they were rejoicing Lou and I were having our butts roasted by crawling over every floor in the four room apartment.

Another "baby in there episode" occurred not too long after that. We had a fire in the Bedford-Stuyvesant section of Brooklyn when the same team happened to be on duty. We were the second due engine company but the first to arrive as the assigned first due company and the hook and ladder company were busy operating at another fire. People in the street informed Lieutenant Mulligan that children were trapped in the third floor apartment. Mulligan ordered Briscoe Payne and myself to check out the third floor where the children were supposed to be located. As we raced into the building a man and a woman on the stoop kept screaming, "My kids are in there". As we ran up the stairs there was no fire evident, just smoke.

When we got to the third floor apartment we sped into the bedroom. The sight we were confronted with got us both sick, yes, and angry too. There wasn't that much smoke in the bedroom, and not much heat either, yet there were three small black kids, all dead. The infant was in the crib and the others, about three and six years old were huddled under the crib. Evidently all had been suffocated by the gases that arose from a fire that was located in the basement. By this time the hook and ladder company had arrived as we started CPR and mouth to mouth resuscitation.

The hook and ladder truck company took over and Briscoe and I went to the basement to join Lou Vaio and Joe Doyle, who by now, had the small blaze in hand. The tragedy is that the fire appeared to be deliberately set, but that would be hard to prove, and had claimed the lives of three small children. There also was a delay in transmitting an alarm. All the bystanders congregated outside, assumed that someone else had turned in the alarm. By the time someone actually called the Fire Department, valuable minutes had passed which resulted in death. What really angered Briscoe and myself was that no one outside, especially the parents, had made any effort to rescue the kids. The fire had been confined to the basement and there was not much heat or smoke in the hallway from the first floor to the roof. These "concerned" parents had left the kids alone and were reported to be having drinks at the corner bar. I can understand the fear that is associated with fire but cannot forgive the parents for not even attempting to get their children out. I am not going to repeat what

Briscoe said as we passed them by, but if I had given them the same "blast" there may have been a mini-riot.

The next "baby in there" incident occurred during my first year as a Lieutenant in Engine Company 44. We pulled up to this building and it was immediately evident that we had a "worker" on our hands. Smoke was shooting out of the front of the entrance door to the building. We were met by three policemen in the street who reported that they were told a child was trapped in an apartment at the rear of the first floor. Firemen Rooney and Andriuolo immediately stretched a line up to the door of the apartment. From the condition of the metal door, which was heavily scorched halfway down from the top, it would be a miracle if anyone inside had survived. As we were about to open the door, we were set upon by a hysterical woman screaming that: "My baby is in there". She was attempting to rush into the apartment ahead of us, preventing us from advancing the hoseline.

I tried to keep her away from the door, but she was like a wild woman screaming and clawing at us trying to break free. If we tried to open the door she would be in grave danger of being burned. I had to call out to the three patrolmen in the street for help in removing her. The combined efforts of the three husky patrolmen and my two firefighters still couldn't subdue her. Meanwhile, we were kept from advancing our hoseline. Her anxiety gave her superhuman strength. Finally the cops had to use force against her, including a punch, to subdue her enough to drag her out to the street.

The blast of heat and smoke encountered as we opened the apartment door was proof enough that there would be no survivor. We hastily put out the fire and began to search for the body. We were now joined by the ladder company which had broken in from the rear fire escape. Thank heavens, there was no body to be found.

What had happened was that the mother had left the apartment for a short while visiting a neighbor on an upper floor. When she heard yelling in the hall about an apartment on fire. She ran downstairs and went berserk thinking her six-year old girl was still inside. What had happened was that when the fire started the little girl ran into the hall and was taken into an adjoining apartment by a neighbor.

From this experience, with a seemingly frail female, I can understand how some policemen can have a very difficult problem in attempting to control someone high on drugs without taking some drastic and forceful physical action.

LEAP TO SAFETY

In my first year on the job all my tours were limited to Engine Company 280 with occasional details to other engine companies in our battalion. I was on the job nearly a year before I was detailed to my first Hook and Ladder Company, ladder 123, which was located in a very busy section of Brooklyn on Ralph Avenue and Herkimer Street.

On a miserable night in February, while I was detailed, we received an alarm for a fire in a six story old law tenement. The dispatcher gave us a specific address which usually meant we had a real worker ahead. As we approached, smoke was spewing out of all the windows but there was no visible fire at the front of the building. As the hook and ladder chauffeur and tillerman were raising the 110 foot ladder to the upper floors, the lieutenant ordered me to take a hook and portable extinguisher and then told me, "You got the rear of the building." Never having worked a ladder company before, without specific training in every aspect of the job, I wasn't sure what the lieutenant meant by that order. Not to appear too stupid, I asked the chauffeur, Fireman Carrol, what the lieutenant meant. "He means you ventilate the rear of the building." That I understood. I was a sorry sight going into the yard, with a truckman's helmet that didn't quite fit, ready to attack with a two and one-half gallon extinguisher and a hook. It was tantamount to attacking a fiery dragon with a fly swatter!

I'll never forget the sight that greeted me as I entered the yard. The fire escape drop ladder was not released, and the fire escapes on all floors were dangerously full of persons fleeing the fire. I put the can aside (two and a half gallon extinguisher), and with the hook was able to release the drop ladder to ground level. People immediately started rushing down the ladder in a frenzy. I couldn't get up the ladder myself to ventilate, as I was fully occupied trying to calm down this disorderly exodus. My presence in the yard at least had a calming influence on them, and somehow we avoided a panic and serious injury. As some had infants, I had them throw them to me from the first floor landing. All this delayed me from accomplishing my primary duty, which was to provide ventilation for the engine men who would be advancing hose lines into the building. I couldn't stop the onrush down the ladder, so I had to climb by the flat metal part on the side of the ladder. As soon as the last person was off the landing, I began breaking any window left closed as I made my way up the fire escape. This was not the proper sequence, however, but due to the time lost in evacuating the people to the yard I didn't want to lose any more time in effecting ventilation. This mistake almost had tragic results for me.

By this time fire was escaping from every window, from the first floor and up to the fifth as the fire intensified. When I got to the top landing of the fire escape, only then did I realize that there was no ladder from the top floor landing to the roof. I was trapped on the landing. There was no way I could make it down the same way I came up. The yard at this time was completely and densely crowded with people that I had helped evacuate. It is impossible to adequately describe the scene. They were aware of my plight and, in unison it seemed, they were all swaying side by side to some indistinguishable chant. This, together with the sight of the reflection from the flames of the burning building off their dark faces and bodies was an eerie sight. It was like a reddish-bronze colored field of corn swaying in tune to a howling wind.

If I wasn't to be roasted there was only one thing left for me to do, and there would be no second chance. The fire escape on the adjacent building was about ten feet away with the landings staggered in height from my position. I took one last look down into the yard and had the feeling that I had died and gone to hell. I could only think back to the times when, as a teenager, I had jumped from roof to roof just for kicks. The heat from the flames licking below my landing made up my mind. act now, and fast! I climbed onto the top rail of the fire escape. I then threw the hook and my helmet over to the adjacent fire escape which was about three feet lower in height. Although only ten feet away, now that I was ready to jump it appeared to be a lot further. I took one more look at the swaying and chanting throng in the yard. Some were shouting encouragement. I made the obligatory sign of the cross and leaped out and down to the adjacent fire escape. This was accompanied by a loud combination of screaming, yelling and cheering from below. I caught the top part of the fire escape and my momentum caused me to slam my knee into the bottom part. Never did pain seem so delicious! It meant I made it safely across. The confidence I had built up as a teenager had paid off. That sympathetic crowd of people in the yard were so happy to greet me, as I descended to the yard, that the back slaps of congratulations eclipsed the excruciating pain in my knee. I hobbled out through the hall and into the street where I was met by the lieutenant.

"What kept you," he said, "and why are you limping?" I didn't have the courage to tell him I had done the ventilation in reverse. Nor did I say anything about the predicament I had put myself in. I only related how the tenants had to first be evacuated, about releasing the drop ladder before commencing ventilation, and how I sprained my knee in the process. I did not tell anyone of my stupid mistake but it was one lesson that I would never forget.

ARSON: ANGEL OF DEATH

It was a cold and nasty winter's night in February. Funny how most nasty fires occur on cold, damp nights and always when you have to stretch hose to the upper floors, making operations more difficult and time consuming, especially when short of manpower as we were that night.

By the time we had advanced our hose line to the fifth floor of this building we were all really sucking wind. There were only three of us, Joe Doyle, Arthur O'Connor and myself. At the time all companies did not have gas masks as they do today. We knew we would be in for a really rough time as we approached the door to the fire apartment. The door showed visible signs of scorching on the upper half indicating that a very hot fire had been in progress for some time. The hall was enveloped in heavy smoke and we had to lay on the floor on our stomachs as the door was about to be opened for us by a hook & ladder man. This precaution was taken because if there was no other avenue of ventilation, then fresh air being sucked into the room could ignite the hot gases explosively thereby endangering all of us in the hall. This phenomenon is known as a "back draft."

The door was opened slowly with care and we advanced our line into the apartment. Some woman from downstairs was yelling that a man was still in the apartment. It was evident from the severity of the fire that anyone in that apartment was probably burned to death even before we had gotten to the location. However, you never give up. We were taking a beating as we advanced and put out the fire in the first two rooms before we reached the last room which was an office and the seat of the fire. Art tried to get into the last room ahead of the nozzle as the hook & ladder men were driven back by the intense heat and smoke. Joe Doyle and I kept a steady stream of water over his head as Artie tried in vain to crawl into the room. It was like trying to crawl into the firebox of an industrial oven. We finally put out the fire. When the smoke cleared, there on the floor out of reach of all of us was the first "roast" that I had seen (there were later to be others).

The man was curled in a fetal position and laying on his back. All of the soft tissues of his body had been burned off, eyes, ears, mouth, private parts, etc . Being fairly new on the job I wasn't prepared for this sight. I handed the hoseline to Joe and rushed to a window so I could lose my last supper as unobtrusively as possible and not show my embarrassment to the old timers including the chief in the hall.

All that we had to show for our efforts was that Art had burns on both his hands and we all had blisters on our knees which were oozing beneath our pulled up boots. Our eyelashes were curled and shriveled from the heat. Our lungs seemed to be bursting from the intense heat and smoke. We had tried for a rescue that appeared to be futile from the beginning.

None of us went on sick call for smoke inhalation either. That was not the fad in the 1940s and 1950s. Joe and Art's faces showed more of the effects of reddening because of their fair Irish complexions.

We thought that Art should be written up for a citation for his last ditch effort in a rescue attempt when all others gave up. However, that was not the primary job of an engineman and paradoxically, his efforts could be the basis for charges being brought against him. Such was the straight jacket mentality of the "powers that be" in the good old days.

It turned out that the man who had been burned to death was a dentist. However, we never did learn how the fire had started or any other details. That was the responsibility of the fire marshals. Back at the firehouse, Art was treating the blisters on his hands and Joe and I were dabbing some antiseptic cream on our faces. I might add that after the local residents heard that all the dentist's records had been consumed by the fire a disproportionate amount of dental work was included on their income tax returns.

On the very next night tour we were called to a fire at the same address. The fire was of no consequence and had been partially extinguished by the occupants before our arrival. This did seem to be an unusual coincidence: two fires in the same building of unexplained origin in such a short time! We put out the remaining smoldering fire and returned to quarters. A few days later, again on our night tour of duty, we were called to a fire at the same address, this time on the third floor. The last was on the fourth floor and the original fire, the one that claimed the life of the dentist was on the fifth floor. These had to be more than just coincidences. This latest fire was in a clothes closet located in the foyer of an apartment. The fire marshall responded while we were still at the scene. After extinguishing the fire in the closet, Gus Guidice and I were tending the hoseline in the hall. We were in the line of sight of a full length mirror that was in the foyer. I could see an angelic looking eleven year old girl, who had been so terrified moments ago, talking on the phone. The fire marshals were in the living room questioning her parents as there appeared to be an arsonist on the loose. I couldn't take my eyes off this "sweet kid" watching as her face changed as she spoke on the phone. Her eyes seemed to sparkle as she spoke excitedly. As she continued to speak her smile seemed to be more devilish than angelic.

I had seen that expression before. It seemed like a long shot but something had to be done. I was hoping to be wrong. However, there was already one death and the fires were still under investigation as "suspicious".

I handed the nozzle to Gus. The girl was still on the phone as I entered her bedroom which was adjacent to the foyer. There she had a sizeable bookcase so I checked out some of the books and magazines she had on hand. I wasn't surprised to find that practically all the literature dealt with fires, excitement, murders, disasters and other eroticism. This seemed to confirm my suspicion. This was not the type of reading material that a normal teenager, especially a girl, should be obsessed with. On a hunch I called one of the marshals aside, told him of the reading material and more importantly, of her reactions while on the telephone and convinced him that the wrong people were being questioned.

When the marshals did turn their attention to her she readily admitted to setting all the fires. She seemed to be almost too anxious to let it all out! She had no remorse for the death of the dentist on the fifth floor. She had set the fire in her own apartment's clothes closet with "exploding matches". Can you beat that! **An 11 year old girl!** That fire in her own apartment was intended to cast off suspicion. In fact, it had the opposite effect.

I might never have seen that angelic face turn into the devil, and she would never have come under suspicion, if her reflection in the mirror hadn't given her away. I never did find out how she had done the dentist in nor for what motive. We never found out either what punishment had been meted out, if any, for such a young girl.

Some of the most normal appearing persons turn out to be fire bugs. I could never understand why. It is usually difficult to distinguish the sick from the normal but after a while, at a fire or other disaster, that unmistakable look comes onto their faces.

THE FAT LADY

We were working the night tour on a November evening. Lieutenant Mulligan was conducting company drill and we were going over a new radio procedure when the company phone rang. The ringing was followed, almost simultaneously, by the box number for the location sounding out. The dispatcher had given us the exact address so we knew we had a tough one going. Especially when informed that the dispatcher had received telephone alarms from various locations. We could see why there were so many calls long before we reached our destination.

There were flames and firebrands leaping at least 100 feet in the air over the roof of this five story brownstone building. Dense smoke was pushing out of the first floor doorway. The battalion chief, stationed by the door, was shouting that there were people trapped inside the building. We were the third due engine company. The first due company was down the block hooking up to a hydrant preparing to stretch a hoseline to the building. As is often the case, the hook & ladder company was at another alarm location. There was also no rescue company responding. Lieutenant Mulligan approached the battalion chief to get our operating orders. As the last due company our job would normally be to advance a line to protect exposures. There was some confusion with some other firemen milling around by an incoming apparatus. Arthur O'Connor and I thought we heard the same thing-that a fireman had entered the brownstone, probably to search for an occupant, and had not come out. The battalion chief was visibly shaking.

Art looked at me and I knew what he had in mind as no one was venturing into that inferno without a charged hoseline. So, as our lieutenant was approaching the chief, Arthur and I ran past the chief and into the building. Inside the building was like an oven and you couldn't even see a hand in front of your face. In order to breathe at all we fell to our stomachs and crawled along the floor, feeling in all directions, as we hoped to come across a body. Soon Art called out that he had a body and was on his way out. He was lucky for he had stumbled onto Fireman Mannino who earlier had gone in to effect a rescue but was himself overcome. I was almost ready to give up, as the smoke was taking on a reddish glow from the rooms at the rear, when about fifteen feet further in I came upon another body. I felt for a way to execute the fireman's carry, we were taught at school, but it was no use. I couldn't get around this bulk. From what I could feel this body was about two foot high, laying down. I had no mask and by now I felt that if I didn't get out immediately they would have to come in for both of us. I didn't care how professional it would appear, I just grabbed her under the arms from behind and unceremoniously backed out of the building, up the three stone steps, and deposited her onto a safe area on the sidewalk. The incoming hook & ladder company and rescue companies took over and worked on her and Fireman Mannino who, up to then had not been revived.

Art was waiting outside and was ready for another sortie if I didn't make it out. I was still retching and gasping for breath. Meanwhile, our company had taken a position on an adjoining roof operating a hoseline to keep the fire from extending to the exposure buildings. Art and I went up to join them. As has often been noted, what Arthur O'Connor and I had done could have been grounds for charges to be brought against us. In the presence of ladder companies on the scene our primary purpose was to extinguish the fire. Of course Lieutenant Mulligan didn't agree with the premise but, on the other hand, he couldn't recommend us to the Honor Board in consideration for an award. Nor did we expect any. Art and I had the satisfaction of having saved two lives. Art had the better of it as fireman Mannino weighed about 175 pounds. After I got the fat lady out the consensus was that she weighed at least 350 pounds.

We later learned that Fireman Mannino and the Fat Lady had both been revived and taken to a hospital. That was great news! Strange, however, how fast news travels and becomes distorted as it is passed along. By this time the fire had progressed to a third alarm. A fireman Duffy, was recounting to another firefighter and myself how Fireman Mannino had made a daring rescue before a hoseline had been stretched. From what he gathered from the street the rescue was to earn Mannino a 1st Class Medal. When I told him what actually happened he was in disbelief. Fireman Mannino did, in fact, deserve a medal as did Art and myself. The irony, however, was that Fireman Mannino was himself an engine man.

Unfortunately, that was not the happy ending expected from this event. After all, two lives were saved, The fire did not extend to other buildings. Art and I came out of this ordeal without an injury, except for a snoot full of smoke and heat. So this episode seemed to be closed. However, it wasn't. Fireman Mannino, because of the exertion he had made in getting the Fat Lady to the point that Art and I were able to reach them had painfully injured his neck and shoulder. He should have gone on sick leave and no one would have blamed him. Instead he accepted a light duty assignment doing building inspection in the district. He had very limited movement of his neck, and in one direction only. It left him in a very awkward and dangerous position, especially in crossing busy streets such as Atlantic Ave. in Brooklyn.

It was shortly before Thanksgiving when we received a strange call for the ambulance in our quarters by the dispatcher. Fireman Habermann, the ambulance driver took the call and was told to "hold". Evidently the dispatcher was getting information from another source. Finally Fireman Habermann was told to disregard the call! What transpired next was an outright disgrace. What none of us knew, was that Fireman Mannino was laid out on a cold street on Atlantic Avenue, fighting for his life with no one to help him. What happened was that as he was crossing the street traffic had resumed, stranding him in the center of this very wide street. A truck coming from his blind side approached and was and ready to pass by him, when by some freak accident some sort of metal hook protruding from the truck pulled the Fireman under the wheels and crushed his body. This is where the stupid and gutless bureaucracy came into play. Here was a hero fireman laying dying in the street, as an indirect result of an injury sustained in risking his life to save a complete stranger, and in his moment of need he was abandoned. He was bleeding in the street upwards of twenty minutes before an ambulance came on the scene.

The department ambulance in our quarters on St. John's Place was only a few blocks away from the accident and we could have responded and gotten to him in a minute. Who knows if that might have saved his life. As it turned out he later died in the hospital.

Getting back to that earlier strange phone call: the dispatcher knew a fireman was involved when he called the department ambulance and then had put the driver on hold. But he had been told that another ambulance had been called and he, therefore, told our driver to disregard the call. Under the circumstances he should have let us go anyway, knowing how close we were. Besides, there are always delays, even for city ambulances. Had he at least told us a fireman was involved, we would have made the decision to respond. What a waste! Fireman Mannino could possibly be alive today. He was scarcely thirty when he died.

As for the woman that we had collectively saved, she survived. No one from her family, brother, sister, mother, etc., or anyone else ever came to the firehouse to express their thanks for our efforts. Not that we expected it but it would have been a nice gesture. Instead, whenever we were engaged in fire operations in Bed-Sty, we were still the targets of rocks, bottles, and other objects thrown at us. One such incident occurred on Election Day when a big bonfire was started in the street. We responded and as I was playing a hose stream on the blaze I ducked as I saw an object coming toward my face. It was a large glass bottle that shattered as it hit the ground. I was so angered that I turned on the deckpipe nozzle and directed it into the unruly mob. Our covering lieutenant, detailed from another company, ordered me to shut it off, saying, as do other apologetic doves like him, "We don't want any trouble." I told him we already had trouble and to call the Police by radio, as we were still under attack. That bottle could have disfigured me or even been lethal. I did not shut down the nozzle and we put out the fire as I held these miscreants at bay. As for our detailed chicken lieutenant, oh yes, gutless wonders can be found, even in the fire department.

HOLIDAY FIRES

At times we would sit in the kitchen and wonder what disaster would be in store for us if a fire involved any of the three buildings to the south of Engine Company 280. These buildings were occupied by a majority of devout Irish Catholic families. They all had large families averaging about six and one-half children per family. With all these children in these old law tenement buildings, an undetected fire in the middle of the night was bound to produce unimaginable horrors, especially during the Christmas season when most all the families had live Christmas trees. These thoughts were constantly on our minds until the holiday season ended and all the live trees were removed from the buildings. In our company drills we would go through the specific actions to be taken should a fire occur in any of these buildings.

One night, shortly after New Years, at about 11 pm, it finally happened. Before we had gotten a signal from the fire alarm dispatcher, Fireman Joe Doyle who was at the watch desk, saw a glow reflected from buildings at the opposite side of the street. He looked out and his heart jumped into this throat as he saw the flames shooting out the third floor windows of one of the apartments. He yelled, "Get out!", and within seconds we sprang into action. The time-saving actions that we had practiced in drills paid off in spades. Our MPO, Seery, had one fireman assist him as he hooked up to the closest hydrant as the rest of us stretched hose to the building. Hook and Ladder Company 132, quartered adjacent to Engine Company 280, ran to the building, banged on every door, and yelled for all to evacuate the building. They also escorted any aged and handicapped people out to safety. At the same time, the truck's ladder was raised to the upper floors to assist in rescue of any occupants that may have been cut off from access to the interior stairs.

These actions were taken with such speed and precision that by the time Engine Company 280 got to the first floor we already had water in the hose line. And by the time we reached the second floor we had water up to the nozzle ready to attack the blaze. We had gone over this very action in our company drills so often that we had every confidence that Marty Seery would be hooked up and have the line charged in time. Meanwhile, the fire had engulfed the entire third floor and smoke was pushing out down the stairs and out the entrance door to the street. We couldn't attack the fire until we were certain all the kids were out. At the third floor, Joe Doyle, Lou Vaio, and Art O'Connor were busy helping kids of all ages to get past us and down the stairs. As soon as we learned no one was left in the apartment we advanced the line. By this time, the fire was so hot, with the heat given off from the burning Christmas tree, that the plaster ceilings in the apartment had cracked and fallen. The paint on the apartment's walls and ceilings was on fire.

In the room where the Christmas tree had been located the paint had burned from the ceiling down to three feet from floor level. Yet to our surprise, in an adjacent room there were two goldfish swimming lazily in a bowl half on their sides. I felt the water with my hand and noted that the water was warm, but not hot as we had expected. I poured out some of the water and had Joe Doyle crack open the nozzle and replenish the bowl with fresh water. We marveled that the fish had survived the intense heat from the adjoining rooms.

Now that the fire had been controlled, Captain Woodrow Franey took stock. After checking with the chief and family members, to our delight there was not even one death nor any serious injury. The only complaints were for smoke inhalation from several occupants. We did not lose a dog, cat or any pet. While overhauling was in progress O'Connor and I went down to the street to take a breather. When we got there, we came across a little red-haired kid about nine years of age, crying uncontrollably. We soon found out that he was the owner of the goldfish in the third floor apartment.

Not knowing if the fish had survived the fire, even with our emergency aid, I rushed up to the apartment and found both goldfish merrily circling the bowl. When the bowl was presented to the little red-head, the reaction we got was worth the beating we had taken as we were searching under beds, sinks, cribs, etc., even as we were fighting the seat of the fire.

This event was a great source of satisfaction for us. It is not usually the case that in a flash fire of this type, in the dead of night, that involved so many inhabitants, that all had escaped death or serious injury. Also to be commended were the adult occupants themselves. They did not panic and made sure to get the last of their kids out of the building. There was no hysteria as members of Hook and Ladder 132 helped escort many over adjoining roofs, down ladders and fire escapes. Unless you experienced it, it would be difficult to understand the feeling of exultation we all had from this rewarding operation.

THEY ARE KILLING MY HUSBAND -- NEW YEAR'S EVE

I had just arrived home after two hectic tours of duty at the firehouse. It was 10:30 am and I was enjoying some much needed rest when I got a call from Slim Trotta, one of the partners of a night spot called "Slim n' Eddys" in Far Rockaway. One of the singing waiters that formed his barber shop quarter had called in sick and a replacement was sorely needed for the big party that night ushering in the New Year. I attempted to turn down the offer as we had already committed to attend our own New Year's celebration party with a host of friends. However, after Slim pleaded that I was his last hope to avert disaster, both financially and to their reputation as the affair had been completely sold out, I reluctantly agreed to fill in.

At the time I didn't have an automobile so I traveled by bus to a train station where I transferred to another bus to within a few blocks of the bistro. I got there at 7 pm and went over a few saloon songs with their head waiter, Bill Puzo and lead singer, George Brosnan. The festivities began early and by 8 pm the last leg of the foursome failed to show up. We were the only three-man quartet working the Rockaways on that New Year's Eve. To add to the misery, this was the most financially unrewarding venture I was ever engaged in. It seems that every parsimonious anal retentive cheapskate in New York had congregated in this out-of-the-way nightclub. The singing was no problem. For one thing, we were so rushed with orders there wasn't much time for singing. The revelers were so "bombed" by 10 pm that no one even cared. We had a big crowd, but they held onto their money as if they expected to live forever.

The festivities finally ended shortly after 3 am. All of the waiters were "stiffed" as tips were in miserly amounts. The bar, however, had done a booming business and the owners insisted on giving a modest bonus to the waiters. What a way to start the New Year! Little did I realize that this beginning was the harbinger of a near deadly episode that was to follow.

By 4 am I was on the bus going to the New Lots subway station. Although the bus was almost full to capacity, it was very quiet. Without warning the bus suddenly came to a screeching halt. It almost struck an elderly woman who had run into the street directly in our path. She was screaming frantically for the bus driver to open the door. Before stepping into the bus she kept screaming, in a thick Yiddish accent, "They're killing my husband." As we looked toward the side street we were met by a chilling sight. A sedan was in the middle of the roadway with all it's doors open. Six black men surrounded the car. The two on the passenger side were punching the old guy as he was being kicked from the opposite side. One was partly in the car and was punching him from behind the rear seat area. He was being beaten unmercifully. The old woman now stepped into the bus and pleaded, "Please help us" and again, "They're killing my husband." I couldn't believe what these animals had done to his helpless woman. One side of her face was completely distorted and so swollen that her eye wasn't visible. There was blood all over her face. I looked around the bus and no one was making a move. This was reminiscent of the old Kitty Genovese case where a young woman was being brutally beaten and raped and finally murdered as 38 persons watched. No one rendered assistance or called for the police.

Finally one man from the back of the bus got up and said, "Well, are we going to help?" Only one other young man joined in as they came towards the front of the bus. I looked back at the busload of people and said, "There are six of them out there. Who else is coming?" It is a sad commentary on the youth of New York when only one other guy came forward. Another started to get up, but a hand on his shoulder by his wife quickly squelched the feeble attempt. That left only the four of us. The driver said, "I would come and help, but I cannot leave the bus." He promised that he wouldn't leave without us. Considering his responsibility, he couldn't be faulted.

As the four of us ran towards the car in the still of the night it must have sounded like a herd of buffalo approaching. Five of the gang ran off. The one in the trench coat who was punching the old guy from behind was so engrossed in his activity that he was still banging away as

I grabbed him by the collar. I said, "We will take this clown with us." What unfounded optimism! Things now started to take place in rapid fire order.

The carjacking muggers, seeing that only four unarmed men had come out of the bus, quickly returned and surrounded us with drawn knives. In the glow of the street lamps the 6-inch blades looked more like sabres. I let loose the perpetrator in the trench coat. Realizing we had painted ourselves into a lethal corner, I attempted to question their manhood. "You guys are pretty brave, six against four. Put the knives away and let's see how brave you are." That challenge was for another era that had long ago expired. The answer I got instead was a swipe toward my gut with a knife from one of the gang. As I pulled back to evade the thrust, the old woman ran towards the car that her husband had moved away. At the same time, "trench coat" took after her with his knife drawn. Instinctively, I took off after him, determined that he not inflict further damage on this woman. It was obvious that she was not going to make it to her husband before "trench coat" got to her.

I caught up to him and grabbed at his coat as it trailed behind him. As I did so he made a wild roundhouse swing at me with his knife which missed. At least I thought it did.[3] As he spun I caught him with a punch at the back of his neck, just below the skull. That sent him sprawling face down onto the pavement. Meanwhile the bus driver was blowing his horn, probably hoping to attract attention or to scare off the assailants.

At the same time the three other would be rescuers who were being held at knife point made a run for the bus. They were being pursued by a screaming, howling horde bent on mayhem and murder. The woman had made it to the car and "trench coat' lay prone in the gutter. The bus driver evidently was blasting his horn to attract my attention to the situation. The three made it to the bus and I, coming from the opposite direction, also made it before the muggers. The bus driver quickly closed the door behind me. Meanwhile, the muggers, still seeking vengeance, were stabbing at the rubber separating the doors attempting to break

---

[3]It wasn't until the next day that I realized that I had come out of this experience with a lasting memento in the form of a slit, just below the buttonhole on the lapel of my suit jacket. This was a sobering discovery on how close "trench coat" had come to scoring big with that wild swipe he had directed at me with his knife.

into the bus. We were in a minority section of town and no one, it seems, had made a call to the police.

By now I had become a full blown maniac with all that had transpired in such a short period of time. I grabbed the pump type pyrene extinguisher mounted at the front wall of the bus and extended the pump handle which made a formidable weapon. I then straddled the well by the door and ordered the bus driver to open the door. Instead he made the proper decision by pulling away from the scene. I was never so angry in my life, not only at the muggers, but also at all the healthy men that stayed behind. For a while, when I ordered the bus driver to open the door I must have gone berserk. My only thought was to inflict serious bodily harm on these mutants for what they had done to the elderly couple and for what they attempted to do to us for interrupting their violent escapade. I couldn't accept the fact that they were getting away with acts of felonious assault and attempted murder. If it wasn't for the presence of the many women on the bus, I would have been tempted to take to task the men on the bus that were content to sit passively and possibly be witness to a carnage.

This was an experience that I have never forgotten. I had nightmares for months in which I was armed with a baseball bat, wreaking havoc on these animals as they were slashing at me with their knives. At times I would wake up in a cold sweat as the horror-filled dreams became increasingly realistic.

On transferring from the bus to the subway at the New Lots Station, I was able to talk briefly with the first man that had stood up in the bus offering to help the hapless couple. The young man was on the soon-to-expire list for appointment to the New York Police Department. Ironically, due to the delays in hiring and affirmative action, it was doubtful that he would be hired.

I wonder if the elderly couple that had escaped with their lives that New Year's Eve would ever have an inkling that they had been spared by the actions of an off duty fireman, an aspiring policeman and two total strangers. I hope that the next time they had occasion to render an opinion on the workings of the police and fire departments their response would be favorable.

On my next day tour I recounted the incident to a couple of the firemen in the kitchen. In my anger I had thrown in a disparaging ethnic epithet. My friend, Briscoe Payne, came in and caught part of the conversation and I apologized to him for the slurs. He had heard enough. He told me I had nothing to apologize for and he added a few ethnic epithets that I had never thought of. Briscoe certainly understood that the invectives, uttered in anger, did not apply to him nor to any other person of good will.

Chapter 9

THE BATTLE OF THE BROGUES

I DEPUTY CHIEF - BURKE,
II DEPUTY CHIEF - MUTO,
UNDER SIEGE

BATTLE OF THE BROGUES

It was a beautiful spring morning. I was doing the 9 am to noon housewatch duty at the quarters of Engine Company 280. The 11-11 signal from the dispatcher's office, which denoted the time 9 am and also served as a test that the alarm bells were operating properly, had just been received. The gong had scarcely ceased reverberating when an explosion broke the serene Sunday silence with a force that laterally shifted the position of the chair I was seated in almost four inches.

Before I could imagine what had happened, Fireman Martin Hanrahan from Ladder Company 132, the adjacent fire company, came running into our quarters screaming, "Fire." For Martin, who was an experienced firefighter, to be acting in such a hysterical manner, after the many "hairy" jobs he had been involved in for the previous ten years, I expected to be confronted by a major catastrophe as I ran to look out past the sliding apparatus doors. I was even more apprehensive after seeing Fireman Hanrahan's condition as he burst into our quarters. His hair was disheveled and was almost standing straight up. It was as if he had seen a ghost or been electrocuted. His shirt was open and haphazardly hanging out past his beltline. He was acting stranger than someone that was simply highly excited.

As my feet hit the sidewalk in front of quarters I could see the cause of Martin's bizarre behavior. Fire was already licking out past the apparatus doors. Everything combustible on the apparatus floor was on fire. I quickly banged out the in-house alarm bells and yelled, "Get out," although everyone by then had slid the pole from the upper floors at the first sound and shock from the explosion.

As is usually the case, there is a fire hydrant located directly to the side of the firehouse in close proximity, approximately a ten foot distance. We didn't waste any time getting our pumper out and hooking it up to the fire hydrant. Instead, we used the fastest hook-up possible and stretched a 1-1/2 inch hose directly from the hydrant and quickly put the fire out. Most of the combustible materials on the apparatus floor were beyond salvage (rubber coats, boots, hats, etc.) There were going to be many unhappy brothers when the damage was assessed. Especially since it was close to the regular semi-annual inspection which included uniforms and turn-out gear. Any article that did not pass inspection would have to be replaced immediately.

Within moments of extinguishing the fire we could hear screams coming from the yard area adjacent to the kitchen which was to the rear of the apparatus floor. It sounded like the wailing of a woman suffering from pain and fright. When we ran to the yard we were surprised that the screams were coming from a young adult male. He was doubled up on the ground and grasping his knees and yelling. His eyes were closed and he was huddled as if expecting the building to collapse upon him. In reconstructing the events that led to the fire and explosion, the explanations were almost beyond comprehension.

Fireman Hanrahan and the tillerman had removed the ladder truck to a position across the street so that they could get at a stubborn and unsightly grease stain located under the grease pan kept on the floor below the motor that was used to trap any oil and grease that might leak past the gaskets and seals. Removing the ladder truck was the most fortunate element in the events that followed.

With the ladder truck out of the way, and the grease pan removed, Fireman Hanrahan began his assault on the oil and grease stains. When the spots would not yield to the soap and grease-dissolving solutions, Martin decided on the very dangerous practice of using gasoline on the ugly stains. Knowing the practice was dangerous, he then proceeded to provide as much ventilation as possible by opening the doors and windows facing the apparatus floor. In the interim, a man from the Department of Water Supply had entered quarters for the purpose of testing the quality of our water. Fireman Hanrahan directed him to the kitchen where the sink was located. Hanrahan then liberally splashed gasoline onto the grease spots and vigorously worked it into the spots with an ordinary corn broom.

In a short while, with unexpected suddenness, a loud explosion resulted. Martin was in shock wondering what had happened until he saw the flames. His shirt was blown open and he was thrown several feet from the area he was working in. That was fortunate or he would have been severely burned by the residual gasoline that had also caught on fire.. In the kitchen the employee from the water department was blown out through the open window and into the yard. It was a minor miracle that no one was killed, or seriously injured, by the thoughtless action of Fireman Hanrahan. However, the only reason for this escape was that he had at least ventilated the area. Had the blast been confined, if the apparatus door and windows were kept closed, it is possible that no one at Ladder Company 132 would have survived. Miraculously, the man from the water company was blown clean through the open section of the window or he would have been more seriously injured. His shoes were blown off his feet and his clothing suffered damage from his unscheduled flight into the yard.

The second miracle was that except for the shock and the disheveled shirt and hair, Fireman Hanrahan also got off lightly. Had the blast been more confined, the brick wall separating Engine Company 280 from Ladder Company 132 almost certainly would have collapsed into our quarters.

We then had the task of trying to deduce what actually had set off the explosion. Was the static spark that was probably produced by scraping the broom against the concrete floor of sufficient intensity to ignite the flammable vapors of the gasoline? Or did the flammable vapors of the gasoline travel along the apparatus floor and into the kitchen until it reached it's optimum explosion range and was then ignited by the open pilot light of the kitchen stove? Either was a distinct possibility and Fireman Hanrahan would be at fault for terrible judgment in either case. This incident, however, was scheduled for an intense investigation, especially since it had the potential for a real catastrophe that could have resulted in the collapse of the building under the proper set of circumstances. This became a very serious business and a date was set for the investigation to begin by the Deputy Chief in Charge of the Borough of Brooklyn, Dickie Burke. Chief Burke had a reputation for meting out hard, swift and severe punishment when established rules were either broken or ignored. To add to the gravity of the situation, the sun hadn't set before a lawyer for the water company employee was on the scene seeking information for a suit being prepared against the city, the fire department and Fireman Hanrahan. Poor Martin was wallowing in deep dodo.

Hanrahan didn't know it yet, but he was equipped with the only weapon at his disposal that was destined to save his ass. It was his thick Irish brogue!

At exactly 9 am the next morning, Deputy Chief Burke arrived. The officers and members of both companies were assembled and stood at attention. By order of the officers on duty, we smartly executed a right hand salute acknowledging the arrival of our tyrannical inquisitor. After the Chief returned our salute, the members were dismissed except for Fireman Hanrahan and the men that were involved during the incident. The officers of both Engine Company 280 and Ladder Company 132 remained for the investigation. Deputy Chief Burke, in his inimitable brusque and intimidating style, beckoned Martin to step forward for questioning.

Chief Burke:"Fireman Hanrahan, explain exactly what happened leading to the fire and explosion." (The question was spiked by his natural, thick Irish brogue.)

Fireman Hanrahan:(In a brogue that was thicker than the Chief's and reeking of the old sod began) "Weeell ayl tell ya, Cheef..." (and began to truthfully relate the events of the previous day).

We could see the Deputy Chief's eyes almost close into a tight squint and his face contorted as it reddened like a fire alarm box. He had no idea of Martin's brogue, and his first thought was that not only was this son-of-a bitch guilty of breaking every safety rule in the fire department, but he had the temerity and cojones to mock the way I speak. Actually, he did not hear a word that Martin was reciting. All he could focus on was the brogue mocking him. He ordered Martin to stop.

The Chief then asked Fireman Hanrahan to repeat all he had said before being interrupted. "Fireman Hanrahan, start at the beginning again." Martin then reiterated his story, emphasizing every detail up to the occurrence of the explosion. Soon Deputy Chief Burke realized that the brogue was indeed Martin's natural way of speaking. The questioning continued but now was not quite as harsh. When the questioning was over with, the Chief stood by the housewatch desk contemplating his next move as he had to make entries in the company journal on the results of the investigation and what punitive action, if any, would be taken. Also, there were to be recommendations made on what actions were to be taken to prevent a reoccurrence.

It was obvious that the Chief was wrestling with conflicting thoughts on rendering a decision. There was really no point in punishing Martin with a hefty fine and suspension. His innocent wife and 7 kids would also suffer by that decision. In Martin's favor, he had told the whole truth in spite of the fact that the truth made him solely culpable. A mitigating factor, however, was that he had the presence of mind to at least provide ventilation or the entire firehouse could have been destroyed. After mulling all the pros and cons, Deputy Chief Burke arrived at a truly humane and momentous decision. He stood on the raised section of flooring upon which the housewatch desk was located and placed his hand on the company journal, almost appearing as though he were being sworn in. He prepared to announce his decision. Chief Burke then turned to Fireman Hanrahan and those of us assembled and proclaimed in the finest brogue this side of the Old Sod: "It mooost hev been a defective stooove."

Thereby the kitchen stove became the convenient culprit and was scheduled for an overhaul. It was then to be provided with an interrupted pilot light to replace the constant pilot that was reputed to have leaked natural gas into the kitchen until it was ignited when the room had a sufficient gas to air mixture. This resulted in the explosion and ensuing fire.

We never did learn how the water company employee made out with his case against the city and the fire department or on his reaction to the fact that now he would have to sue the kitchen stove in place of fireman Martin Hanrahan.

BATTLE OF THE BROGUES-II

One day we had an unannounced and unexpected visit to our quarters at Engine Company 280 by Deputy Chief Muto. A few days earlier a tragic mistake at a fire operation by the Motor Pump Operator (MPO) of the first due engine company caused the death of a firefighter and injury to several other firemen operating a hoseline on the fire floor. The MPO had inadvertently shut down the wrong hoseline from the several lines stretched from his pumper. It turned out to be the very hoseline being used to combat an extensive and stubborn fire on the upper floors of a tenement building. As a result, the fire had overwhelmed the men on the hoseline, resulting in serious burns to the first due engine company. The burns later proved to be fatal to the man on the nozzle.

Anyone who has witnessed a major fire scene can visualize the seemingly haphazard arrangement of the many hoselines in the street stretched by the various companies. It can, therefore, be understood how an error could occur in correctly identifying the proper hoseline and its actual location for use in fighting the fire. The scene takes on the semblance of a twisted and entangled web of spaghetti. By the time that the error was discovered, it was too late to prevent the resulting tragedy. The pump operator who had committed the error was devastated, but it was too late. The only course left was to assure that such a mistake would not be repeated. Upon investigation of this unfortunate incident, it was discovered that the error had been made by the alternate MPO who had worked a mutual exchange of tours with the regularly assigned MPO. This was hardly irregular and was a common and necessary practice in training. Due to this tragedy, however, a concentrated drive was on to acquaint **all** firefighters in the proper operation of a fire department pumper.

On the day that Deputy Chief Muto visited our quarters, our company officer had been detailed out to another company and the senior man, Charlie Deza, was the acting Lieutenant. At the time I was also a designated alternate Motor Pump Operator, substituting for Victor Vitale who was on vacation. Firefighters Joe Doyle, Frank Ricciardi and a man detailed to us from a Ladder Company, Bob Smith, completed the working group for this day tour of duty.

When the Chief announced the purpose of his visit and the subject we were to be questioned on, we were gathered in a semi-circle on the apparatus floor. Chief Muto was a very able and competent commander, however, he had a very definite Italian brogue and spoke with a broken English dialect that reminded me of the Italian comedic actor, Henry Armetta.

The question and answer period went along smoothly with Chief Muto demonstrating his knowledge of the subject matter we covered. The brogue wasn't too noticeable at first but became thicker as the session progressed. When we got to the specifics of the engines' pumping capacity, it had developed into a full blown brogue. He started with the first man situated to his left and inquired about the **stages** of the pumps on our fire engine. It may have been more clearly pronounced in the Chief's mind, but what came out as he asked the question was, "How many stages isa gotta this pumba?"

First Fireman: "Two stages, Chief."

Chief Muto: "Ok, thatsa your answer." (Then to second fireman)

Chief Muto: "How many stages isa gotta this pumba?"

Second Fireman:"Three stages, Chief."

Chief Muto:"OK, thatsa your answer."

I was the third in line for questioning and by now it was all I could do to stifle a laugh that was fighting to break out. Afraid that a repeat of the question, and a terse reply by me would betray me, I volunteered to answer before he could ask the question. "This is a 1000 gallon, four stage pumper, Chief." The Chief just nodded and then turned to Charlie Deza, the Acting Lieutenant.

Chief Muto: "OK, you are the acting officer, tell me how many stages isa gotta this pumba?"

By now it was more than I could bear. Especially when Charlie went through an embarrassing long pause and looked in turn at each of us who had answered. He figured that since he was the designated acting officer it made sense to add a stage to the last answer given. When he finally answered, "Dees poms eez five stages" in his South American accent, sounding more like a Mexican bandit than a New York City firefighter, I could hold out no longer and broke out laughing.

Not to appear disrespectful, especially given the seriousness of the circumstances that brought about the importance of expanding knowledge on the operation of a fire department pumper, I feigned a coughing seizure to cover my insensitive outburst. It almost appeared that Chief Muto himself was somewhat amused by this unexpected dialect-à-deux.

After I contained my seizure we resumed. The brief hiatus smoothed out the Chief's dialect appreciably and we continued. "OK," said the Chief. "We have four men here and I got four different answers. I see by the entry in the journal that there is one man out investigating a complaint. Are we to expect an extra stage to be added?" He then declared that three stages was the correct answer.

However, I insisted that four stages was the correct answer as we had a 1000 gallon pumper, not a 750 gallon pumper. This brought about a three-four, three-four exchange between us until he concluded the drill. He advised us to bone up and the visit would be repeated at a future date. As he pulled away in the Chief's car I didn't score any brownie points when I called out, "Four."

"WE'RE UNDER SIEGE"; BED-STY ENGINE CO. 280

In the early to mid-1960s, fires in the predominantly minority areas of the Bedford Stuyvesant sections of Brooklyn as well as mindless attacks against firemen began to reach epidemic proportions. The excuse at the time was that it was in protest to the Vietnam War and other domestic civil rights issues. The more these incidents were tolerated by failing to exact swift and harsh punishment when perpetrators were apprehended, the more brazen the lawless acts became. Incidents of arson were definitely on the rise starting in the mid 1950s.

So widespread were these acts of anarchy that the busy companies in the Bedford Stuyvesant area where I was assigned didn't bother to return the apparatus into quarters after responding to an alarm as they would only lose time waiting for apparatus doors to be reopened and traffic cleared in front of quarters for the next run which was soon to follow. On one such night the alarms were coming in faster than the dispatcher could assign units and the forces were spread thin to cover most of the affected areas. Fireman Gus Guidice of Engine Company 280 had been detailed to drive the 38th Battalion Chief. When they arrived at the tenement building involved in what appeared to be an intentionally-set blaze, he noted that the first due engine company had not arrived. They should have been at the scene well before the Battalion Chief and the responding ladder company. Valuable time was wasted in waiting for the later assigned units as fire conditions worsened. Battalion Chief Franey ordered Fireman Guidice to contact the first due engine company by radio, surmising that they had broken down en route to the fire scene.

When Gus finally contacted the Captain on duty with the first due engine company he inquired as to the company's location and the reason they had failed to respond to the fire alarm. Gus was amazed at the response. The company was still in quarters and failed to respond as they were "under siege." This was a new excuse to Gus and the Chief until it was explained. As the firefighters were stopping traffic in an attempt to leave quarters in response to the alarm, they were pelted by rocks, bottles, garbage pails and other dangerous missiles from the roofs of adjoining buildings. They made several attempts, all with the same result. The deadly barrage would not let up. Rather than expose his men to this impossible situation, the Captain notified the fire dispatcher to send police protection.

Meanwhile, Gus and the Battalion Chief were faced with a fire that was beginning to spread rapidly. Only one other engine company had responded, as all other first alarm units were operating at other locations. Chief Franey immediately transmitted a second alarm.

When the police cruisers arrived at the company that was "under siege," they too were the recipients of various dangerous missiles thrown from the adjacent roofs. They had to take refuge inside the fire station. The police cars sustained damage as the officers retreated into the building. The miscreants, and the arsonists probably among them, aware of the administration's policy of restraint in dealing with these so-called civil upheavals, persisted in their attack to keep the company from responding to the alarm and resumed the barrage as the company tried in vain to emerge from the building. As a last resort, the police officer in charge, after making various notifications, called out the Tactical Command Force. When they responded they too were attacked by missiles from the closest roof. The tactical units now moved to a location out of reach of the barrage and attempted to reason with the perpetrators, in calm, measured tones. The result? More debris from the roof. The perpetrators were then notified that they would have one last chance to get off the roofs and allow the company to leave quarters, or stronger measures would be taken to assure their removal. This announcement was met with vile language and accompanied by yet another barrage from the roof.

There was now a long pause. As was the liberal policy of the times, the Commander of the tactical force was probably in contact with City Hall to get permission for their next move. (They should have done this from the start.) They gave one last warning (again a last warning) to get off the roofs. When that too went unheeded, they finally advanced with clubs and weapons drawn towards the buildings. Like magic, the roofs were cleared and the engine company and the police that had taken refuge were able to leave quarters. Once that was accomplished, the mistake was that no effort was made to apprehend those responsible for the willfully unlawful behavior. This assured a recurrence with impunity.

The fire? Oh yes, the fire! It was finally contained before spreading to adjacent occupancies by the second alarm assignment. It could easily have gotten out of hand by the unanticipated delay caused by the "siege" of the quarters of the first due company.

FIREHOUSE CHARACTERS

THE SLACKERS, LE VOYEUR VEGETARIAN, EMBARRASSING MOMENTS

This type we usually refer to as "the Lump." Of the thirty-two firemen assigned to Engine Company 280, we were saddled with two of these. At a fire they did the minimum. They were rarely, if ever, found on the nozzle when fighting a fire of any consequence but would volunteer to take the nozzle in minor operations such as trash fires in the street. They are also known as "kink chasers and butt tighteners" which at least was of some use by keeping hose from being entangled in the hallway and preventing water from dripping past the hose couplings.

After a working fire was extinguished, Lumps would invariably take the nozzle to "wash down". One of these Lumps, let's call him fireman Humpty, as he was built like a giant bowling ball, actually missed a run on a day that I was the acting lieutenant. He was polishing the brass pole when an alarm came in. When he failed to get to the apparatus floor within fifteen seconds we took off without him. Luckily we weren't needed at the fire as it was easily contained by the first due company. The Lump wouldn't have been of much use anyway. When we returned to quarters I couldn't believe the excuse he gave. He claimed he got jammed in the space between the pole and the floor through which the pole extended. On another occasion we forced him up front with the nozzle man at a fire in an apartment building. Things were ok in the hall until the door to the fire apartment was opened and the heat and smoke filled the hall. Fireman Humpty knocked over the firemen who were trying to keep him in position by the nozzle like they were ten pins at a bowling alley. At another fire we had occasion to stretch hose over an eight foot fence to reach the rear of a building that was fully involved in fire. The Lump never made it to the other side of the fence.

However, he later claimed a shoulder injury from this operation and was subsequently retired on a "line of duty" injury. Although all who had worked with this Lump were outraged by the injustice of the department rewarding gross incompetence we were glad to see him out of the job. In private enterprise he would have been fired as soon as it became evident he wasn't doing the job.

The other lump was equally useless. In addition he had a repulsive habit of passing lewd and filthy remarks when a pretty girl would pass by. I first became aware of this while still a probationary firefighter. As no one else paid him any attention I just walked away. Sometime later this behavior led to a direct confrontation with this character. Besides his dirty mouth he had other revolting behaviors that no one bothered to challenge. The lieutenant disliked this man's conduct but was too much of a gentleman to chastise him. I had no such qualms and took him to task at sexually oriented remarks he was mouthing as two teen age girls were passing by the firehouse. Hopefully they didn't hear him. It was the start of "bad blood" between us.

The day of my confrontation with this Lump started peacefully enough. I was busy in the kitchen frying onions for a meal I was preparing. It was near noon when we got a visit from our battalion chief. Everyone initially snapped to attention, the hood of the apparatus was opened for inspection and "all hands" made themselves busy at some chore. If the chief was making a formal visit we would all "fall in" until the inspection was complete. I shut off the gas stove and started towards the hose wagon when the chief notified the lieutenant that this was an unofficial visit since he was stopping only to pick up company papers.

As I approached the hose wagon, the Lump was dusting it off with waste rags. As I got close he tossed the rags at me with the remark, "You're the driver, you dust it off." I tossed the rags back and warned him not to be throwing rags at me. He now threw them overhand, and forcefully, right at my chest. I considered this a direct challenge. I took the waste rags and smashed them into his face. The chief had already left before this took place. It got uglier when the Lump's foul mouth got into the act. I then invited him into the cellar so we could settle our differences. I could see Lieutenant Mulligan racing up the stairs to his office and the floor cleared of everyone except the house watchman. There obviously were not going to be any witnesses. Now that I had called his bluff his aggressive posture was changing as I now had him by the shirt and had thrown him against the ambulance which was assigned to our quarters. The bombast was replaced by olive branches. I further urged him on by reminding him of his army fights where he claimed he was felling giants and I was only a welterweight. To no avail! I then let go and returned to the kitchen to resume my cooking. The floor was alive again as the reluctant potential witnesses returned with the apparent "all clear". I resumed sauteeing the onions when in walks the Lump. Again the floor was vacated as it appeared round two was about to take place. I had just put a cigarette to my mouth and was checking my pockets for a match. I had no matches and I couldn't believe what happened next. The Lump had seated himself at the table, and aware that I had no matches, he jumped up and lit my cigarette. I had no further problems with him after that.

Even with all that had transpired here, Fireman Oscar (the actor) continued to fear this guy and allowed himself to be dumped on. He wasn't a typical fireman. There were other incidents of conflict here as I'm sure there were in other companies. That's not surprising since the fire service attracts lots of people with aggressive personalities. Since antiquity there have been clashes between firemen. Most of the cases were between companies on arrival at a fire where they'd be fighting to see which company was to be the first one to hook up to a hydrant and get water on the fire. This zeal and rivalry is a hold over from the days before the horse drawn steamers, in the 1800s, when almost all companies were staffed by volunteers.

There are cases on record of buildings burning down to the ground while competing companies were engaged in full fledged battles with fisticuffs, and an occasional baseball bat, cast in the glow of the flames from the building in dispute. It took years of organization and regimentation to assure that such aggression be directed towards fighting the fire instead of each other. So it is the duty of a fire officer to manage these various temperaments in a company and to form a cohesive and effective fire fighting unit.

OVERZEALOUS WILD MAN

In this mode a firefighter is almost as useless as is the slacker. This is a throwback to the time when we had wooden hydrants and firefighers were rumored to have iron lungs impervious to fire and smoke. The danger is when this character blindly charges into a fire building without a charged hoseline and is oblivious to conditions inside. Unless these steps are taken in an attempted rescue they are foolhardy. Such actions have proven to result in injuries and, at times, fatalities. After over zealous firefighters have been toned down by training and experience they are valuable additions to the force. They are the ones often involved in daring rescues and who give the fire department its well deserved reputation. In some cases they take up the slack for the occasional "Lump" encountered on the job. They also turn out to be very dedicated firefighters. Many of them would take the position of firefighter even without pay. Given two of this type firefighter in a working group, and an officer would be confident he could attack any fire or emergency situation.

THE UNDESIGNATED QUARTERBACK

Practically every company has experienced this player in one form or another. Until all hands became wise to his act this cutie has a routine, so smooth, that it goes undetected for some time. Usually when a company stretches hose to a fire in an apartment building each man takes three folds of hose which is the equivalent of a little more than a fifty foot length. As they advance up the stairs the hose is played out until they reach the fire floor. In a good aggressive engine company everyone vies to be the nozzle man. To accommodate each man in the group this honor is normally alternated among them.

Aware of this propensity, the quarterback, with a minimum amount of expended energy will take only one fold as he drapes the nozzle over his shoulder as the line is advanced to the fire floor. Once there, under the cover of smoke and heat, the quarterback laterals the nozzle to the first arriving firefighter who had stretched the hose to the fire floor. He then retreats to the landing below while busily straightening hose in the stairwell. He then resumes his position at the nozzle after the heat and smoke is subdued.

LE VOYEUR

In every large group of men a couple of these may be found. In one of the companies that I worked a drama unfolded in an apartment house opposite from the firehouse that held the interest of three of the crew. In a repertoire befitting the movie REAR WINDOW one scene stood out. Without benefit of binoculars, or hindered by shades or blinds, Les Trois Voyeurs were witnesses to an act of infidelity that was almost laughable. A young, sexy married woman left her husband, reading or watching TV on a lower floor. She would then go to a bachelor's apartment on the floor above and engage in sex acts. She would later return to her apartment and to an unsuspecting spouse. This act played out until the cuckold became aware of the subterfuge. One day he confronted the guilty bachelor in the street. The confrontation escalated into a fist fight with the husband getting the worst of it. The house watchman, seeing the unequal battle, called out and two of us ran over and broke up the fight. I felt like taking a poke at the bachelor myself as he was betraying a supposed friendship. The wife, of course, was more to blame. I have a dim view of voyeurism. I also shun the occasional porno flick that one of the truckmen would sometimes show. I'm not exactly a prude but I don't think much of the guys engaged in these pursuits.

THE VEGETARIAN

Late at night, probably to break the boredom, or as an outlet for the perverted nature of some of the troops, some outlandish banter takes place in a firehouse kitchen.

On this night, Engine Co. 280 had just returned from the last of three consecutive runs since midnight. They were mostly routine runs. The first was a false alarm, the second an auto accident with gasoline leaking onto the roadway. The last was a fire under a stairwell that could have developed into a major problem had it not been discovered early and an alarm transmitted. We quickly put that blaze out after some tenants had retreated into the street and others were alerted to the possibility that they may have to evacuate the building. However, there was no extension of fire and the tenants were relieved to return to their apartments although uneasy as the fire was of suspicious origin.

On return to quarters, Captain Franey, as usual, made sure that the MPO washed, with a long handled brush and a bucket, each and every tire, wheel and wheel well of the engine. This practice is no longer followed. He then retired to his office to log the results of the previous company activities in the fire record journal. With hardly a respite between runs most of the working group remained in the kitchen and the bottomless, ubiquitous pot of coffee was getting most of the attention.

One of the group on this tour was an engine man from another company detailed to Engine 280 to fill in for a regular who was on medical leave. He was a very quiet fellow who hardly ever spoke unless spoken to. He was in good condition and had at one time been an amateur boxer with an impressive record. He certainly "held his own" at a fire and was well liked by all the men. He had one failing, however, that the perverted inquisitors soon exploited. Beside being on the bashful side he was also naive and didn't like to discuss matters of a personal nature. What's more, our hapless detailed fireman had recently been married and was celebrating his sixth month of wedded bliss. After the usual small talk on the subject of marriage, Bill Kamerling, an instigator of the first magnitude, posed questions of a strictly intimate and personal nature to our beleaguered detailed fireman. He climaxed his lecture on marital responsibility by asking our newly wedded fireman the ultimate contrived question. Feigning seriousness, at his irreverent best:

Bill:"Now that you have been married six months, have you given your spouse the benefit of oral sexual gratification? (Of course, the actual question was posed in other words.)

Detailee:"If you don't mind, I don't like to discuss personal matters."

Now that Bill sensed that the detailee had taken the bait as evidenced by the reddening of his cheeks, he doggedly pursued this line of inquiry much to the discomfort and embarrassment of his target.

Knowing that Bill Kamerling was an ace salesman, I realized it was only a matter of time before the reluctant fireman would succumb to Bill's merciless onslaught. Bill then conducted a mock poll of everyone in the kitchen as the poor detailee was gradually broken down. Finally, in the wee hours of the night tour the detailee finally admitted that he, indeed, consummated (as Bill put it) his marriage in an exploratory act after his fifth month of marriage. The poor soul was bashful beyond belief about this admission but Bill still wasn't completely satisfied and went on:"

Bill:"OK, so you finally consummated the marriage. But one thing you haven't said was the extent of your olfactory sensation during your obligatory act" (though not in so many words). The popular notion, he went on to say, was that the sensation was of a piscatorial nature. Bill Now demanded the detailee's version.

Bill:"Well, what did it remind you of?"

The Detailee: now red faced, looked up sheepishly and blurted out, "BRUSSELS SPROUTS"

This declaration and confession caught us all by surprise. It was all we could do to keep from rolling on the floor. We must have laughed for an hour. After a while the detailee himself sheepishly joined us in laughter which caused a resurgence of our intense laughing. After a while the laughing subsided and another pot of coffee was started on the stove. The laughter finally began to die down until the detailee, now composed, came out with "I knew I should never had told you." This brought on another round of rib-cracking laughter. No one really wanted to embarrass our temporary guest so we went out of our way to make him feel secure as "one of the boys" until he returned to his regular company. His surprise secret was safe with us and was never revealed to his regularly assigned company. However, I believe that all of us in the kitchen that day will never forget the vegetarian fireman who had been detailed to our company that night.

Thankfully, most firemen have a great sense of humor. It is a good escape from some of the sad and sometimes grisly conditions we are faced with in the normal performance of duties.

EMBARRASSING MOMENTS - LOST IN BROOKLYN

It was shortly after the 7 pm drill at the start of a night tour on a hot summer's evening that we received a cryptic alarm for relocation by the Brooklyn dispatcher. At the time I was the MPO in Engine Co. 280 and a newly promoted captain from Queens, NY was covering for our vacationing regular officer. He appeared very nervous. It was his first unfamiliar assignment in an unfamiliar borough. To make matters worse our regular pumper was at the shop for repairs and the replacement must have been scraped up from the bottom of the pool. It was an American LaFrance that was so old it actually had solid rubber tires instead of pneumatics. It didn't even have a windshield. If that wasn't discouraging enough, every time it was started it belched flame from the exhaust that extended clear to under the back step. It also had a tendency to backfire that sent a cloud of black smoke to mix in with the flaming exhaust. At times the grease in the undercarriage would catch on fire during start up and we had a man stand by with a dry chemical extinguisher to guard against the fire extending to other parts of the rig. When it was underway it appeared to be a flaming chariot from hell on its way to the moon or beyond.

All this only added to the extreme discomfort of our nervous covering captain. Of course, we had complained to the shop that this rig was an outright hazard if not a fire trap. But we were ordered to make do for a couple of days. To add to the ongoing fiasco the dispatcher ordered us to relocate to a section in Brooklyn that none of us in the working group ever heard of. I called the dispatcher back for clarification, but the order stood. Captain (Shakie) couldn't believe all this was happening to him on his initial sojourn in Brooklyn. After twenty minutes of driving we still couldn't find the location given us. In fact, we stopped some surprised and sometimes frightened pedestrians and asked for directions always with the dry chemical extinguisher at the ready. No one ever heard of the location. After about a half hour the covering captain could stand no more. The radio on the rig was inoperative so we stopped off by a pay telephone booth and called the Brooklyn dispatcher for further information. During our misguided trip we never came across a firehouse that may have provided a clue. One patrolman had given us a lead that sent us to a dead end street.

The captain was too excited and embarrassed to make the call so he asked me to contact the dispatcher. To the unbelieving citizens we had passed along the way we must have appeared to be the fire department's version of the Keystone Kops, what with the antique fire apparatus, open cab, no windshield and flaming trail frequently punctuated by loud, smoky backfiring. We must have appeared to be an apparition; in a time warp from the past.

When I finally got the dispatcher on the phone he was all apologies. He explained that there had been a snafu and that he tried to get back to us immediately after we made the last call from the firehouse but we had responded too quickly. There had been no way to contact us en route. We had no radio.

Next he tells me to disregard the whole assignment and to sneak back to our own firehouse as if nothing happened. I was to call the dispatcher upon arriving back at quarters. Imagine sneaking back with a flaming, exploding excuse for a fire engine, manned by a, by now, comatose captain, rumbling along on solid tires which made sounds on cobblestone streets like the approach of a displaced IRT subway train. By this time it was dark which made the flame from the exhaust more noticeable. We now had to contend with the further indignity of having pedestrians yelling out to us that the truck was on fire. One wise ass kid called out to us to pull the next fire alarm box. Most of us took the passing taunts good naturedly. Not so the covering captain. I'm certain that he was ready to transfer back to Queens. Who knows, maybe he thought this was a routine occurrence in the crazy borough. After all it was the home of the Brooklyn Dodgers and all Yankee fans knew that Dodger fans were abnormal especially in the days of Casey and Marv Throneberry. After the Dodgers and the Symphony what ever else would one expect a fire engine in Brooklyn to look like?

EMBARRASSING MOMENTS

The members of Engine Co. 280 had built a decent four wall handball court which covered most of our yard area at the rear of the firehouse. Playing was a real good way to stay in shape. A lively twenty-one point game, especially during the hot summer months, resulted in working up a healthy sweat. It was a warm September day and

I had just completed three games in succession. I decided it was time for a nice shower. During working tours of duty only one fireman at a time would be taking a shower so the remainder of the crew would be "at the ready" in the event of an alarm.

So as not to be caught short, the accepted practice by the one in the shower was to lay out his boots, with the pants legs fitted over the boots. In this way there would be hardly any time lost when responding to an alarm. All that had to be done was to step into the boots and pull up the trousers as you made your way to the pole hole.

I was in the shower this day, all soaped up, when the alarm hit. I just had time for a fast incomplete rinse of my face and stepped out to where my pants and boots were laid out. But some prankster had taken my gear away! To miss responding with the rig was unthinkable so I slid the pole, reasoning that the sadistic jokester had relocated my gear on the apparatus floor. The MPO had started up the engine. As I landed on the apparatus floor, dressed only in some lingering soap bubbles, I saw that there was a bunch of second grade school kids, accompanied by their female school teachers, gathered by the open door. Imagine my embarrassment! Luckily the clothing rack was nearby and I quickly grabbed any turnout coat nearest to me to preserve what privacy was left me in this situation. In the same motion I stepped into the closest set of boots and redfacedly made it to the back step, all the while disregarding the tittering by the unexpected guests and the unrestrained laughter from my bosom buddies as we made our way out with bells and sirens blasting away.

Visits by teachers and pupils from local schools are not uncommon and in many cases are welcomed as the wide-eyed kids make a very good audience. At times we would simulate a response and some of us would execute a couple of pole slides which the kids enjoyed. On this visit, however, they were treated to a lot more than they expected. I don't recall seeing the same female teachers in later visits. I never did find out the name of the fiendish jokester who hid my gear. You never saw so many innocent and hurt looks as I tried to ferret out the culprit!

EMBARRASSING MOMENTS, SUMMER WATER FIGHTS

Firefighters display an aura of strength, trust and professionalism. During hot summer months however, any semblance of dignified behavior within the confines of the firehouse evaporates. Firefighters then metamorphose into frivolous, inane juveniles characterized by the indiscriminate splashing of water either by squirt gun, pail, garden hose or the ever popular brown or plastic bag. During these splash frenzies no one is spared including the officer on duty.

On one such day, after having thoroughly soaked each other, the trap had been set to get the officer on duty. The stage was set when the working group disappeared from the apparatus floor after calling the officer, Lieut. Mulligan, to inform him, as a ruse, of an impending visit by the Chief in Charge of the Borough of Brooklyn. When the lieutenant got to the floor and saw no one he became suspicious and went down to the basement where he would be impervious to flying aqueous missiles. In the meantime, who should enter quarters unannounced, but Borough Deputy Chief Muto. Seeing no one on the floor he went across the floor to the yard area expecting that a drill may be in progress. Poised above the yard area on the first floor, armed with a pail of water and a full #3 size brown bag, were Joe Doyle, Lou Vaio and Gus Guidice as the bombsight director. The chief's white hat appeared briefly in the yard but, at that moment the lieutenant emerged from the cellar and called out to the chief who stepped back just in time to evade the flood from above. Had the lieutenant not called out at that exact moment, the borough chief would have been the unintended victim. He quickly sized up the situation, and luckily had a sense of humor, which may have disappeared had he suffered a direct hit. He let us all off with a half-hearted reprimand, signed the journal and was off to brave the vagaries of yet another company. The moral is that during the hot summer months, let the visitor beware when entering a firehouse. The lieutenant was not as gracious after this incident. If the attack had not backfired, he, Lieutenant Mulligan would have been held accountable. He did not relish that thought because Borough Chief Muto had a reputation as being a tough "cookie" regarding discipline.

Chapter 11

MUCHO MACHO

ATTEMPTED MURDER, SHIP FIRE, LADDER CO. DUTY, GAMBLING COMPANY, INJURY, CHINESE RESTAURANT

July 1954. I got to work early for my 6 p.m. to 9 a.m. (next morning) tour. Around 5:30 p.m., I was visited by the battalion chief and notified that our captain was to be detailed to a double company to cover for the vacationing officers. Being that I was on the promotional list for lieutenant, I was designated as the acting lieutenant for the tour. This was common practice at the time. There was always a shortage of officers since the city was slow on making promotions, probably to keep the budget in balance.

I had reported in early that evening, expecting to relax a while, as most of the day I had spent helping my older brother on Long Island paint the exterior of his house.

We were on the apparatus floor at 7:30 p.m., during the company drill period, practicing cardio-pulmonary resuscitation on our life-like dummy called Resusi-Annie. Suddenly, there were excited sounds of screaming and hollering from outside. The house watchman ran out to check on the source of the commotion. He returned immediately, beckoning us to come out quickly, as there was a murder in progress. When we got outside we were greeted by an ugly and violent spectacle. There was a gang of about eight men surrounding a young male. There was a lot of yelling and cursing, mostly in Spanish, as they were beating the man with fists, while kicking and stabbing the unfortunate victim who himself was screaming blue murder. This incident was playing out across the street and was about 200 feet from the fire station. The house watchman stood fast while the remaining four of us ran to assist the unfortunate victim.

As we drew close to the gang a few of them turned in our direction as if they were ready for a confrontation, until they noticed that we were armed with an ax, a claw tool, and a hook. They then decided to run off leaving their victim lying in a pool of blood. He was bleeding profusely from multiple stab wounds and kept repeating that he was going to die. We got some compresses from our first aid supply, and while two of my crew were attempting to stem the flow of blood with the compresses, I called the police department on the company phone. I told them to have a police car and an ambulance respond immediately, as a man was bleeding to death. I got an okay and went to check the victim, notifying him that help was on the way. After ten minutes, there was no sign of the police nor the ambulance. I got back on the phone again, stressing the urgency of the situation, as the man was bleeding profusely despite our efforts. He must have had twenty stab wounds. When there was no response in the next ten minutes we decided to put our asses on the line. The hospital was about a half mile away. We got our stretcher and two of the firemen broke all records in getting to the hospital on foot. By now, the victim was in deep shock from loss of blood and exposure despite the July heat.

This decision on my part (we all agreed, but I was the acting officer and would shoulder the responsibility), was a gamble to save a life. We were left seriously undermanned and could be placing many lives in jeopardy in the event of a full scale emergency.

We were lucky, as no alarms affecting us were received in the next half hour. By that time my men returned. They would have been back sooner but had trouble having the hospital staff accept the hapless victim. And still, neither police nor ambulance arrived. I didn't bother to call them again. No one there would be interested in what I had to tell them this time around. Later, when it was evident no one was coming we assumed they had gotten a call from the hospital covering this incident. So we put this episode behind us, satisfied we had helped save (maybe) a life, and had not been needed elsewhere in the interim of vulnerability.

The remainder of the night was relatively uneventful. I was tired from the day's activity before reporting for duty but had to get company papers ready for the chief to pick up at 8 a.m. At 11:30 p.m., while knee deep in preparing the papers, the house watchman called up to the office on the intercom.

When I got down to the apparatus floor, there were two policemen at the house watch desk. I reasoned that they had gotten all the information at the hospital and wanted to get our deposition, and maybe a description of the assailants. Also, we thought they may have information on the victim's chances of survival. We were ready to forget our earlier frustration at the delay in response. That all changed when the younger cop asked me, "What happened?" I said, "What do you mean, "what happened"?" Then, "We came to investigate an accident."

Me: "That was four hours ago and it was attempted murder. You mean to say that you are only now responding to that emergency call?"

The cop was mouthing some kind of combination excuse and explanation none of which embraced the fact that not even an ambulance was sent as requested.

The truth is, I was not even listening at this point. I only knew there was no excuse. What I went on to say after that is not fit to print. However, they both left hurriedly before I was done.

Now in 1995, there is serious talk about emergency responses involving both police and fire departments, supposedly in an effort to improve services and save the taxpayers money. My feeling is that "if it ain't broke, don't fix it." The New York Fire Department is probably the only emergency force that still makes house calls, AND PROMPTLY.

The exaggerated delay in response by the police as related above is certainly not the norm. There had to be some snafu in the line of communications. However, it does point out the fact that when someone reports a fire or other emergency to the fire department they can be confident there will be a response without any undue delay.

SHIP FIRE - LADDER CO. DUTY

In January, 1955, I was transferred to a very busy truck company in Red Hook, Brooklyn. After seven years on the job, all of which was spent working mostly in engine companies, I felt like a johnny again. The lieutenant that I worked my tours of duty with in this company had, ironically, come off the same promotion list that I did. He had been promoted a couple of years before me since he had lots of seniority. For some reason he resented me from the start. Here was this young upstart passing the first promotion test with high marks, which were the highest in the division, and he had had to struggle for many years, with many failed attempts before he finally just barely passed the last promotion test for lieutenant. Of course this was no fault of mine.

We got off on the wrong foot the first day that I was on duty. Unbeknownst to me, this company had a duty roster for committee work, another name for the housecleaning detail. The working group from the previous night tour had a tough worker. As a result the apparatus was left in a sorry state after having been out nearly the whole night and subject to smoke, ash and debris. All of the tools had to be cleaned and the hook and ladder truck itself had to be cleaned and waxed. This was the first order of business as we started our day tour. I was kept busy on this task without a break, from before the time my tour started, 8:45 a.m., to almost 1 p.m., when it was time to break for lunch. At this point, one by one, the men would leave the apparatus floor, and go to their lockers. Before I realized what was going on, I was left alone, and the lieutenant and most of the men were in the kitchen having their lunch. I wasn't used to this arrangement. All the companies that I had worked in had someone cook and we all ate together. Or, at least we were asked if we had brought lunch or wanted something from the store. Here, not a word! Everyone had brought their lunch.

I went into the kitchen to find out what the score was on lunch whereupon the prematurely grey-haired lieutenant (let's call him Lieutenant Choker) informed me that everyone brings their own lunch. He then took this occasion to inform me that his office had not yet been cleaned, dusted and mopped, and why hadn't I checked the Committee Work Roster to see that it was my duty on this day. And that it had to be done before lunch time, to boot!

The men, of course informed him that I was busy cleaning the rig and the tools which was a lot more important. This SOB lieutenant would have none of this as an excuse to deviate from the Committee Work Roster. So as not to make a scene on my first tour of duty in this company, I went up and cleaned the office. When I got down to the kitchen after I was done, I asked the lieutenant where was the nearest place to get a sandwich. I couldn't believe the reply! He said no one was permitted to go to the store and that I should have brought my lunch. I could sense where this was heading but that was all I was going to put up with. I then told this SOB that I was going out to get a sandwich and that he had better not try to stop me, and if he wished, he could bring me up on charges. Boy, what a start!

The next day tour that I had with this creep was really a beaut. We responded to a fire on board a Collier type ship out in the bay. The only transportation available was by a small police department launch, so our heroic lieutenant took the only smoke mask we had and told me, "You come with me," whereby we were taken to the ship to assess the situation. The one crewman left on the ship took us to the deck hatch where most of the smoke was coming from. As he removed the hatch he informed us that just below the deck there were ten five-gallon cans of gasoline stored. At this point, our heroic lieutenant dons the only mask we have, a Scott Air Pack, and says, "Follow me."

As we got below the first deck he told me to remove all the gasoline cans while he checked for the source of the smoke. With every can of gasoline that I handed up to the crewman above I was able to take in a mouthful of air, until I got all of the cans of gasoline out.

It was then that Lieutenant Choker called for me to come down to the next lower deck. When I got down there he was trying to break a wooden chair which was in his way. He ordered that I get the chair out. There was really no sense in expending precious time and energy on this stupid order but I did it anyway. This wasn't the proper time for a dispute. Meanwhile, the heat and smoke were building up below. The smoldering fire was coming from behind the cork wall tiles of a refrigeration room and acrid black smoke was pushing past the seams. I told the lieutenant I couldn't hold out much longer; that we should call for a fireboat and get more manpower before things got out of hand and the fire extended. It was then that the bell alarm from his Scott Air Pack went off as it was almost expended. By this time I felt that my lungs were about to burst, when to my surprise, our heroic lieutenant started acting kind of crazy after removing his face mask. I couldn't figure out what was wrong. He should still have some time on the air pack. Before I knew what happened he collapsed and passed out. I was so choked up from the smoke that my first impulse was to make a run for some air and get some help. I called for this guy on deck for help but there was no answer.

My mind was alternating between feelings of panic and complacency knowing we were alone two decks below on this ship with no back-up on the way. The one crewman above deck couldn't be counted on. I again got no answer to my call so he may have left his position at the hatch. I had the strange sensation that our actions were in slow motion. It is a feeling that is very difficult to explain. Of course it must have been from the effects of the carbon monoxide which was constantly mixing in with the noxious fumes given off by the smoldering adhesive behind the cork tiles. You know what is going on, and that you have to get the hell out immediately, and yet you feel no sense of urgency. Luckily, I hadn't gotten to the point of being completely oblivious to the plight we were in.

The next step, when overcome by the pernicious effects of carbon monoxide poisoning, would be that you know what to do but that you would be completely helpless. The body would not respond.

I was already feeling a bit woozy - what with the ridiculous effort expended in breaking apart the chair in the fire room plus removing the gasoline cans. At least with that removal I was able to suck in some much needed air. It's a wonder I wasn't in worse shape than our intrepid lieutenant.

When my calls for help went unanswered, for a moment the feeling of fear and urgency must have taken over. There was only one thing left to do before I too passed out. In desperation, I grabbed the lieutenant and somehow made it up two decks to the open hatch where I was able to lift him to the waiting crewman above. To this day I don't know how I was able to make it! There was still no other help to arrive. I just stood with my head above the open hatch sucking in gulps of air, stinking though it was, before I was finally able to lift myself out with the help of the crewman who hadn't deserted us after all. Shortly after, the launch came by again with the Deputy Chief in Charge of the

Borough on board. Meanwhile, a fireboat had been summoned to the scene by the chief's driver.

I was still in a daze. I could see the crewman's mouth moving but couldn't understand a word. I wasn't too sure how I got to the deck. I didn't remember going up the first stair from the second deck below. All I remembered was having flashbacks to the days working in construction and carrying hods full of brick and mortar up the steep vertical, twenty-five-foot ladder to the bricklayers in the tower. How I had vowed not to quit even as the hod had pulled the skin away from my shoulder and the lime leaching from the mortar in the hod was burning onto the open wounds. I was new at the job and they all expected me to quit but whatever the pain I was determined to see the job through. In my semi-dazed condition, that is what I visualized instead of saving that abusive and ungrateful lump on my back.

It took a little time to regain my senses as I was sucking in air by the mouthfuls. From this account let's not get the impression that one man can tolerate lots more smoke than another. Every fire fighter knows that is not the case. I believe that our intrepid leader had gone directly from breathing the oxygenated air of the mask to the carbon monoxide laden air, mixed in with the poisonous, noxious fumes and, in panic, hyperventilated causing him to pass out.

Shortly afterwards, I was met on the deck by the deputy chief and his driver. The heroic lieutenant was starting to come to, so we put him a safe distance from the hatch and left him sitting there until the ambulance arrived. The chief asked me if I had left my mask below. I told him I did not have a mask. "You mean to tell me that there was only one mask, and the lieutenant took it himself?" I replied that that was the case. "How come he had the mask and you had to carry him out?", he said. I told the chief he would have to ask the lieutenant about that.

As it turned out, the deputy chief was none other than Dickie Burke of the thick brogue whose chief's car, the Desoto, I had fixed when he had broken down near Engine Company 280 only six years ago.

By this time the fireboat came alongside and we had plenty of manpower. The only problem was the firemen from the boat were falling like flies. It seemed that for everyone that ventured down the hatch, without a mask, it took two firemen to carry him out. Chief Burke asked me, "What in hell is down there?" I told him there were no open flames just smoldering from the cork and adhesive in the refrigerator room. Obviously, there was now a heavier concentration of carbon monoxide below from the time I had escaped. No one was permitted below without a Scott Air Pack Mask, until the overhauling and extinguishing operation was complete. The cork tiles had to be stripped from the walls causing the adhesive to glow as it become exposed to the air. It was a messy job, left to the fireboat. Luckily, I was spared that end of the operation. The ambulance arrived, and our hero was taken from the ship by the launch. The chief suggested that I also go to the hospital and be treated for smoke inhalation but I declined. The ambulance driver was Bill Kamerling from my regularly assigned company, where the ambulance was quartered. Bill was urging me to go along, at least to keep him company, as we had not seen each other for some time. I told Bill I didn't relish the idea of going to the hospital together with the lieutenant. No way was I going to give him that satisfaction. I finally persuaded the chief and Bill that I was okay and wanted to return to duty.

I never got to work with that lieutenant again. I was put in another group working with the captain. Our hero lieutenant went on sick leave and did not return for weeks. I'm sure he didn't want to face me after the fiasco at the ship fire. Although I never found out, I wonder if the deputy chief in charge, Burke didn't have something to do with keeping us separated; or maybe it was the doing of the intrepid lieutenant himself. It didn't matter. However, the fun at this company was only beginning.

GAMBLING

Never in my time in the fire department did I ever hear of a company where gambling was so prevalent. Not that I had led such a sheltered life that I was against gambling but I was against gambling for sizeable amounts of money on the job. Late one night, when alone in the kitchen with one of the company's high rollers, he asked if I would like to pass some time playing cards. I said okay. He then suggested Hollywood Gin Rummy. I said I played Gin Rummy, but never Hollywood. With out much further ado, we played for a nominal amount of one dollar and another seventy-five cents a box. That seemed sociable enough or so I thought. At the end of the first round he declared I owed thirty-eight dollars. That to me didn't sound like a nominal amount so I had him explain how it was arrived at. After the sneiders, double, and tripling of boxes were explained, we continued playing. After three more games he owed me sixty-five dollars. He then suggested we continue on the next night tour for higher stakes. Now I declared that he could forget the sixty-five dollars and from here on we play for nominal stakes not to exceed one dollar a game. He declined and insisted we continue so that he would have a chance to make it all back. At the end of the week he owed Three Hundred and fifty dollars. He now decided we change the game to One-On-One Pinochle at ten dollars a hand. He was doing fairly good at this for a while.

I knew my way around a deck of cards and some of the plays made me a bit suspicious especially after he always picked out the same deck of cards from the cabinet. Rather than change decks I decided to check if there was another reason for his success. While alone doing the three a.m. to six a.m. house watch, I took out this deck and checked each card for any subtle marks. On three of them I found what could be distinguishing marks. On two others I was not too sure but kept them in mind. From that time on, whenever I got any of the three suspect cards in hand, I would hold onto them whether needed or not. The same with the other two. This disrupted his game so much that at one point he exploded with, "Why were you holding such and such a card when you didn't need it?" That gave him away and he knew it. That was the last time that I played any card games with him. I was not only angered but very disappointed that he would cheat a brother fire fighter.

One night, while I was on the six p.m. to nine p.m. house watch, I kept seeing officers from our and other companies accompanied by some strangers, going up to the top floor and no one seemed to be coming down. I asked one of the firemen what was going on. He was surprised that I didn't know that after every pay day there was a big crap game on the top floor. Well, after my watch was over I went up to the top floor and was greeted by a sight reminiscent of Las Vegas. The full size billiard table was fitted by a backboard for shooting craps and there was hardly a spot open to get at the table. When one guy checked out I decided to try my luck. After all, I only had twenty dollars, and who knows, I might get lucky? About an hour later we had a run and all the on-duty men responded. When we returned to quarters, I checked the bills that I had hurriedly stuffed in my pockets and to my surprise I had won three hundred and seventy-five dollars. At the time, that was more than a month and a half of a fire fighter's salary so I wasn't going back up that night.

By next payday, I was looking forward to the crap game. Most of the time the big winners were two plumbers from the neighborhood that had been invited into the game. They usually won because they came to the game with the most money and always were wrong betters. The next time out, I had a real lucky streak and even had the two plumbers on the ropes. I was on the verge of breaking the whole game. I never had such a run. I was throwing ten and twenty dollar bills around like they were Ronzoni coupons. During the last part of the session, some firemen had asked for a loan so they could remain in the game. Against my better judgment I did lend a few of them money. I soon learned that a couple of these guys were funneling money back to the two plumbers thereby keeping them in the game. Right then I should have quit and kept my winnings which were over three thousand five hundred dollars. A year's salary, plus! Instead, I set a time limit to give some of the brothers a chance to recoup. As so often happens in gambling, the tide turned completely against me and at the end of the game I came out winning a mere four hundred dollars. What angered me was the fact that my comrades borrowed from me under false pretenses to keep their plumber friends in the game. That was the last crap game I participated in. It was a good thing, too because I was getting addicted to the action. Also, I did not have a good feeling, even in winning, knowing that some of the brothers had lost most, and sometimes all, of their two weeks' salary.

Sometime later, after I had left the company, I learned that the game had been raided on a complaint from of all people, the captain's wife. She had enough of this officer - at times losing his entire paycheck - and wasn't going to take it anymore! In a way, although charges were pressed against those permitting the game to go on, I was glad to see it come to an end.

One quiet Sunday, as I was standing by my second floor locker changing into my turnout gear, I could hear the familiar clicking of pool balls from the top floor. The table was also in service for playing pool. It was only converted to a crap table on paydays. When I got to the top floor, there was a fireman practicing alone at the table. We exchanged greetings and he asked if I played pocket billiards. He then asked if I was any good to which I replied that I could hold my own. He suggested we play a fifty point game of straight pool for a quarter. I agreed, thinking to myself there was finally a guy in this company not looking to hustle a brother, and just looking to pass time.

"Okay," he said, "I'll break." As we played I could see he was a pretty good shot. After I ran a few balls it started. "You know," he said, "that around here when we say a "quarter", it means twenty-five dollars."

"No," I said, "I didn't know that." I then put down my stick and told him, "I don't play for that much with a fellow fireman."

"Okay," he said, "Let's play a game for one dollar." That I agreed to. I don't try to hustle a brother and I resent when a brother tries to put the hustle on me. Again, he broke the balls. As we played I could sense he missed some shots on purpose, so I did likewise to see what he was up to. When it became evident to me that he was indeed missing on purpose I really got angry.

"Okay," I said, "I see that you can't play for only a dollar so let's play for the twenty-five." Again he said, "I'll break." I said, "Go ahead." I made a long shot that was left and proceeded to run the fifty balls in two trips to the table, and was still shooting. In the interim he had run off seventeen consecutive balls. You should have seen the look on his face. The hustler got hustled!

I said, "Let's play a return game, and this time I will break." He weakly agreed. He saw that I allowed him to win this game without my saying so. After this game was over I said, "We are now even. Now, how much would you like to play for? Name it. Fifty? One hundred?" He replied that if I still wanted to play it would only be for a dollar.

The lesson here was that no matter how much of a hustler you think you are, there is always someone who can take you. What he didn't know was that I had played exhibitions with some well-known professional billiard champions. At age sixteen I was already capable of running up to fifty balls at a trip to the table.

I soon finished my two month tour at this company and I can't say that I was sorry to leave. It was quite an experience, and one I was not to forget. What a difference in fire houses, and both in Brooklyn!

Carl at the wheel, Mom in the   Angelo and Carl - 1927 (c)

back seat and brother Slim

(Angelo) on the passenger side.

Temporarily located to upstate farm after being evicted
from apartment in New York City.

Carl Chiarelli 1940 - New York Welterweight

Oct. 1943 Shore
Patrol (Sp) Duty at
"Coney Island"

Fireman George Mueller and Sparky

Homeward bound "the hard way"

Home with wife to be
Natalie on matrimonial
leave.

The Normandie aflame at North River Pier in 1942.

Tony Monterossa (Left) - Laid Off
Retired Lieutenant Carl Chiarelli (Right) with
Sparky on Closing of Engine Company 44.

A truckie removes part of plane which crashed into the Empire State Building in 1945.

President Nixon, on a visit to New York City, smilingly accepts a warm welcome from members of Engine Co. 1, Engine Co. 10 and Engine Co. 24.

Welfare Island became
major training center
in 1960.

Above: Chief McGinty
directs operations at
68th Street Training
School.

Horse drawn steamer displayed in
1948 at the N.Y.C. Golden Jubilee
Parade.

Cross RIP L/S
Enroute to Nantucket
Overturned during
hurricane with loss of
"All Hands" 1943-4

Lieutenant Carl Chiarelli, Paul Lotti, Herb Purcell, Larry Rooney, Harry Byrne, George Wojiula, Larry Monachelli, Lieutenant John Cavanagh, Frank Dodd, Artie Walka and Tom Byrne

Motor Pump Operator (MPO) Training Larry Rooney, Lt. Chiarelli, Tom Rogers

Fire Drill - East 78th Street Pier George Wojiula,
Lieutenant Chiarelli, Bill Dickensen

Riding the "Back Step" Bob Andriuolo, Herbie Purcell,
Larry Rooney

Caines Warehouse Fire where members of Engine Co.
44 narrowly escaped collapse of building interior.
February 1960.

1965 - Fireboat FDNY aquatic
display.

1962 - Welfare Island
Probationary Training
Center.

Engine Co. 280 and Ladder Co. 132. "Eye Of The Storm"

1966 - Engine Co. 280 and Ladder Co. 132 in remodeled quarters - lunch time.

Engine Co. 44 responding to an alarm.

March 1948 - Author - Jump to life net training school - East 68th
Street, New York City.

Captain McGinty teaching the inner workings of a "positive
displacement" pump.

Engine Co. 44. Quarterly Inspection.

Probationary Firemen Training School New York
Fire Department. December 1963.

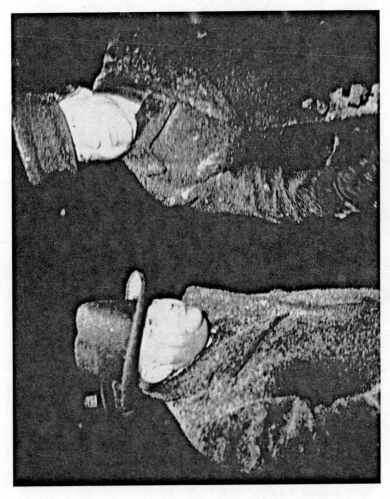

Mayor LaGuardia and Dr. Archer at a major alarm in New York City in the middle of winter.

Pompier (Scaling Ladder) Drill.

20th Annual Convention held by the International Fire
Buffs Assoc. at the Div. of Trng. on July 15, 1972.
Volunteer organizations brought their ancient prized
apparatus, some dating back to 1918.

A: Scene of Brooklyn crash in densely populated Park Slope. B: St. Augustine's Church, and School containing 1700 children. C: Downtown Brooklyn, the business and shopping center of the Borough.

Somber remains of four-engine Constellation lies in snow at Army's Miller Airfield in Staten Island after fire had been extinguished.

Section of wall is all that remains of Pillar of Fire Church.

Police Comm. Kennedy, Council Pres. Stark, Mayor Wagner, and Fire Comm. Cavanagh being interviewed by T.V. reporter Gabe Pressman.

Tail section of DC-8 Jet sprawls across intersection of 7th Avenue and Sterling Place in Brooklyn, where it narrowly missed truck halted at Stop sign.

CHINESE RESTAURANT, BKLYN

It was after 6:00 pm roll call. The air was heavy with a fine mist that made driving over the city's cobblestones an adventure. We received an alarm for box 1095 which was for a fire at a Chinese restaurant on Franklin Avenue in Brooklyn. On arrival the first floor of the restaurant was completely involved and heavy smoke and flames were pouring out of the second floor windows.

To make matters worse, as was often the case, we were short handed that day. Our full response was a lieutenant, our MPO Vic Vitale, Neil McGroarty and myself on the back step. The lieutenant had us stretch a 2 1/2 inch hose line up the fire escape at the front of the building while preparing to attack the fire in the kitchen on the first floor. We were the only company on the scene and our MPO was doing double duty by assisting with the hose stretches after hooking up to the nearest hydrant. Meanwhile, the lieutenant transmitted a second alarm as the fire intensified.

I was on the 2nd floor landing of the fire escape when the lieutenant ordered me to advance the line into the building. The windows were jammed in the down position so I had to climb over them to effect entry. After getting in, I advanced the line to a door leading to the first floor and the kitchen. I opened the door and was met by a full blast of open flame. I opened the nozzle fully and was winning the battle with the fire devil when suddenly I was without water. I immediately shut the door and went to the window to see that the hose had burst in the street. Neil unsuccessfully attempted to stop the leak with a hose jacket. I climbed down to the street and together we succeeded in snapping the hose jacket in place.

I again climbed over the window into the building. With all of these sorties I kept tripping over what appeared to be a tool box. The box had become a nuisance only after I had moved a bed in the room to the window to facilitate my trips over the jammed sash. Meanwhile, help arrived and I remained at my position and was able to beat down the fire that had previously chased me down to the street. I was then able to put out the fire that had extended to the second floor.

As the smoke was clearing I was again faced with the box that I was continually tripping over. Being curious, I flipped open the lid and was faced with dollar bills in large denominations neatly crammed into the box. I immediately snapped it shut and went to the window to inform the lieutenant. I was greeted by excited yelling, in Chinese as the restaurant owner was being escorted up the one remaining stairway by a policeman. He grabbed the box and without opening it proceeded to scramble down the stairs. I then wondered how much actual cash was in the box? Was it reported income? Would it have been destroyed if the fire had spread to the second floor? In later years, when known ex-cons were allowed into the job what might have been the fate of that cache?

This operation resulted in my first injury related sick leave. I initially wrenched my back severely as I slipped on the trolley tracks while simultaneously stretching two 2.5 inch hoselines. This happened as I jumped off the back step of the pumper while it was still in motion. My injury was further aggravated by the action of the hose stretches up the fire escape and the awkward entries over the jammed windows. After the fire it was pure torture as I helped replace the hose back onto the rig.

When we returned to quarters we washed and placed the used hose in the hose tower. We were seated in the kitchen when I decided to go the bunkroom as I had the midnight to three am watch. By this time my back was very sore and I found that I could not budge from the chair. With some help I made it to the bunkroom feeling that some rest was all that I needed. I was on my back in the bunk when the alarm sounded for a location we responded to. I practically crawled to the pole hole and attempted to slide to the apparatus floor. However, my legs couldn't grasp the pole and I went crashing down to the mat. I was helped onto the back step as we raced out the door. Luckily, we weren't needed because I would not have been able to get off the back step. When we got back to quarters the lieutenant asked if I wanted to go on sick leave and he would call in the department doctor. Sick leave was a dirty word in those days so I declined. Instead I told the officer I would be OK if allowed to lay down for a while. I was again helped to the bunkroom floor.

After a short time on my back the pain got progressively worse. I found it difficult to breathe. I couldn't even call out for assistance. After about an hour Mike Siegel came up to check on my condition. I told Mike I couldn't move and to tell the lieutenant to call the department doctor. I couldn't believe the sequence of events that followed. Just as sick leave was a dirty word for firefighters, report writing was to be avoided at all costs by some fire officers. When a member is injured the officer on duty is responsible to immediately enter the incident in the company journal. He then must follow up with two subsequent reports and notify the department doctor. It was my misfortune that night to be working under such a report shy officer.

The lieutenant came up to the bunk room to check my condition. Satisfied that I couldn't move, he asked if I had ever hurt my back in the past. I said I had once hurt my ribs while in the sanitation department and was out for a couple of days. He then advised me to tell the doctor that this was an injury sustained in prior employment. Thinking in terms of "line of duty" injury was never on my mind. I had no reason to believe the officer would do anything to hurt me just to escape writing a couple of reports. While he was on the phone with the department doctor, Mike Siegel, who had come in to spend the night with us, couldn't believe what he was hearing. He tried to stop the lieutenant from telling the doctor that I claimed a recurrence of an injury before coming to the fire department. This circumstance was to haunt me later when I had suffered additional injuries on the job.

When Doctor King arrived he examined me and ordered that I not be moved until the next morning and then taken home by ambulance as I adamantly refused to be admitted into a hospital. Later on, when I was able to have x-rays taken, they proved positive for two ruptured disks in my lower back. After notifying the doctor the lieutenant also had to notify the deputy chief on duty. I was still on my back unable to move at 4:30 am when I could hear the responding Deputy Chief Curtis, from the apparatus floor. He knew me from various operations and had once complimented me at a particularly punishing fire where I had wound up alone on the nozzle. From what I could hear the lieutenant had not operated in my best interest at all. The whole working group could hear Chief Curtis as he berated this self-serving and lazy man.

Chief Curtis: "I see you made no entry in the journal after the fire that Fireman Chiarelli was injured."

Lieutenant: "He told me he was OK and would be able to resume after he was rested."

Chief Curtis: "O.K., you had another run later when he had to be helped. You saw he couldn't be moved, why didn't you call in then."

Lieutenant:"He told me he had hurt his back in the sanitation dept."

Chief Curtis:"Tell me, is this a bad fireman and you are getting back at him?"

Lieutenant:"No, he is a good fireman, but that is what he told me." (He didn't mention that he coached me on what to tell the department doctor). Then came the blast from the Chief.

Chief Curtis: "You stupid son of a ....., just for the sake of avoiding a couple of reports can't you see how you have loused up this mans future." At least the doctor had the decency to write in the journal that the injury was incurred "After operation at 3-3-1095 and 986." Nothing specific. Only then did I realize the disservice this lazy officer had done me. From this lesson I vowed that if I ever was promoted that I would be sure to protect the interests of all members under my command.

Some years later after being injured at a major alarm, an overzealous doctor suggested that I be retired from the job on a non- service connected injury that had recurred. Just desserts?

BACK TO NEW YORK CITY

THE MECHANIC, SONGSTRESS, WET WASH, GHETTO GARBAGE, RAT ATTACK

If there was one part of my past that I wished could be hidden from the New York Fire Department it was the fact that I had been previously employed as an auto mechanic. As was the case with the hook and ladder truck that I resurrected at the training school, my dossier followed me to all ensuing assignments.

On any given day tour there was always a mechanical problem waiting for me. It started shortly after being assigned to Engine Company 280. One of the lieutenants had an ongoing problem with the front end of his car, a 1937 Chevy. He already tried having the condition repaired by his local mechanic and at the dealership, but the condition persisted. Before my arrival he had seen my personnel file and noted that I had placed number two on the list of a field of 34,500 for the position of auto mechanic. On reading that entry this lieutenant must have believed he was to witness the "second coming." On my first day tour I was told of the ongoing problem. Naturally, I volunteered to check it out. That was the beginning and from then on I was never free from extracurricular charity operations. It was a complicated knuckle like assembly and we annexed the adjacent yard and took the system apart for examination. That was the first mistake. I was sure not to miss a run while working on the car. We then ordered replacement parts and I completely rebuilt the entire front end system. The job took two full days and when finally completed the front end problem disappeared. That was the second mistake.

The word got around and from that day forward there was not a day tour that at least one vehicle was awaiting my attention. On one day tour the Deputy Chief in charge of the Borough of Brooklyn broke down two blocks from our quarters. He was responding to an alarm when his DeSoto just quit and wouldn't start up again. His driver was left with the car and Deputy Chief Burke walked to our quarters to use the department phone and report in to the dispatcher. He was then going to call the repair shop to have the car towed away. On duty at the time was Lieutenant Mulligan. I had recently corrected a chronic problem on his personal car. So it was with extreme confidence that he volunteered my services. It went something like this:

Chief Burke:(extremely agitated) "This is the third time this month that this car has been to the department shop and we still have this same terrible problem."

Lt. Mulligan:(I could see it coming) "Look Chief, we have a new man in the company that is a crackerjack mechanic. Why not have him take a look before calling the shop?"

Chief Burke:"I don't know, three times in the shop already must be a serious problem. Besides, he may cause a problem. It's not his job classification." (I'm breathing a sigh of relief).

Lt. Mulligan:(Undaunted) "What do we have to lose, the man is right here. The shop had three tries, maybe it needs a fresh opinion."

Chief Burke:"Well, OK, but I can't be out of service for too long before calling in." (Great, now I have a time limit).

Lieutenant Mulligan sent two men to the car and, together with the driver, they pushed the car into the adjacent yard. Of course, by this time I kept a full line of tools at the firehouse so I set to work. I could see what was replaced by the shop and, from the symptoms, it appeared they changed components in column "A" while the complaint seemed to point to a problem in column. "B."

After about twenty minutes of cleaning, scraping and testing contacts I told the chief the car was ready to roll. He didn't appear too convinced that the problem would not recur but he thanked me as the car was idling smoothly. He waited a while and then returned to his quarters. After he left, Lieutenant Mulligan told me that if the car didn't break down again, Chief Burke will never forget you, even ten or twenty years later. He had a memory like an elephant. He did in fact have a brogue twice as thick. We didn't hear from him for some time so the problem obviously had been solved.

About this time, in the 1950s we were on our way to having a second child. We were still living in a dingy uninsulated apartment in Jamaica. The heat in summer was unbearable and in winter the apartment was so cold that clothing had to be preheated before donning. Blue jeans, washed and hung to dry from the previous day, had to be preheated in the gas oven as they would be as stiff as a board.

Later an apartment would be available in a building that was owned by my brother-in-law in downtown Manhattan. There was only a slight catch. The building had been involved in a fire that almost totaled out the top three floors. I could have the apartment on the fourth floor provided I could make it habitable. I was so desperate to escape the Jamaica apartment that I quickly accepted. It had gotten so cold that whenever my infant son wet his diapers in the crib, mist would arise. The first time that had happened my wife panicked and woke me from a sound sleep screaming that the crib was on fire. It wasn't a healthy environment for two infants. I began the demolition and repair work in earnest on my new apartment. Before long I was doing charity demolition work in the other burned out apartments.

I didn't want to charge my brother-in-law for my labor as I was grateful that I would have an apartment with some degree of privacy for a change. I finally reached an accord with him where he would apply five dollars towards my monthly rent for days that I performed work on the other apartments. I completely refurbished the apartment within weeks and made it the showplace apartment for the building.

Meanwhile, the freebie auto repair work at the firehouse was booming and going into major repairs. I now had to charge something to discourage further growth, but also to put away something for a down payment on a house being built on Long Island. I started charging five dollars for labor, per day, for any major job accepted. My butt was starting to drag and my four wall handball game slowed considerably. Finally a situation arose that made me decide to quit altogether. For one of the brothers I did the following: 1- rebuilt carburetor. 2- removed cylinder head and replaced two burned out valves. 3.- Replaced heat riser (30 dollar job), and 4- replaced defective hand brake. 5-removed broken stud in manifold. Total cost of parts with my 40% mechanics discount was $12.50. I then added my five dollars for labor. His tank read empty so I added in two dollars for gasoline. The total time for the job was seven hours. When I saw my friend Mike that night he was elated that I had rebuilt the carburetor (he was told he needed a new expensive unit). When I said he owed me $17.50 plus $2.00 for gas, I couldn't believe his reaction. "You mean you are charging me for gas?" That did it. That job was worth over $150.00 and he complained about the $2.00. From that day on, no more freebies. At first I was angry then glad that I now had cause to stop what was becoming almost full time employment much to the dismay of long lost friends and relatives.

I was only back in Manhattan, the borough of my birth, a year before I realized it was a big mistake. The neighborhood on East 10th Street, east of Avenue A, had deteriorated rapidly. What had been a bona fide bath house and sauna, directly across the street from our apartment house, was now a front for other unsavory activities. The only decor missing was red lights at the front entrance.

If that wasn't discouraging enough, my apartment was broken into three times in the first year. The burglars in the first break-in struck a bonanza. I had just cleaned out the savings account to pay for a 15 inch tv set that I was to pick up the next day, TV was very new at the time and, that evening we were at my parents house inviting them to attend the unveiling of the large screen TV the next day. Everyone was excited at the prospect.

When we arrived home that evening the apartment didn't look right. I went to the rear window, facing the yard, where the fire escape was located, as my wife rushed to check the dresser drawer where she had stashed the $480.00 in cash for the TV set. What a shock. We had never been robbed before. Welcome to the barrio. Next came the jewelry box. Gone were the diamond engagement ring and everything of value. No costume stuff. My son's piggy bank with over five pounds of silver coins was also gone. If you have been robbed, you know it may take years before you discover all that is missing.

The robbery was reported to the police who couldn't disguise their disinterest. They didn't bother to take the nine distinct fingerprints on the window sill. In 1950 that was a big haul, at least it was to us. After that my wife never felt secure at home, especially during my night tours at the firehouse. I attempted to make entry more difficult by drilling holes and installing bolts through the window frames and by putting double locks on the doors. As an added precaution I went to the sign maker on First Avenue and had him make a 6 inch X 12 inch sign which I affixed to the entrance door from the hall. Some neighbors were not amused as the sign read,"Warning. These premises protected by attack roaches." Well the sign must have had the desired effect as they never touched the door. Instead, three months later, they broke through the door facing my apartment and robbed my neighbor. Then from the common fire escape they broke through my window, bolts and all, and feasted on the spoils. Although pickings were a lot leaner this time they did however, pick and choose all my best mechanic tools.

I was so outraged by these intrusions that might have escalated to physical danger to my family, that all I could think of was catching these burglars in the act. For weeks when I was not working my night tour, I would make a big display of leaving in my 15-year-old convertible Plymouth, with the top down and some luggage, giving the appearance that we would be gone for some time. I would then sneak back alone, under cover of darkness, and lay in wait, armed with a baseball bat, hoping to confront the original perpetrators on the fire escape. It never happened and my wife was tired of spending those evenings at her sisters. After a month of that nonsense I gave it up. Two months later they struck again while we were really visiting my in-laws on Long Island for the weekend.

I returned home alone as I was due to work that Monday evening. On the way home I stopped by my insurance broker's office and added burglar insurance to our policy. When I got to my apartment all appeared neat until I saw the rear window bolts were missing. I didn't bother to check for missing items nor did I call my wife Natalie with the news. I called the broker and told him what had happened. He asked if I wished to put in a claim. I told him to forget I had even called as it would appear to be contrived. Besides, I told him as President Nixon so eloquently put it, "I am not a crook."

10TH STREET TO ROOSEVELT

In addition to the exposure to burglaries the neighborhood was fast becoming the drug center of Manhattan. Parking was an ongoing problem then, as it still is now. Even my old convertible parked in the street was vulnerable to attack by various liquids and other foreign matter thrown from adjacent upper floors and roofs. After the second canvas top had been slashed to gain entrance to the car interior I gave up replacing the top and patched the slashed areas with duct tape. So as not to have subsequent vandals break a window or make additional slashes I just printed "OPEN HERE" on the duct tape protecting the last slash on the canvas top. It was evident that this was no environment to raise my two very young children.

Meanwhile the development in Roosevelt, L.I. we were interested in was in full swing and we put a deposit down on a unit in a nice location very close to a park and a lake. Next came a visit to a bank for a FHA mortgage loan. We were shocked to learn that no bank would provide a loan on a $15,000 home on a first grade fireman's salary. It was only after I brought in proof that my promotion to lieutenant was imminent that the bank hesitantly approved. But, only after a down payment of $4,000 which no bank would lend for the purpose. The money had to be borrowed privately for the down payment. By this time my old convertible had died of abuse and old age and was replaced by an even older 1937 Plymouth Sedan with a "blown" engine which I had to resurrect in my spare time. I eventually had it running like new. I was now working extra jobs to pay off the loans and to save to buy furniture for the new home when it was ready for occupancy. In an effort to make a "killing" I began to frequent some locations where covert gambling operations were held. I had no success in "craps" so I tried my hand in a gut wrenching, suspense filled, card game called "Zigginette." It is a card game frequently played in Italy and that is where it should have remained. By the end of one night I had borrowed against my reborn 1937 Plymouth to the tune of $500. When I was unable to repay the "nut, plus the vig" by the end of the following week I had to surrender the car which was worth $480 at the time. I explained to Natalie, my wife, that a car wasn't necessary in New York City with the bus and subway service. Besides we were no longer subject to parking tickets and damage to the car. No more early morning risings to beat the opposite street parking restrictions.

After her reaction to the fate of the wedding envelope "bounty" still fresh in her mind, I dared not tell her the method of the untimely demise of our reconstituted relic. My ill-disguised coverup was soon uncovered as our home in the suburbs became ready for occupancy.

MOVING TO ROOSEVELT "AUTO A MUST".

To live in the suburbs of Long Island an automobile was no longer a luxury but a necessity.

I was cruising along Queens Blvd., which at the time was the used car action center, when I spotted an old 1942 Dodge convertible that had my name on it. The dealership, Carol Motors, was run by a fine gentleman with attributes seldom found in a used car salesman. We arrived at a fair price and the car was held for me with a nominal deposit. While I was trying to figure out where the remainder of the purchase price was to come from I noticed that his car lot was in desperate need of repaving. I sold him that job as fast as he sold me the car. It became one of the first paving jobs my brother Angelo, who was now a paving contractor, signed up. From this association, Mr. Carol gave many other jobs to A.C. Paving at other locations for years. The work afforded me as a mechanic, laborer and operating engineer, at these jobs, also helped pay for the Dodge Convertible with the new fangled "fluid drive".

It wasn't too long before what I had visualized as the American dream was fast resembling a nightmare. The closing held at the bank that had granted us a mortgage was quite an experience as every first time mortgagee soon finds out. With every unanticipated payment doled out we were left with exactly $5.00 in cash at the table. As a messenger from the county clerk's office reported in to one of the bank's lawyers I decided on a "grand slam" and gave the $5 to him, much to his astonishment.

A fireman's salary still wasn't cutting the mustard so after completing the radio and tv repair course by the National Radio Institute (NRI), I added another source of income to keep the suburban dream alive. I wasn't alone in this bind. I didn't know of one fireman with children, who was a homeowner, that didn't have to "moonlight". The exceptions were the ones whose wives were employed. The so-called union at the time was a joke. From our meager salary 13 1/2% went towards a pension along with the other deductions. The union execs then were more or less figureheads who enjoyed some "perks" which were increased in direct proportion to the decrease in the "waves" generated.

With my past union experience with Unions I seriously contemplated a run for a position in the union but this was immediately discarded. I was already wearing enough hats. Besides, the union lacked the only weapon the city officials feared. And that was the right to strike. Nor did I, and most firefighters, feel that it was morally proper for the fire and police departments to engage in a strike. It was a catch 22 affair. That loyalty was repaid by city officials who limited pay raises to minuscule amounts more as a gesture than to keep abreast of other departments and outside prevailing wages.

SONGSTRESS – WET WASH

In the building next door to the firehouse on St. John's Place there lived an Italian middle-aged couple who had a teenage daughter. She was taking opera lessons and during the summer months, with all the open windows, her beautiful voice filled the alleys and back yards as she practiced her scales. She was a sweet kid with an even sweeter voice with a sound so uplifting that we adopted her as our resident canary. At the time she was about fourteen years old and her hard working parents were spending a good deal of money for her musical education at Julliard and with private tutors. All in our company were convinced that she would someday be a prima donna. Her father was a laborer doing seasonal work and the mother worked full time to further her musical education.

One Saturday afternoon while I was standing outside the apparatus door, I spotted this frail lady as she rounded the corner of our street. She was struggling with a big laundry bag of "wet wash". The bag was bigger than she was and probably just as heavy. At the time I don't believe there were any dryers in the laundromats. Seeing her distress I ran up to meet her and offered to take the bag of wet wash up to her apartment on the fourth floor. Against her protests I took the bag and started up the stairs with her following. The bag must have weighed one hundred pounds. As I reached the fourth floor landing I could hear the fire engine's siren sound off, meaning that we were responding to an alarm. I went down the four flights so fast I hardly touched half the steps.

I caught the rig which was on the way out of quarters. I already had my gear on the apparatus so all went smoothly. Well you couldn't believe the appreciation this family showed for that small favor. Her husband came down to thank me personally and wanted to know if there was something that they could do for the firemen. All this for a bag of wet wash. He was so persistent that I had to come up with something.

"O.K.", I said, "you can do this for us: have your daughter Mary sing a couple of our favorite pop tunes which she can mix in with her practice". Well every now and then she did just that and the whole neighborhood benefited. Later on, on a Sunday when I was working a day tour, Mrs. Caruso (if I remember the name correctly) brought in a real Italian feast for the entire crew. She made a big batch of blue claw crabs cooked in a delicious sauce and a pot of linguini in marinara sauce. As if that wasn't enough, she added a big bowl of salad with everything in it. Her daughter followed with a couple of large loaves of fresh baked Italian bread. Lieutenant Mulligan and the gang were in heaven. They wanted to know what I had done to deserve this heavenly larder. They would not believe this was all over a bag of wet wash.

Of course, I understood they were trying to show appreciation. But now I had a feeling of guilt. This had gone too far. She must have blown the weeks food budget on the delicacies. The big bowl of salad alone with the imported cheeses, sopressata, olives, and whatever, was a meal in itself.

I told her how we all appreciated the sumptuous meal but PLEASE do not repeat this act of generosity. I made her promise. Still on some special holidays she would drop in with some cookies or pastries she had baked for the occasion. Another time her husband dropped off half a bushel of blue claw crabs, plain boiled. He claimed he caught so many they would only have gone to waste. We got along with all the people in our neighborhood, especially on St. John's Place. That was later to change along with the neighborhood. I never did find out how our resident canary progressed, as shortly after I was transferred out of Engine Co. 280 to a hook & ladder company to gain experience prior to being promoted to lieutenant. That turned out to be a learning experience but not in the way I had expected. It soon became evident to me that all firehouses are not alike nor were firefighters welcome in every part of the city.

RAT ATTACK

In the early to mid 1950s rat infestations were becoming quite a serious problem in our fire district and in many other sections of New York City. A fire department order was circulated in our Brooklyn district to report any rat sightings and make appropriate entries in the company journal. All other factors taken into account, it was generally acknowledged that rats thrived and proliferated in areas where housekeeping was lax.

One evening late in June, Engine Company 280 responded to a call for fire in a tenement building. When we arrived we discovered the fire had been confined to the garbage dumbwaiter shaft but was beginning to extend past the shaft where the sheet rock had been broken. There was a full three stories of garbage in the shaft.

There was an obvious conflict between the landlord and the tenants. The tenants complained that the dumbwaiter had been inoperative for weeks, so in spite they continued to throw garbage into the shaft. The building superintendent claimed the dumbwaiter couldn't be repaired because whenever the workmen arrived to effect repairs, they were hindered by large amounts of new garbage in the shaft. When the situation reached an impasse either the tenants or agents of the landlord decided that the best solution was to dump the problem into the lap of the fire department by setting the garbage on fire at various floors. It became a smelly and trying task as the garbage had to be removed to the street and washed down.

Captain Franey ordered me down to the basement to check for any extension of the fire. Once in the basement, I was ankle deep in more garbage. In checking the basement, I noticed that the metal clad door to the boiler room had been removed and was laying on the floor.

As I directed the beam of my flashlight to the crossbeam at the ceiling of the boiler room, I was startled when a rat leaped from the beam towards my face. I could see his teeth and the eerie glow of his eyes from the reflection of the light beam. I ducked and the rat landed on the metal clad door with a thud that sounded more like it was struck by a Shetland pony rather than by a rat. I never got a good look at him but he was huge. There was no extension of the fire and I returned to the messy operation in the street. There must have been a whole nest of rats residing in that filthy basement. We gave the super violations to replace the boiler room door and to clean out the basement. Big Deal! They got the stinking garbage cleaned out of the shaft, courtesy of the fire department, when no workmen would touch the job.

At another fire in the same area we were treated to an unexpected surprise. When we opened the 4 1/2 inch cap from the hydrant, before "hooking up", out flowed a dead rat. That was a departure from the usual objects thrust into hydrants such as rocks, metal objects, etc...designed to impede fire extinguishing operations. Who said everyone likes the firefighters?

It was a warm summer's evening. The working group was seated in the kitchen except for the house watchman who was seated at the desk thumbing through the latest copy of WNYF (With New York Firemen). It was a nice quiet night, up to now, and four of us were enjoying a game of bridge in the kitchen. The game had been introduced to the company by Paul Julian, a migrating Texan.

A pleasant breeze was wafting through the kitchen from the open apparatus floor door and the open window in the kitchen. We were in the middle of a "penny a point" contract bridge game. I was sitting North and Lou Vaio, my partner, was seated South. Art O'Connor and Paul were the east and west opponents. Lou and I had lost the last game and weren't doing too well in this set.

I had opened the bidding and Paul, sitting east had "doubled". Lou, my partner, redoubled. O'Connor passed and the bid came back to me. I had not played much with Lou as my partner so I was puzzled as to my next bid. While I was deciding I could feel a light rubbing against my left ankle. What is this? Is my partner giving signals? Even in a friendly game I frown on cheating so I didn't look up. Paul, getting impatient says "Come on Carl" along with a wisecrack regarding a bed pan. I was just about to make my next bid when again I get a nudge at the ankle of my left leg. Now I am really annoyed. I always knew Lou to be honest and forthright. I was very disappointed and was going to tell him off after the game. As I started my bid, from my peripheral vision, I thought I saw something roll towards the kitchen sink from under the table. I turned to look and saw that it was a rat as big as a tom cat. It scurried into a four-inch space between three water pipes, and the wall and remained there. The tail extended out another thirteen inches.

I alerted the others to the presence of our nocturnal visitor. That's when Paul Julian took over. Where he came from in Texas, there was a

bounty on rats. He organized the attack. Lou was to sneak out and bring
the long handle snow shovel to Paul. O'Connor was to stand guard at
the apparatus door armed with a shovel. He and the house watch
immediately closed the sliding apparatus door. I got a short spade shovel
and was stationed directly outside the kitchen. Charlie Deza jumped on
the table and Harry Hirsch jumped on the closest chair. When Paul
signaled, the attack began. Like a spear he tried to cut the rat in two
with the shovel edge between the pipes. Instead, the rat that had
appeared lethargic sprang out of the niche and ran for daylight. I was
ready as he came towards me and swung down with my shovel. He was
too fast and ran under my legs as the shovel missed with a loud clang
and the rat hid under the department ambulance parked in our quarters.
Paul, having missed the "coup de grace," came out and formulated a new
plan.

We were redeployed and were now joined, reluctantly, by Harry
Hirsch. Charlie Deza, our import from Argentina, never left the
kitchen. I was now positioned at the far side of the ambulance in the
direction of the apparatus door along with Paul Julian. Art and Lou
blocked off the door to the kitchen in the event the rat decided to
return. Harry was given a pot from the kitchen to bang against the wall
and the ambulance. The banging had the desired effect and Monsieur Rat
shot out from under the ambulance and made a beeline for the apparatus
door by the house watch desk.

When he got to the apparatus door and discovered it was now closed
he turned back and was going to head for the kitchen but was faced with
four shovels banging on the apparatus floor. The cornered rat ran back
to the apparatus door and was attempting to squeeze through a gap, less
than an inch wide, between the wall and the metal apparatus door.
That's when Paul struck the fatal blow plus a few extras for good
measure. He then picked up the dead rat by the neck and went towards
Charlie who was still perched in the kitchen. He was now standing on a
chair. He bounded off the chair and ran outside.

After it was all over we had a good laugh at Deza's expense. When I
went on to tell about the nudges at my ankle and how I thought Lou was
trying to give me signals on the bidding they all really had a good laugh.
Except for Lou who was miffed that I could even think that he could
stoop so low as to cheat his friends in cards.

We now turned our attention to the house watchman. He was to survey all that passed into quarters. His story was that he did see something out of the corner of his eye as he was reading but thought it was a cat. Cats did sometimes venture in and out of quarters so he thought nothing of it. However, he said he knew it couldn't be a rat because it was too big.

MANHATTAN OPERATIONS ENGINE CO. 44
(PART I)

PROMOTED TO LIEUTENANT, ASSIGNED ENGINE CO. 44, MAN IN CEMENT (SAINTLY SOUSE), SLEEPING BEAUTY, PHARMACY PARK AVENUE FIASCO, THE LOVER, BLACKOUT IN MANHATTAN, BUILDINGS UNDER CONSTRUCTION

In April, 1955, I was finally promoted to lieutenant and assigned to Engine Company 44 on East Seventy Fifth Street between Second and Third Avenues in Manhattan. In between my last two tours of duty with Engine Co. 280, I threw a big party as was the custom in those days. I rented out the back room at a local tavern. Our MPO, and good friend, Marty Seery handled the catering except for the meats which were provided by my father-in-law's meat market, adjacent to Engine Co. 5 on East 14th Street, known as Geraci's Prime Meats. He provided the finest Italian cold cuts and three fully cooked and sliced roast beefs. Everyone from Engine Co. 280 and Hook & Ladder 132 were invited and the party lasted until the wee hours of the morning. The members of Engine. 280 presented me with an inscribed gold ring with a diamond inset which I still proudly wear today. Gone would be the carefree days on the back step and operating the pumper. Gone too, would be the days that an altercation could be settled by a trip to the cellar. Now I would have to act in a manner befitting an officer.

I had mixed emotions on leaving after my last tour of duty at Engine Company 280. I had spent seven years here and made some lasting friendships. We had shared some happy and sometimes sad experiences together. In leaving Brooklyn I felt I was leaving for another country although I was born and raised in the "big city" of Manhattan. Unlike many other jobs, and I've had many and various, being in the Department is like having a second family. Ask any firefighter. For some, it is their only family. I know of firefighters who had worked thirty-five years on the job and wouldn't retire even though it would mean more "take home" pay than if they stayed on the job. That's how much the camaraderie on the job meant to them. In Engine Co.44, I met one such character. His name was William Purcell but everyone called him Herbie. He had played the clarinet in the fire department's marching band. He worked mostly as an MPO (Motor Pump Operator) in my tours of duty with him and he got plenty of razzing from the guys as he practiced on his "licorice stick".

That "Herbie" moniker caused me problems in making out the roster sheets. Only he could get "Herbie" from William. As much as we all loved this animal the troops belabored him mercilessly, telling him to get the hell out of the job, find a nice woman and get married. After more than thirty-five years he finally got out and found a fine woman but Herbie never got married. Until this day he is a good friend to all who had worked with him. The only happy men he left behind were the ones who couldn't stand his snoring in the bunkroom.

I will never forget the events that greeted me on my first day on tour of the "Big City". I got there at least an hour early to get the "lay of the land" and meet with our Captain, Tony Burke. Captain Burke was a big husky tough Irishman. If one had to envision a prototypical fire officer, it would be Captain Burke.

After the usual pleasantries, he introduced me to the members and we went over the administrative duties of the company which all of the officers shared. The physical layout was very similar to my previous quarters of Engine Company 280 in Brooklyn. The kitchen was located on the first floor to the rear of the apparatus. The Company Officers were quartered on the second floor as was the bunk room. The third floor at this time was occupied with civil defense equipment for use in the event of nuclear attack or other catastrophe. Otherwise, this room was unoccupied. It was later to be the quarters of the deputy chiefs of the 4th Division.

Our company district extended from 72nd to 79th streets and from the East River to 5th Avenue and Central Park. It was a nice district and during my off time I cruised the area to familiarize myself with the various occupancies.

Being newly appointed, and coming to the "Big City" from Brooklyn, it wasn't long before I was tested by the captain and the men themselves. There was a general inclination by some of the senior "brothers" to see how much they could get away with. For instance, one day tour the crew was busy changing hose on the apparatus floor and one of the self-styled salty firefighters kept addressing me as, "Hey You". After the next, "Hey You" I told him to drop everything and meet me in my office on the second floor. I sat him down and asked if he had a problem in addressing me as either "Lieutenant" or the informal "Loo." He just sat there without answering.

I then advised him that the next time he referred to me as "Hey You", whether alone, or in the presence of others, that he was in for a swift kick in the ass, and if he wished to take it further from there I would be glad to accommodate him. He got my meaning, apologized and in parting gave me a "Thanks, Loo."

The next encounter was with my MPO. He reported in one morning and right after roll call complained of a toothache. I asked if he wanted to report sick and see the department dentist, but he declined. Instead, he asked if I would allow him to visit his own dentist and he would return immediately thereafter. I respected his decision to spurn sick leave and, against my better judgment, I let him go. He was to advise me if there would be any undue delay in which case he would call back and report to the medical office. It was a stupid move on my part as I was left with only three men, one of which would have to serve as the MPO. I was on edge the whole time he was gone from before 9:00 am to 1:30 pm. when he returned. He really took advantage of my misguided trust in him. When I questioned him about the delay it was only then that I learned his dentist was located in the Bronx. That was item number one with this guy. Number two came shortly after when his lack of "hustle" in response to a fire to which we were first due allowed the second due engine to hook to the hydrant ahead of us. That cute move did not go unchallenged and he was put on notice that a repetition may result in his removal from the seat. Number three came two weeks later when we got a "courtesy call" that the Assistant Chief of Department was visiting quarters in our area, unannounced. This was comparable to General Patton coming to inspect a platoon in the field. Everything had to be in perfect order: apparatus, quarters, equipment and all members had to be neat, clean and accounted for. I alerted my crew and noticed that my MPO was across the street doing some adjustments on his personal car.

I summoned him back to the firehouse and told him of the impending visit. Since his shirt was smudged and spotted with grease I suggested he change to a clean shirt. He balked and said the shirt was OK. I asked him once more and this time he said the shirt was good enough for him. He was deliberately flouting my authority. Now anyone knows that when infractions are treated with feeble slaps on the wrist that, henceforth, your authority will be either treated with contempt or completely ignored. The ensuing exchange followed:

Lt. C.:"I asked you nicely twice. Now I will tell you only one time. Either you change to a clean shirt or you will be brought up on charges for insubordination."

MPO:"This shirt is clean enough for me."

Lt. C.:"I'm going up to my office. I will be down in five minutes or earlier if the chief arrives. In either case, if your shirt is not changed there will be no further warning."

I now proceeded to the office. Once there I realized the frustration of being an officer. Had this been a one-on-one flap as firefighters, I would have punched the uncooperative SOB. Now if he didn't follow my orders, I'd have to press charges which I found to be very distasteful. Still, I had clearly stated my position and couldn't retreat without losing credibility. I never hooked up anyone. I didn't even know how. I was ready to get out the "book of rules" for procedures to follow.

In exactly five minutes I went down to the apparatus floor and was relieved to see that the MPO had on a sparkling new shirt. I nodded in acknowledgment and put the matter behind us. He even went so far as to put some finishing sparkle to the pumper and offered a weak apology. When the Assistant Chief of Department arrived the inspection went off without a hitch.

I had another encounter with a working group that had failed to follow my orders at a fire and had improperly acted on their own. It didn't have a negative effect on the operation, luckily, but it could have. That was it. When we got back to quarters I read the riot act to this group. No more Mr. Congeniality. When I came in the next day to relieve the captain I went into his office and informed him that, amongst other things, I was requesting a transfer back to Brooklyn.

Had it ended there, I would have had a very bad impression of Engine Co. 44. Luckily, I soon worked an exchange of tours with other officers in the company and found that the three lumps that Captain Burke had assigned to my group were the only stiffs in the entire company. Having discovered the true nature of this outfit I withdrew my transfer request. I then confronted the captain with the suggestion that there be a readjustment in the working chart to redistribute the talents within the company. With that accomplished, I once again enjoyed working at my job.

Later, when Lieutenant John Trainor transferred out of the company his replacement happened to be a redheaded Irishman from my old neighborhood, John Cavanagh. I didn't know he was on the job. When I last saw him we were teenagers and he was associated with a group on East 34th Street called the "Ferry Gang". At one time there was a ferry service, at the East River that was later discontinued. I remembered John immediately. He was one of the gang that had thrown me into the East River when I had ventured onto their turf, south of 34th street. He didn't remember me until I brought up that incident. There were gangs then such as the Gas House Gang, Ferry Gang, Such and Such Boys, etc., but nothing like today. We would exchange cute names like, Dagos, Irish Micks, Wops, Shanty Irish, etc., but no ganging up and mutilating one another as is often the case today. Later in life we were all good friends. John and I got along very well especially when I discovered he shot a decent game of billiards.

I was closer to John than any of the other officers. His brother Robert was also a firefighter in Manhattan.

But the many years of sucking in poisonous fumes without the benefit of a face mask took its toll on my good friend. Sadly, John passed away shortly after he retired. He suffered from emphysema for many years but continued to work. I believe he could have retired earlier on a disability pension and at least enjoyed a few years of retirement.

The records bear out the fact that life expectancy for firefighters after retirement is pitifully low. Yet many firefighters delay retirement to the last minute. Such is the attachment many have for the department.

MAN IN CEMENT

The company was returning from operating at a fire in a retail fish store when we were hailed by a gang of kids. They were running in the middle of the street towards the fire engine. They were all yelling excitedly that a man was drowning in cement a few blocks away. It has always been the policy in the fire department that no matter how outlandish or ludicrous a story may sound, that it at least be investigated. Some of the boys were known by many of my firefighters. They were also more believable as they were enrolled in the Cub Scouts. And we all know "scouts honor" is not to be disregarded.

I pulled the leader into the cab with me and the others ran behind the engine as we raced to the scene of the reported event. They were telling the truth all right. There was a building in the process of being renovated. As was the custom with most builders, a plentiful supply of prepared mortar was stored ready for use in the morning. A large open storage bin was created by stacking and securing two inch thick planks. The resulting bin was approximately eight feet wide by twelve feet in length and was filled with mortar (cement slaked with lime) to a height of six feet. In the middle of this "pool" sure enough, there was a man thrashing about and yelling as he was sinking into this gook. He was already up to his armpits. In New York City you can be screaming bloody murder and seldom would anyone pay any attention.

At first it appeared that this would be a simple rescue operation. First, we tossed him a rope in an attempt to bring him closer to the platform but that didn't work. Meanwhile, he was complaining that he believed his leg was broken. This stuff was a lot more tenacious than quicksand. And this situation was not covered in the Training Manual. Whoever heard of a person drowning in cement in the middle of Manhattan? Seeing that the man was in pain I got on the radio and called for Hook and Ladder Company 13 for assistance. I had them place a ladder across the top of the enclosure and place a rope under his arms from above to keep him from sinking further and to provide for a more direct upward lift. The guy did nothing but moan, groan and complain. He didn't try to cooperate in the least. He was as drunk as a skunk and his lethal breath was making the rescue crew groggy. That mortar just wouldn't let go. It was thick, unyielding and very caustic.

Next, we ripped away a few of the old doors that the construction companies use as makeshift fences. A couple of these were placed on the mortar close to, and around the victim. I then had Fireman George Mueller jump in and test the doors for stability as a charged hose line was brought to the platform. George then opened the nozzle gradually, underneath the mortar and close to the man's body, as the door panel was slowly sinking into the mortar. We threw in additional door panels to keep Mueller afloat until he had loosened the mortar from around the man with the hose stream. He was then lifted out gently by two men pulling from the ladder above and another man pulling him towards the platform by the rope we had tied around his waist. He cursed at us every inch of the way as we got him safely onto the platform.

Meanwhile no one was paying attention to Fireman Mueller who was standing on the door panel which by now had sunk a foot below the surface of the mortar. More door panels were thrown in and relieved of the hoseline, he gingerly jumped out of the bin. We had an ambulance standing by to take the victim to the hospital. He was checked on the spot but didn't have a broken leg as he imagined. He graciously cussed out all of us, singly and collectively as he was being escorted away in the ambulance.

Many years later I received a telephone call from a lawyer representing the City of New York. He asked if I recalled the incident. (How could I forget? It's the only one of it's kind in my experience).

This guy was suing everyone he could think of. He claimed he was returning from a late night mass and while walking home he had fallen into an unprotected hazard. I wondered what they were serving at Mass that night. The priest must have shared much more than the sacramental wine and it had to be at least 90 proof.

The Cub Scouts that had alerted us to this memorable event became heroes for some time, as their pictures and an account of the rescue was in the next days newspaper. I never found out how he made out with the suits against the city and all participants.

SLEEPING BEAUTY

It was a clear, cold night with the temperature below freezing when we received the alarm. When we arrived at the location there was no visible fire or heavy smoke. We were met at the curb by the building superintendent who had turned in the alarm. He explained that although he couldn't locate the source that the odor of smoke was noticeable on every floor of the five story building.

In his own apartment, which was on the first floor, he seemed to think that the odor of smoke was emanating from the "dummy" fireplace. This disclosure was of serious concern as it was possible that the fire could be advancing through the concealed spaces. The building had been renovated some years ago and the original fireplaces, which were operable at the time, had been faced over for decorative purposes by sheet rock. A "dummy" fireplace had been created. If the ensuing vertical concealed spaces had not been fire-stopped at each floor, even a minor fire could have serious consequences.

On arrival, Engine Co. 44 was the only fire apparatus on the scene. We were later joined by Hook & Ladder Company #13. As the super had reported, the source was indeed difficult to locate. As a precaution we stretched a hoseline to the front of the building. I then dispatched one firefighter to each floor to check for visible signs of smoke before I would make a decision to evacuate the entire building in the middle of the night. The super was sent to check the basement and I took the second floor. There were four apartments on each floor and at the door of one apartment the odor appeared to be stronger. A dog inside was barking loudly. I knocked on the door, gently at first and then harder when there was no response. It's amazing how indifferent New Yorkers can be unless they're faced with a real calamity. None of the tenants opened their door to see what was causing the ruckus in the hall. Meanwhile the dog in the apartment was barking louder as I banged even harder on the door. Still, there was no response from inside.

That's when I stepped back and dealt a forceful kick at the lock and the door flew open. I was surprised and shocked at the sight which greeted me. There was a beautiful young woman, stark naked, on the bed. At first I instinctively closed the door, to where it was only slightly ajar, probably to afford her some privacy and maybe to keep the dog from running out. Who knows? Instead the dog retreated under the bed.

I checked and saw that the young woman was breathing and then saw that wisps of smoke appeared to be coming from the dummy fireplace. By now the truckmen had arrived.

I called down to the officer of the truck company that I needed a wall to be opened. As he came up with two husky firemen and their tools, they stopped in their tracks, jaws agape, as they entered and saw the naked beauty on the bed.

I immediately announced that no "mouth to mouth" resuscitation was necessary and for one of them to fetch a blanket that had been draped over a chair in the far corner of the room to cover her. She still had not awakened. She either was a very sound sleeper or was heavily sedated by sleeping pills. Thinking that she may have possibly been affected by the fumes generated from the concealed space, I rubbed her hands and wrist and gently slapped her on her cheeks (the face of course). She then woke up in a daze and pulled the blanket tightly around her and retreated to the chair in the corner of the room. Had there actually been a fire in her room she may very well have perished before help arrived.

Meanwhile, the sheet rock facing that concealed the original fireplace was removed and revealed some smoldering electrical wiring that led to the fixture over the fireplace. We got there none too soon as there already was charring where the junction box for the wiring attached to the wooden stud. The fuse for the circuit was located in the basement and removed. The area was "overhauled" for safety and the Super was instructed to have an electrician rewire the circuit in accordance with the Code. He thanked us profusely for the consideration shown in not evacuating the building and for the minimum damage to the building interior.

"Sleeping Beauty" was still huddled in fright in the corner chair. Her brave large terrier that she had taken in for her protection never came out from under the bed. I did advise her that if she was such a sound sleeper, or a frequent user of sedatives, that she should install a loud sounding combination heat and smoke detector.

In later years, when I was assigned to the Division of Training as an instructor, I had occasion to interview and review the "dossier" of probationary firefighters as they were enrolled in the school. One had me wondering how he had gotten to the stage that placed him in the training school as I went over some of the felonies that he had on his record. Two were quite serious, but the one that was really bothersome was where he had been convicted of rape. I wondered how the above scenarios would have played out if he was the one that had encountered "SLEEPING BEAUTY" alone in the apartment?

ARSON

This is a crime that occurs more often than people realize. The reasons for commission of this crime are varied. Some are hired arsonists and do it for pay. Some wish to relocate a business, usually a failing business, to another neighborhood. Some do it for revenge, others may be strapped for cash and decide to defraud the insurance company. Whatever the reason, arson is usually very difficult to prove. It appears that unless there is loss of life or very extensive property loss, the insurance companies rather than go through a very expensive and prolonged investigation and trial, pay the claim. If the circumstances appear suspicious in nature, the insurance companies cancel the client's policy.

On one occasion, while on duty in Engine Co. 44, we received a box and phone alarm, simultaneously, for fire at a pharmacy located only three blocks from our firehouse. My men and I were all on the apparatus floor when the alarm was received and we were on our way in less than fifteen seconds. In less than two minutes we were at the scene of the fire. Yet, when we arrived, the entire stock area was fully involved with heavy smoke and flames blowing out the side door. The door from the stockroom to the customers entrance on the avenue side of the building was closed so the fire had not extended to the front of the store yet. We advanced a 2 1/2 inch hoseline to the front entrance and attacked the fire, pushing the heat and smoke out the side door.

During this entire operation, my men and I had the counter and cash register in full view until the time we advanced into the stockroom. No one entered the store until after the fire was completely under control, which took a few minutes. We didn't have masks and had to suck in some wicked fumes from whatever unknown chemicals were involved in the fire. About the time the fire was completely under control a bottle on an upper shelf exploded. As I instinctively looked up, what appeared to be a liquid splashed into my eye. Whatever chemical was in that bottle caused intense pain. I am relating all the details so that you may understand the anger I felt from the events that followed.

As soon as the store was safe, the pharmacist accompanied by a policeman entered. He was explaining how he had been on the telephone when he saw a "wisp of smoke" coming from the stockroom and immediately called the fire department. (So far, OK, so it was an unaccountably fast spreading fire as we were there in less than two minutes). He then goes to the cash register, opens it and exclaims "the cash is gone." By now my eye is swollen and the pain radiating to my ankles. My men and I were having trouble breathing normally from the effects of the toxic fumes. This last implication was that someone stole the cash. I stepped up to the cop:

Lieut. C.:"OK officer, I want you to take down his statement. The cash register was never out of my sight. No one came in until you two did now, and I want you to put that in your report."

The pharmacist is now attempting to "fudge" on his story. However, I am so angry that I insisted the officer make a note of the implied accusation. The pharmacist suddenly remembered he hadn't put in the "big bills". Such unmitigated greed! This was a suspicious fire to say the least. He wanted to milk it to the last buck with the disappearing cash story.

Shortly after he was at the front of the store and my men and I at the side of the store on the side street. I had them "crack" the nozzle to spray some water into my eye. We could hear this conversation from just around the corner:

Stranger to Pharmacist:"Hi, this is the public fire adjuster that I was telling you about".

Pharmacist to Adjuster:"I'm glad to meet you. It looks like everything went up in smoke. You got here quick enough."

Stranger to Pharmacist:I told you he was good.

Of course, they were unaware that we could hear all this from just around the corner. How could this adjuster be at the scene within ten minutes after the fire was extinguished? From the conversation, when did the stranger tell the pharmacist about the public adjuster? Who was the pharmacist calling when he noticed the "wisp of smoke"? When did the stranger contact the pharmacist and the adjuster?

I went to the battalion chief in charge at the scene and related all that had transpired. I wanted to be on record that in my opinion the fire was the result of arson to defraud the insurance company. The battalion took it from there. I doubt if any investigation followed. There was no concrete evidence and as is well known arson is difficult to prove.

When we returned to quarters, the condition of the eye worsened. After cleaning and replacing the hose, I appointed an acting lieutenant, notified the battalion, and left for Lenox Hill Hospital to have the eye treated. I then returned to quarters and finished out my tour of duty. I reported my action to the fire department medical office including the medication prescribed. However, I declined the doctors suggestion that I go on sick leave and finished out my tour of duty. Eye drops, three times daily for a week. Stupid jerk!

PARK AVENUE FIASCO

We were shorthanded on an evening when we responded to an alarm for a fire at a Park Avenue apartment building. To add to the problem, when we arrived then Fire Commissioner Edward F. Cavanagh was outside at the front of the building with the concierge. Heavy black smoke was pouring out of a third floor window at the front of the building onto Park Avenue. When we got to the third floor the metal entrance door to the fire apartment was scorched from the top to half way down the door. Smoke was also pushing out past the door saddle. The available fire fighting attack force consisted of a new arrival to our company, Jim Logan, and a fireman that we had inherited from the minority hiring program in effect at the time. Due to past experiences with the second fireman, where he had proved to be totally unreliable, I stationed him at the foot of the stairs of the third floor where he would not be exposed to the full effects of the heat and smoke, This all happened before we opened the door to the apartment.. The commissioner was observing every move we made up until the time we opened the door to attack the fire. The only task that I entrusted to the other fireman was to remain at his assigned position and feed in the 2 1/2 inch hose when I called for it.

Jim and I advanced the line into the apartment which was fully involved in flame and smoke. The heat was so intense in this fireproof apartment that the concrete ceiling was shooting off chunks of concrete at us; a condition called "spalling".

Things went along fine as we put out the fire in the first two rooms we encountered. When we had to advance further I removed my MSA mask and yelled out for the man at the stairs to feed in more hose. I got no response. I went almost to the hall to call out again. Again, no response. (Remember that this operation is being monitored in the street by the deputy chief and the commissioner).

I then had Jim shoot the hose stream directly forward and overhead at the ceiling to create a "water curtain" as I ran into the hall and fed in some extra hose. We then extinguished the fire in the next room until we again ran out of hoseline. Hoping the other fireman had returned to his post, I again called out for more hose. Again, no response. This time I took over the hoseline and sent Jim to feed in a few more feet of hose, as we only had one more room that was still on fire, .

Without warning, the last room was flooded by a deckpipe high pressure stream from the street. (That is something that should never be done at a fire operation unless the firefighters in the apartment are first allowed to back out). Jim, who was on his way to the hall, was practically blasted down the stairs. I took the full effect of the blast and must have tried to escape before being rendered unconscious. The next thing I remembered was laying face down on the floor of the landing below the fire, semiconscious. I was part angry and part embarrassed at not being able to complete the job without the interjection of the killer stream from the street. I got up and Jim and I returned to the apartment for overhauling. We were now joined by the missing leg of the team as the danger had passed. It was all I could do to keep from punching out this SOB on the spot. I may very well have except for the presence of the deputy chief and commissioner.

Because of his failure to fulfill his part of the operation, minor though it was, Jim Logan and I were exposed to a situation that could have caused us serious lasting injury from the effects of the deckpipe stream. The excuse this lump of drek gave was that he had held his position but did not hear any orders to advance the hoseline. That was a deliberate lie!

When I met with the chief in the street, challenging his use of the deckpipe while we were at risk, it appeared his action had been influenced by the presence of the Fire Commissioner. He commented on how smoothly the operation was going until there was only that last room facing the street. When we returned to quarters I informed him that he could have sent in a couple of men from the incoming force to help feed in the heavy 2 1/2 inch hose. I then informed him that I was going to bring up the "phantom fireman" on charges for cowardice. His immediate reaction was that he would not approve of the charges. I then advised him that this last transgression was the culmination of at least five instances in which the phantom fireman had either abandoned a brother at the nozzle or had not entered a hazardous environment at all. I told the chief that sooner or later someone would be seriously injured or killed by this inaction. It is an unwritten rule in every fire department, whether paid or volunteer, that no one be left alone at the nozzle fighting a fire. I decided something had to be done. The effects of the assault of the deckpipe blast were felt for weeks to come.

The next day as I reported for duty I was on my way up the stairs to my office when I overheard part of a heated exchange taking place in the kitchen. The working group between my tours of duty had become aware of this botched up operation.

I could hear Tom Byrne, one of two brothers assigned to Engine Company 44. He and his brother, Harry were assets to any company. When it appeared that the exchange escalated to the point that Tom was about to punch out the lump, I went into the kitchen and put a stop to the altercation. I appreciated Tom's concern but resolving the problem was my responsibility. Had Tom assaulted the phantom lump he himself could be in trouble.

Later, I summoned the "lump" into my office and we went over the record of his actions that had either put others at risk or added to the burden of others, as evidenced by yesterday's fiasco. He was also reminded of his hysteria at the Caines Warehouse operation where he refused to take his turn at the nozzle and the countless other problems he was involved in. After the discussion I told him that if he decided to ask for a transfer that I would not stand in his way. Tom Byrne who later became an officer candidly told me I was being too easy. Of course this was true. Later he too would feel the constraints that go along with being an officer in a company. In the past, as happened when I was a fireman in Engine Company 280, I did have to resort to violence with a problem fireman. However the situation changes when one is a fireman and the other an officer. Knowing Tom, I didn't think that rationalization made any difference.

At any rate this liability to the company did eventually transfer out. He realized he was not suited to the rigors of firefighting. Later, through some outside influence, he was made a full time building inspector where he wouldn't have to fight fires. I worked with many other minority firefighters who performed their duties as well as, or better than the average. The only distinction separating these men from the lumps encountered was that they had earned their way into the Department and not thrust into a job that they were ill suited to perform.

THE LOVER

This denizen, in various forms, is surely to be found in every large organization. The Fire Department is no exception. There may have been more than one at the time I was assigned as an officer in Engine Company 44, but one young man in particular gave me cause for concern. Some of his escapades were harmless enough and did not affect his performance on the job. He seemed to draw the attention of women like moths to a flame for reasons that none of us in the company could fathom.

He seemed to relish being involved in situations fraught with danger and perplexity. That part of his nature, at least in many cases, was a plus on the job as he was an excellent firefighter. However, at times his efforts at a fire or emergency had to be stifled as he would sometimes approach a challenge with reckless abandon. At one incident we had a fire in a row of stores in Yorkville. The cover for the coal chute located on the sidewalk had been removed resulting in a heavy outpouring of smoke. Fireman Romeo (name changed) was preparing to slide down the chute in an attempt to locate the origin of the fire without benefit of a mask or charged hoseline. I had to restrain him from this reckless, actually stupid, action. This was witnessed by Deputy Chief Contrastano, of the 4th Division, who asked: "What do you feed your men? Raw meat?" We then found an alternative method of entry and put out a punishing and persistent cellar fire. I warned Fireman Romeo to refrain from such foolhardy actions in the future.

He was involved in a surreptitious romantic affair with a divorcee who was already engaged to a policeman from an adjacent precinct. He first met this southern belle at a time when she lived in an apartment across the street from our firehouse. She was a very pretty young girl, in her early twenties, and spoke with a melodious southern accent. On one occasion, in the summer of 1961, she ran into our quarters seeking refuge claiming she was being beaten by her husband. There was physical evidence on her face and arms to substantiate her claim.

She was clad only in a negligee over her undergarments and begged me to escort her back to her apartment to protect her from her husband, so that she could dress and pack her belongings. She decided that she had absorbed her last beating and was going to return to her parent's home in the Carolinas. I empathized with her but advised her that this was a police matter and it would be improper for us to intervene in a domestic squabble. I then offered to summon the police and she could remain in our quarters until their arrival. The house watchman at the time was none other than Fireman Romeo. He was champing at the bit, anxious to confront the "wife beater". I had a man bring her a light watch coat to wear until the arrival of the police. She then collected her belongings and thanked us before leaving in a police car.

That was the last we heard of her until two years later when she returned to New York. She evidently was seeing Fireman Romeo. But she was also engaged to a Policeman. It seems that a game of "musical beds" was being played!

According to Fireman Romeo on many mornings after his night tour, "Honeysuckle Sue" would unlock the door to her apartment and return to bed awaiting the arrival of our dauntless fireman. The game of "musical beds" came to a head one morning when an unanticipated knock on her door announced the arrival of the other leg of this triangle. When the knock went unanswered her policeman friend almost knocked the door down. Fireman Romeo and the girl were in a compromising position at the time so he dressed hurriedly while the door was being vigorously attacked.

Knowing her policeman friend would be in a jealous rage if he discovered she was "two timing" him, and knowing he would be armed, Fireman Romeo positioned himself at the side of the door. If the unwelcome suitor succeeded in breaking in, Fireman Romeo was ready to punch him in the face as a delaying tactic, and make a run for the stairs. Fortunately, cops are not as adept in kicking in doors as firemen or a violent confrontation was inevitable. The cop however, gave up and left. After this near calamity "Honeysuckle Sue" presented Fireman Romeo with an ultimatum. Either he promised long term commitment with a promise of marriage or they end their relationship. If all participants in this incongruous triangle acted in good faith, I told Fireman Romeo it was a reasonable conclusion. However, I suggested a hiatus of three months, without any intimate contact, before making a decision. Fireman Romeo agreed, and so did she, although reluctantly.

He never had to make that decision however, as the "musical beds" had taken on additional players. The incongruous triangle had progressed to a lopsided polygon. Among countless liaisons she cohabited with an unsavory character. After a while, Fireman Romeo never heard from her again.

BLACKOUT

On August 17, 1959, a vast area of Manhattan was deprived of electricity and for a while went back to the candle light era. Five days of intense heat had caused an overload of the "feeder" cables affecting the Hell Gate generating system.

Over a half million people living between 59th street and 110th street on the East side were directly affected. Engine Company 44 and almost all of the 4th Division's district felt the brunt of the outage. Engine companies 22, 47, 53, 56, 74 and 91, and Hook and Ladder companies 13, 22,25,40,43 and Marine Company 5, besides our own Engine Co. 44, were within the blacked out area.

The fire department immediately called up sixty additional firemen detailed to the 4th Division. In addition, seventy probationary firemen were ordered to remain on duty. Also three Civil Defense pumpers were fully manned and put into service for the duration of the emergency. Thus, the safety of the city was well provided for by the NYFD. In all 23 officers and 210 firemen were on duty to cope with the emergency. Searchlight units were in high demand and dispatched to hospitals in the area.

Engine Company 44 left quarters to patrol the area from 90th Street to 99th Street, from 5th Avenue to the East River. The CD pumpers and other units did comparable patrols. This action, no doubt, had a calming influence in the affected areas, showing that the situation was well in hand by the police and fire departments.

Whether it was the result of the extra patrols and the constant presence of the police cars and the fire apparatus patrolling the streets, it was notable that no significant instances were experienced in the high crime areas of the city. The only unexpected incident reported was the bombardment of the firefighters of Engine Company 91 while they were busy supplying the Metropolitan Hospital in Harlem with lighting.

Ungrateful patients, and maybe some of the attendants, rained various missiles at them, which included kitchen knives from windows on the upper floors.

Fortunately no major fire or emergency developed during the period of the electrical outage. Relatively few persons were trapped on elevators. Fortunately, at 3:55 am the lighting system went back on line and was fully restored in the affected areas. All units returned to quarters. Many New Yorkers felt that the reason there was no rise in crime as in past history, was that a feeling of sharing misfortune made people work and live together in harmony.

My feeling, shared by many others in the front lines, is that the outage was in effect for a relatively short time, from 2:49 pm. to 3:55 am. of the following day. Also, the saturation of the high crime areas by the combined police and fire patrols must have been a factor. However, an electrical outage that would have lasted for a prolonged period of time may have presented a different outcome. On this occasion, good fortune prevailed for the residents of New York City.

BUILDINGS IN RENOVATION & CONSTRUCTION

Buildings under construction present unique and dangerous problems, because of their unpredictability. You don't know what hazardous materials may be stored on floors by the various tradesmen. You may encounter flammable liquids, acetylene and oxygen tanks and, more often, propane tanks. All gases stored in tanks under high pressure making them extremely dangerous.

There is a case on record where a propane tank, involved in a fire at a building under construction, had blown off the valving mechanism and became jet propelled, air borne, for three city blocks. A waitress working behind the counter at a restaurant was struck by the deadly missile and killed instantly. Of course, that was a freak occurrence, but it doesn't lessen the inherent danger involving gas under pressure.

We averted disaster when Engine Company 44 responded to an annex in the Cornell Medical Center when it was under construction. Fire alarm boxes were pulled from many blocks away, north and south of the actual fire. It was no wonder, for as we approached it was more like responding to a bombing site than a fire. It was impossible to see more than ten feet in any direction. I had two of my men walking ahead of the pumper to guide us into the block and two others searching for a hydrant for us to hook up to. Propane tanks on the upper floors were exploding and steel fragments could be heard bouncing into the street and off of the buildings across 68th Street. As I headed towards the fire building, to size up what we were faced with, I bumped into a hard hat workman fleeing the building. He said he was one of the foremen on the job and that everyone had gotten out of the building. That was welcome news.

He also told me that the concrete floor above the fire had been poured early that morning. It was now late afternoon. The fire appeared to be concentrated on the last floor to be completed which was the fourth floor. There was no life exposure or danger of extension to adjacent properties by the fire itself, as it appeared to be confined to the center portion of the fire floor. The immediate danger was from the exploding propane tanks that were exposed to the flames. The incoming battalion chief ordered my company onto the roof of an adjacent building where we could direct a hosestream onto the fire floor. We succeeded in cooling off the remaining propane tanks on the fire floor thereby lessening the explosion hazard. Soon there were no more tanks bursting. However, there was fire in one small section, deeper into the interior, that we couldn't entirely extinguish. Now that there was no longer an explosion hazard, or so it appeared, I was approached by the battalion chief:

Batt Chief:"Lieutenant, would you stretch a line to the fire floor and put out the remaining fire?"

Lieut. C."Chief, is that an order or are you asking me?"

Batt. Chief:"What's the difference?"

Lieut. C:"Well if that's an order I will take my men up. But first, if you don't already know, the concrete floor above the fire was poured sometime this morning. The wooden forms have been exposed to lots of flame and may no longer be able to sustain the weight of the floor."

Batt. Chief:"In that case, keep hitting it from here." (He then ordered a ladderpipe stream from the street to put out the remaining small pocket of fire.)

The ladderpipe stream extinguished the remaining fire in short order. Shortly after the fire was out a small section of the floor directly above the seat of the fire gave way. It was followed by most of the fifth floor collapsing onto the fourth floor.

The battalion chief just looked at me with an expression of relief. The real hero was the construction foreman who took the time, first to get all the workers out and then to seek me out to warn us of the newly poured concrete floor. By the time that floor collapsed my company could have been on the fire floor and probably caught under tons of concrete.

It was at a mishap similar to this one that there was a multiple loss of life. The new sports arena (the Coliseum) on 59th Street and Columbus Circle was under construction when an overhead floor collapsed onto the workmen below. Several workmen were trapped. Not all survived. These experiences point out that buildings under construction present special hazards. Extra precautions must be taken especially where there is no life hazard involved.

THE TOWERING INFERNO

We had an unusual and physically challenging fire in a building under construction late one evening. As we arrived we were met by the nightwatchman who had turned in the alarm. The fire was glowing and lighting the sky from the 22nd floor of the skyscraper. No problem, we figured! Well we figured wrong. To start with, the temporary elevator could not be used as it could only be operated by a union man from the engineers local, and he was long gone. All we had to do now was lug a couple of lengths of rolled up hose to the floor below the fire and hook up to the standpipe there before advancing to the fire floor. Each rolled up length is about 72 pounds but gets to feel heavier in direct proportion to the number of stairs climbed. Once we got to the floor below it would be a "piece of cake". No exploding tanks. No danger to adjacent buildings.

As I said, piece of cake. Right? Wrong! When we got to the fifth floor, the MPO had hooked up to the standpipe and started pumping so we would be able to hook up to a charged outlet when we reached our destination. Suddenly we could hear a strange rumble as we continued to climb. It sounded like Niagara Falls, and we soon found Niagara was coming down the stairs to meet us.

The steam fitters had neglected to cap the standpipe on the last floor they worked on as they were required to do by the building codes. We now had over 550 gallons of water a minute cascading down at us. We quickly called out for our MPO to shut down. I sent three men down to the pumper for extra hose as I continued climbing with one of the rolled up lengths of hose until reaching the 20th floor. I kept most of the hose, enough to reach the fire, and stretched the rest down to the landing below. Each man in turn, upon reaching the butt of the hose above them, hooked up and stretched down until they met with the hose length that was stretched from the pumper outlet. As I said, "a piece of cake."

The fire itself was just that. But I had some tired firemen on duty for the remainder of the tour. It makes me shudder to think of how this operation, which is certainly not routine, would have played out if I had three firemen that night like the one that I had encountered when I was later detailed as an instructor at the Probationary Fireman's Training School. The standards for the physical requirements had been reduced when a federal judge decreed that physical strength is not required to be a firefighter. That brilliant edict resulted in the hiring of some firefighters without enough strength to lift a single length of hose.

Not long after this I was involved in an episode that could have ended in tragedy. We responded to an alarm for fire in a building being renovated. A building undergoing extensive renovation is even more treacherous in fire conditions than when under construction.

When an alarm was received in quarters, the house watchman on duty would call out the box number and the location. He would then check the large color coded response board to ascertain if our company was the first, second or third due at the fire. He then activated the interior alert bells and out we go.

On arrival at the location the deputy chief in charge had the first due engine company stretch a hoseline to attack the seat of the fire which was on the first floor. He then had a Hook & Ladder Company raise its aerial ladder to the top floor, which was the ninth floor of this building. The chief then asked which was the second due engine company. I asked the house watchman. He stated he had checked the response board and that we were the second due company. The officer of the other company wasn't sure either (second or third due), which isn't unusual. Everyone knows when they are the first due company. I thought we were third due, but didn't think this was a subject for debate, so I told the chief I was his man and asked what he wanted done.

I was to climb the 110 foot ladder to the 9th floor to check if there had been any extension. On the way up I would make a visual inspection of each floor. This was a routine procedure when stairways were not intact, or I would have used the stairs. When I got to the top floor I climbed into the window and reached down to feel if there was a solid floor underneath.

This simple precaution is stressed time and again during company drills. Especially since there had been a recent case where a firefighter had stepped into a window at night without first probing with his foot. He had stepped into an elevator shaft and fallen to his death. There have been other such cases that eventually resulted in laws requiring elevator shafts to be clearly marked on the outside of the building.

When I felt a solid floor, as far as I could reach with my foot, I started walking into the building. It was very dark. Meanwhile, without stopping, I reached into the pocket of my turnout coat for my flashlight until I felt the floor get "spongy" underneath. I immediately stopped dead in my tracks got out my light and shone it down to the floor. Instead of shining onto what I expected to be a solid floor my light was shining down into a black void, down towards the ground floor which the beam of light never reached. The sight was so unexpected that I became dizzy and fell to my knees. After this initial shock I probed with my flashlight and found that I was standing on a 5-foot wide by 9 foot long plywood board spanning a seven 7 foot wide opening in the concrete floor that ran almost the complete width of the building.

I became so disoriented that I didn't attempt to stand immediately. Instead, I crawled to the center section of the 5x9 board as I had been standing about two inches from the side edge when the floor became "spongy". Talk about luck! Had I been walking in any direction other than onto the plyboard; or if only one of my feet contacted it, I don't think I could have survived a nine story fall nor would I want to. I didn't dare try to stand up but crawled to the other side of the opening. Finally I called down to the chief that all was OK

I was still shaken and didn't want to cross that plywood board again. Instead I made my way to an adjoining building and down the interior stair. I did not tell the chief or anyone else of my narrow escape. He would only lecture me on what I was already lecturing myself. For a long time after I always made sure where the next step landed.

When we returned to quarters I checked the response board for our due status. We were the 3rd due company. I should never have been exposed to that incident. I gave the house watchman a little hell. He was apologetic but the mistake was already made and in the end the final responsibility rests with the officer on duty. There was another reason I wasn't too harsh with him. After the scary experience I began thinking; what if the lieutenant of the actual 2nd due company had gone up and made the same mistake I did? Suppose he wasn't as lucky as I was and fell into the gap and down the nine floors. How would I have felt then?

Chapter 14

MANHATTAN OPERATIONS ENGINE CO. 44
(PART II)

TRUCK FIRE, GOLD DUST TWINS, FISH STORY, YOUR GOOSE IS COOKED, COURT JUSTICE, CEMENTING RELATIONS, BROADWAY BEAT, REVOLT OF THE TRAINED BEARS

It was not long before I realized that the performance of one of the MPOs (Motor Pump Operators) assigned to my working tour was woefully inefficient. He would become so excited during a fire situation that it wasn't unusual for him to screw up the operation by making a wrong hook up to the pumper.

On one occasion we had two lines stretched off the pumper during a training exercise we were conducting. Instead of charging the line laid out in the street, he charged the line leading to the neatly folded hose in the hose bed of the pumper. It was quite a sight seeing the hose in the bed being lifted into giant loops, much to his embarrassment. It was comical then but would have been a very serious problem at an actual fire. It could be life threatening to men at the nozzle advancing into a fire and waiting for the line to be charged.

On another occasion the improper operation of the pumps by our lax MPO almost caused serious injury to two of my men. We responded to a truck fire on Third Avenue near 78th Street in Manhattan. As we approached, the truck was obviously completely enveloped in flames. In addition, there was a trail of gasoline that was endangering automobiles parked along the curb. In a fire of this type there is imminent danger of the gas tank exploding with catastrophic consequences. It was a bright sunny day in July and many passersby had gathered at a not-too-safe distance watching the drama unfold. To speed up the operation, I had detailed Fireman Kelly to assist the MPO in hooking up to the hydrant which was close at hand. Meanwhile, I helped Firemen Bob Andriuolo and George Mueller stretch a line.

Bob was on the nozzle, while George, having completed the stretch, was approaching Bob's position. Unexpectedly, and without warning, the MPO opened the gate and started the water before they were on the line together. To make matters worse, the pumper was set at the highest pressure with the engine racing. That is a potentially deadly combination.

It was all Bob could do to hold onto the nozzle as he was being lifted into the air by the excessively high back pressure. George immediately ran and jumped onto Bob and he too was being lifted. I yelled for the MPO to shut down the pumps as I added my weight to theirs. It took the combined efforts of the three of us to control the line from getting away until the pressure was reduced. Fortunately, even as the line was in danger of getting away, all the water was directed at the truck.

Having been an MPO myself, I was both angered and embarrassed by the ineptitude of our MPO. With the line now under control we extinguished the fire without further complication. Like having an explosion! Meanwhile, Engine Company 22 which was the second due engine company, arrived and stretched another line from our pumper to extinguish incipient fires that had extended to two automobiles parked at the curb.

Luckily, the high pressure fiasco occurred before Engine Co. 22 arrived or the "needling" would never have been lived down. The public audience never realized the dangerous situation that had unfolded before them. If Bob had not been able to hold onto the nozzle with its initial unexpected surge we would have had a runaway nozzle. There could have been lethal consequences.

If both men had not been strong and powerful enough the line surely would have gotten away. I shudder to think of what may have happened if that fiasco had occurred with a 105 pound firefighter on the nozzle. True this is an isolated case and unpredictable. But the nature of fighting fires itself is unpredictable. It was now time to deal with this mishap occasioned by an unacceptable error on the part of the MPO. From that day on, during drills, we would go over the proper operation of the pumps. It was also stressed that water should not be started until called for.

Every firefighter knows that an unexpected surge from a high pressure pumper could be deadly and uncontrollable. The motor pump operator is strictly in charge of the pumper during a fire. He does not go into the building but his performance at the pumper could be a matter of life or death during a serious fire condition.

It is sad to say that I have personal knowledge of an incident where an inadvertent shut down of the water at the pumps was responsible for the death of a brother firefighter. Then there is a "full press" crackdown on training when it is too late. In the Fire service there is no such thing as being over-trained in any aspect of the job.

THE GOLD DUST TWINS

Less than a year after I had been assigned to Engine Co. 44 after being promoted to lieutenant, I was sent two probationary firemen for "on the job training" prior to permanent assignment to a company.

I was first introduced to the pair during a particularly smoky and stubborn fire in our district. The fire was partly under control when the chief's driver climbs the ladder to the third floor that we were operating on, with the news that there were two probies on the street with orders to report to Lt. Chiarelli. I stuck my head out the third floor window and there were the two, in borrowed firefighting gear, crisply saluting and requesting orders. The fire wasn't completely under control and heavy black smoke was blowing out the window over my head. I didn't want them to climb three floors on a ladder, as yet, so I told one of them, Joe Harty, to stand fast. The other was Mike Nolan. He never forgot that the first order I gave him was to get me a pack of Pall Malls as I threw a quarter to him which he deftly caught. After the fire was under control I took the pair to the fire floor and had them assist in "washing down" during overhauling operations. From that first day these guys were inseparable. For a while we even had them in the same working group and they spent most of their spare time together as well. They were real outdoors men. They especially enjoyed fishing and hunting. I was especially apprehensive during the duck hunting season when I learned how they would be camouflaged by a duck blind in a row boat and covered with straw as they blared out "duck calls" and were surrounded by decoys which they had made during the off season.

I was on edge during the whole duck hunting season as I would visualize these crazy bastards springing out of their blinds on the rowboat and blasting away at the prey flying overhead. I was sure that someday they would tip the boat and possibly blast themselves out of the water with their own shotguns. Miraculously, that never happened.

Nolan and Harty were so closely bonded together that I inevitably dubbed them the "Gold Dust" twins which was the logo of some cleaning product of the time. Joe and Mike had lots in common. First and foremost both were very good and dependable firemen. They also shared a most bizarre and outrageous sense of humor. Outside of the serious business of firefighting the only thing you could expect from this pair was the unexpected. So it was on a day that the company had been summoned to the Welfare Island Training Center for yet another rating session. The previous year my group was the first from our company to attend these rating exercises and I had passed along the information that many of the rating officers were devious, had no tact, and were often scathing in their criticisms.

This was the scenario when the officer with the nastiest reputation on the "Rock", as the training center was affectionately labeled, was conducting a test on the brass fittings. Mike Nolan was in the midst of the fittings solving a requested "hook-up" when the rating officer, a Captain Nasty (name changed), thought Mike was taking too much time and became overly critical and abusive. That is when Mike went into his "escapist" mode. It took everyone by surprise including Lieutenant John Cavanagh, the officer on duty in Engine Co. 44. Captain Nasty stood transfixed as Mike metamorphosed before him. First his eyes rolled back into the sockets until only the whites showed. He then convulsed into a state of epilepsy coupled with the symptoms of a massive heart attack along with the groping, flailing and incoherent utterances peculiar to both of these attacks. The test was abandoned as all were administering to the victim who appeared to be in desperate straits. Miraculously his condition started to improve as a call was going out for an ambulance and he was placed in a comfortable position. Captain Nasty left the building and did not return fearing that his presence might trigger a recurrence or exacerbate the present attack. Of course, Mike was excused for the remainder of the training session. It was only on return to company quarters that Mike confessed to Lieutenant Cavanagh that he had put on an act.

FISH STORY

I was still reeling from the anxiety of having been exposed to the crazy antics of the Gold Dust Twins (Nolan & Harty), some more bizarre than the comedy team of "Laurel and Hardy", when I was granted a hiatus as they had gone on vacation together. Some sanity was returning to my working tours as we returned to the normal function of extinguishing fires and protecting life and property.

At about the same time another probationary fireman, Bill Dickinson, had been assigned to our company and, as is the custom, he was assigned to the captain's group. He appeared to be of above average intelligence and performed his duties competently. But (as the captain reported) he had a "wacky" sense of humor. So naturally, as is my lot, on the next change of "working groups" he was assigned to work with me. Except for his intermittent "quirks" he was a very competent and welcome addition to my crew. He also was very proficient with numbers and before long was doing tax returns for many in the company.

On one occasion we dropped our probie Bill, off at the local fish market with "orders" that he purchase and bake enough fish to feed six firemen. The local fish monger recommended the fresh catch which was flounder. When Bill asked for the suggested baking time required, the monger recommended that eight (8) minutes to the pound would yield the proper results. Whereupon six (6) 1 1/2 pound flounders were neatly wrapped up and Bill proceeded to the firehouse to prepare our main course.

As noted earlier, he was very proficient with numbers. So he multiplied the six sacrificial flounder by the 1 1/2 pound each and came up with the proper figure of nine (9). He then multiplied that by the recommended eight (8) minutes per pound, and deduced the fish would be done just in time for our return to quarters. He also knew only two oven settings, low and high. Being a gung-ho type, he opted for high. About an hour later as we rounded the corner approaching the firehouse we could smell the products of the cremation. As we were fighting our way through the smoke on the apparatus floor (slight exaggeration), the probie was explaining his "modus operandi". What Bill was subjected to then was almost inhuman. There is no one as unforgiving as a hungry firefighter, especially as we had to settle for baloney sandwiches which had to be eaten "on the run". I actually pitied the poor kid. However, as the officer in charge, I had to accept the final responsibility for the disaster, and duty bound, I had to join in the attack. Bill was never allowed to forget his blunder. In order to escape the torment he got into the books and studied hard and was rewarded when he was promoted to lieutenant and later to captain.

The stigma of this event was not easily erased however. It followed Bill into every company that he was subsequently assigned. Starving firefighters are a very vindictive lot. Having been burdened with the responsibility as the officer present at the scene of the cremation, I carried out my mandate by following Bill to, and alerting, his assigned companies.

He was dutifully reminded of his transgression until he was forced to retire to escape the humiliation of the unforgivable event. Now after thirty years he never misses the Christmas parties at Engine Company 44 so that he can be reminded of the fish story.

There is always something good that follows a horror story. This case is no exception. It proved that Bill Dickinson was far ahead of his time gastronomically. All you gourmets who enjoy eating "blackened fish, filets, or steaks" owe the delicacy of your eating experience to our intrepid probie. The only caution, if you decide to adopt our probies innovative "blackening formula," is that the resulting mass becomes inextricably wedded to the pan.

YOUR GOOSE IS COOKED!

It was a winter in the 1960s, around the Christmas holidays, when we received an alarm for fire at a location on 58th St. and the East River. We were the only company to respond because the first due engine company was occupied at another location in their district.

When we arrived we were greeted with the sight of two hysterical women on the high stoop of a brownstone building, beckoning to us and yelling in a thick accent, "Mein Goose". With the distortion from the accent it sounded like "mongoose". There was only a faint odor of smoke as we approached and a caretaker from an adjacent building, trying to be helpful advised us, from what he deciphered, of the hysterical wailing, that a mongoose was loose in the apartment. I rushed into the building with two of my men and had the door closed behind us to prevent the animal from escaping. Of course, I thought this was quite an unusual situation. However, after having been exposed already to vicious guard and attack dogs, rats larger than full grown cats, crazed black and brown bears, bulls escaping from the former slaughter house at the present site of the UN building, horses stuck in a manhole, and other unusual situations involving animals, the prospect of a mongoose on the loose was not too far fetched.

Once inside however, the cook, a Mrs. Frieda Romano Bombaci, a buxom fraulein and the household manager, a Ms. Waltraut Sczesny, hustled us into the kitchen and led us to the cause of the frenzy. There was smoke pushing out past the oven door. The cook had tried to open the door slightly and had her hair singed by the escaping flame. That's when they decided to call the fire department. What she was trying to convey was that "mien goose" (her goose), which was for a gala party for that evening would be destroyed. She begged us to try to salvage the bird fearing that using an extinguisher would ruin any chance that the goose might still be edible. After all, many believe that firefighters, in their zeal to put out fires as quickly as possible, become uncaring destructive monsters. With this in mind we decided to use an old trick employed by old time experienced chefs. We escorted the women out of the room. I then had each of the two firemen take a heaping handful of common table salt and stand at the side of the oven. I was going to open the oven door, first a crack, then slowly to prevent a blast outward. Then as it was opened wider one of the men would throw in the salt, in a scattering motion over the goose, and then quickly close the door. We then waited a minute before opening the oven as this operation was prone to rekindle. Much to everyone's satisfaction it worked the first try. When the smoke and flame subsided the cook and the household manager were called in.

The cook nervously peered into the oven. By now she was in tears contemplating a completely ruined main course with dinner only hours away. Her expression slowly changed as the large roasting tray was removed. Not only did the bird appear edible but from the combination of heat, smoke and salt shower it took on an appetizing golden brown, slightly salted and smoky glow. I wouldn't however, recommend the afore-described roasting method unless you want a house full of smoke and the fire department at your door.

I could understand the cook's and house manager's concern. The list of guests for the festive dinner read like a who's who of literature, music and entertainment. It was then revealed that the building was the residence of Mr. Richard Avedon, the internationally famous photographer, whose clientele ran the gamut from presidents and heads of state throughout the world to inconspicuous paupers (as subjects). His studio at the time was and still is, located only a block east of Engine Co.44's firehouse.

This incident was all but forgotten until just before New Years when both these women appeared at the firehouse with a large tray of homemade cookies. I was not on duty at the time but they told the house watchman that the cookies were a small gift in appreciation of the care and consideration shown by the men that had "rescued" her goose. From that time on this act of gratitude was repeated annually. On one occasion when I was on duty (they were now Waltraut and Frieda and I was called Mr. Fireman), I told these women that all their attention wasn't necessary although we appreciated their thoughtfulness. But to no avail. A tray continued to be presented to Engine Co. 44., every year until either the women had retired or Mr. Avedon had sold the building. They always accompanied the tray with an almost prayerful declaration of, "God Bless All the Firemen." It is impossible to relate how good we all felt, especially when this thoughtfulness was in contrast to the often uncomplimentary comments sometimes directed at firefighters.

Now, 30 years later, a neighborhood resident happened to tell one of the firemen that Frieda, one of our benefactors known only as the "Cookie Lady" to the younger firemen, was now over 80 years old and had suffered a massive stroke.

When I heard of Frieda's problem I spoke to one of the firefighters that still remembered her and decided to do something to cheer up this fine, unselfish woman. A big beautiful fresh flower arrangement in a beautiful basket and adorned with two candles signifying Frieda and her co-benefactor Waltraut was sent to her. The card that accompanied the basket, mailed to her on Thanksgiving Day, stated simply, "God bless

Frieda" and "get well soon." It was signed Members of Engine Company 44.

Although this story had a happy ending, the lay person or homemaker should not under any circumstance attempt to tackle this type of fire. The most prudent action is to keep the oven door closed and call the fire department. Keep in mind that the fat has reached it's auto-ignition temperature and, although no flame may be present, as soon as the oven door is open permitting air to enter, the fat ignites violently causing flames to leap out past the oven, sometimes with explosive force.

We had a tragic case in our district where a young lady attempted such an action alone. The oven had a glass faced door and there was little or no flame evident. As she opened the oven door, flames shot out enveloping her face and upper body. To compound the tragedy her loose clothing also caught fire. She ran out into the hall screaming and a neighbor extinguished the fire. However, it was not before the ghastly damage had been done. Her face, arms and chest were seriously burned and for a couple of years she underwent numerous skin grafts. We later learned that this young, vibrant and healthy woman could cope no longer and had taken her own life. What had been planned as a surprise dinner with her parents had resulted in a nightmarish horror story all because of taking a rash action, in a panic, to save a roast.

COURT JUSTICE IN NYC

Early in the summer of 1961 I had Fireman Coughlin detailed to Engine Co. 44. He had been placed on limited service and was to do house watch duty only. He was an early middle-aged gentleman with graying hair and very distinguished looking. To meet and talk with Fireman Coughlin, with his modest and scholarly demeanor, you could easily mistake him for a diplomat or a college professor.

It was a hot day in June when Fireman Coughlin, in full uniform, having completed his tour of duty, was parked on 125th Street near Lenox Avenue waiting for a fellow fireman who he shared rides with. He was seated in the driver's seat, with the window wide open, and reading a newspaper. He wasn't parked for long when he was approached by a man who asked Coughlin if he could spare some money. At first he paid no attention to the intruder. But when the demands became more persistent Coughlin politely asked to be left alone and said that he didn't have anything to spare. The guy now became menacing and said "You better give me some money, man." When he was ignored he reached into the car window and, with what Fireman Coughlin thought was a punch, swung his arm into his chest. It was not until he saw blood all over the newspaper, and then on his chest, that Coughlin realized he had been stabbed. Instead of being scared and intimidated he was enraged, which scared off the assailant, who took off down the street. He was caught by the fireman and held against a metal railing hoping for some assistance. Instead a crowd started to gather menacingly. Luckily a police patrol car happened by and the assailant was taken to the station and "booked" with Coughlin pressing charges. Coughlin was then taken to the hospital and had the wound treated and dressed. Appearances before a judge were announced, postponed, announced again, postponed again. This went on for a couple of years, meanwhile Coughlin was receiving threatening calls at his home and warned to drop the case and not appear in court to testify. Instead of being frightened, as is usually the case, he became more resolute that this guy be brought to justice. He had been stabbed by a six inch blade that could very well have been a fatal blow. Finally, the case was presented in court.

The assailant showed up accompanied by a lawyer who went through the standard routine of underlying causes, discrimination and racism before getting into the actual attack which he greatly "watered down" for the judge's benefit. Coughlin was then allowed to tell his account, which he did. He also produced the hospital report which showed he had been lucky that a vital organ had not been penetrated. In addition, the wound had resulted in his being unable to perform his regular duties as a firefighter.

The judge, after listening to both sides, leaned forward in his bench, looked Coughlin square in the eyes and with a declaration tinged with contempt flatly stated, "What's the matter, fireman, didn't you ever play football when you were in college?". Then he rapped his gavel and sounds out "Case Dismissed". Coughlin just stood their dumbfounded by the decision and more so by the judges remarks. He had survived an unprovoked attack, endured countless threatening phone calls, suffered a potentially life threatening stab wound and, to the judge, this was comparable to a college football game.

When he recounted this story to me a couple of years later he still had not gotten over the ordeal, nor the anger. He asked me, "Lieutenant, maybe I am missing something in the meaning of the judges remarks. I still don't get it, maybe you may have some idea of what he meant". To be honest, I told him I had absolutely no idea of what he meant but I certainly believe that the judge in this case definitely did not belong in our court system.

This is not just one isolated case of a judge's incompetence. To open the fire department to under-qualified individuals, didn't a federal judge decide that "strength is not important" for the position of firefighter. How about the judge, "Turn em Loose Bruce" who lets off without bond, an assailant who had slit the throat of a NYC policeman. Is it any wonder that the laws and morals of the land are being held in contempt? There are countless other similar cases, many of which have tragic results, especially for those entrusted to maintain law and order.

CEMENTING RELATIONS

Every fire company in the New York Fire Department keeps a record in company quarters of every building in its administrative district. A card is kept on file giving approximate date of construction, occupancy, and other details including any outstanding violations. Especially during fire prevention education month, there is a renewed emphasis to attempt to remove all violations, which is next to impossible given the reluctance of some individuals in the various occupancies and the limited manpower in the NYFD.

What rankles me is when I am confronted with a tradesman who is quick to offer a bribe, almost as a conditioned reflex, when presented with actions to be taken to comply with regulations, especially with the storage of highly flammable materials or other materials of a dangerous nature. On one such occasion I met with a paint contractor who owned a tenement building in our district. According to zoning, he was permitted a certain amount of paint storage for his business, provided he obtained a permit. When I asked him to display the permit as required he took me aside and thrust a fifty dollar bill into my hand. When I asked what he was doing he started to tell me, "Well, all the others" ...."Hold it" I said, "I don't want to hear anymore." I gave him

back the money and told him I was going to do him a big favor. Instead
of him paying out tribute to everyone from building inspectors, cops,
insurance inspectors, etc. I was going to send a firefighter to him with a
blank permit application for him to sign which was only going to cost
him a nominal amount. From there on in, after he had the permit,
anyone from any department who solicited, or was ready to accept
money, regarding his storage facilities, should be directed to contact the
officers at Engine Company 44. He became forever grateful to us. Who
knows how much he was saving yearly from the illegal payments. He
also felt relieved knowing his storage was within the law.

In the rear office he had a small, well stocked liquor bar. Sometime
after the permit incident my company was involved in a fire close to
his business that kept us out for hours in freezing weather. The water
spray froze over our rig and turnout coats and icicles hung from our
helmets. This contractor came to me at the end of our operation. He
asked that my company stop by his paint store, which was on the way
back to quarters, after we "took up" from the fire. We did so and at his
bar he had lined up double shot glasses of whiskey with chasers at the
side. We were, by this time, chilled right to the marrow of our bones and
that thoughtful offering was greatly appreciated. Instead of being looked
at with suspicion whenever his place came up for inspection he proudly
displayed his permits. We had made another friend in the district. He
was so thankful, in fact, that he offered us an open invitation to his bar
whenever we passed by. I thanked him and promised that we will take
him up on his offer the next time "we have icicles hanging from our
helmets".

TIK TAK

Two blocks from our company, on 77th street and Second Avenue,
there was a cozy little mom and pop Hungarian restaurant called Tik
Tak. They had a small deep fat fryer in the kitchen that was not
provided with an automatic dry chemical or CO_2 extinguishing system.
During the course of our inspection I advised the owner, cook, waitress
and dishwasher, Maria, a full-bodied and buxom female that she would
have to install an automatic system. It was an essential requirement
where deep fat frying was conducted. The response was quite

unexpected. She started to pull on her hair and burst out crying. I said, "Hold it, Maria, this can't be so bad. We can find an alternative.". She continued to cry hysterically and in her almost incomprehensible Hungarian accent, I could make out something to the effect that "everyone in the country is trying to put her out of business." I assured her that she would still be in business after our inspection. She then confided that her main problem was with the building department. The week before our visit a building inspector had confronted her with what he termed was a very serious violation that could only be corrected by extensive renovations to the building fronting the sidewalk. If it wasn't done within a month the building department was going to condemn the occupancy. I told Maria I would look into the matter and get back to her in a few days. Meanwhile, since she seldom used the deep fat fryer she discontinued its use and the vented hood already provided was acceptable.

With the protection for the deep fat fryer resolved, Maria stopped crying long enough to thank us for the inspection. Before I left she gave me the name of the building inspector. The plot now thickened. She now confided that this inspector said he would "forget" about the building violation if she would have seven hundred and fifty dollars cash available to give him when he returned before the month's deadline.

When I returned to quarters I checked the administrative code for the City of New York. There was no such violation!. The next day I called the inspector in question, identified myself, and warned him not to again threaten the people in this mom and pop restaurant. They were very industrious immigrants working sixteen hours a day, seven days a week to eke out a "none too luxurious" living. The amount of that bribe was a lot of money to them, or they probably may have paid it and still lived in fear that others would discover their "building violation". I also advised the scam artist that if I had any future reports affecting anyone else in my district I would deal with him personally. I also had him call, Maria and her husband and inform them that there had been some error and there was no problem with their stores construction.

On my next day tour, when we were resuming building inspections, I stopped by the restaurant with the working crew to check on the status of the kitchen protection before they were to open for dinner. As we came into the store, Maria came charging out of the kitchen, rushed towards me and engaged me in a bone crunching bear hug and planted a kiss on my cheek. She kept repeating "the vunderfool firemens". She invited all of my crew to bring their families in for a special dinner she was going to prepare, a thoughtful and generous offer which we declined to accept. Being from repressive countries she and her husband couldn't fathom the fact that there were persons in uniform that didn't portend bad news. And yes, she did get rid of the deep fat fryer.

SHORT TAKES-BROADWAY BEAT

Engine Company 44 is located in a high profile residential section of Manhattan surrounded by every type of occupancy imaginable.

There are old law tenements (OLT). single room occupancies (SRO), town homes, brownstones, high rises, hospitals, factories, etc. Most important culturally are the famous art galleries and museums. Each of these various occupancies have their own unique characteristics as far as fire protection and fire fighting is concerned.

In the brownstones and town homes especially, but also in the high rises, many tenants are famous and highly recognizable people from theater, show business and politics. It was inevitable to bump into some of these people during the normal course of fire department activities. This was especially true during fire prevention education month where each and every occupancy within the district is visited.

On one such occasion the door at one of the town homes was answered by one of the country's most famous and well liked actors, Henry Fonda. He was very receptive to the program and graciously invited us inside his home. After a complete inspection, which included the boiler room and storage areas, Mr. Fonda thanked us and promised to comply with all of the fire safety recommendations that were made. In fact, he was so pleased with the conduct of our inspection that he suggested that we also check out his daughter's, Jane Fonda's residence which was also in our administration district.

When we subsequently got to Jane's apartment building, she was in the midst of "script reading" and, understandably, she couldn't be bothered with broadening her education in the fire prevention field and she politely begged off.

On another occasion, during an operation at a fire, a few of the tenants from an adjacent building stepped out in curiosity to check on the progress of our operations. It was late at night and the hoseline we had stretched into the fire building wasn't very visible in the darkness. This resulted in one of the kibitzers to tripping over the hose and almost falling.

I was getting ready to break his fall when he regained his balance. He was apologizing for his clumsy action when I noticed that it was Mr. Bennett Cerf. At the time, Mr. Cerf and Ms. Kitty Kallen had a very successful television show which ran for many years in the 1960s. The show was called, "What's My Line".

When I recognized that the clumsy kibitzer was Bennett Cerf, I said, "Watch your step, Mister, because that's my line.". He heartily enjoyed that quip and we shared a little laugh.

During the time that I was temporarily assigned to theater detail duty, there were some light moments and on one occasion a dangerous one.

MISTAKEN IDENTITY

On this evening I was backstage at one of the TV studios when I was approached by a pretty Oriental girl.

GIRL:"Aren't you tanner?"

Me:"I guess I am." (Having spent time in my yard tending my tomato plants. Besides you are never surprised by talk back stage).

Girl:"I will be back in a short while."

Me:"That's nice."

Girl:"I'm going to have to do something about your shirt and cap, and maybe your teeth too. The shirt and cap must be dusted."

Me:"What are you talking about?" (sensing something screwy here).

Girl:"This is your uniform, isn't it?"

Me:"Yes, it's my uniform but what's this about dusting?"

Girl:"They will show up too brightly. Why don't you let me dust them now before the last act is over, while we have time?" (She is now approaching me with a brush and powder).

Me:"Hold it. Are you serious? I'm here on duty and don't you touch my shirt".

Girl:"I have to do something or it will take away from your act"
Me.:(this girl must be nuts, I just said I'm on duty) "What act, I'm from the fire department."
Girl:"But I asked if you were Tanner" (She's still not convinced). Before I could answer, a guy comes up the stairs that puts some light on the Abbott & Costello like banter.

The guy is decked out in summer dress in a fire lieutenant's uniform. The resemblance is striking. I felt I was looking into a mirror. The girl is doing a double take with an incredulous look. Then it started again.

Girl to new arrival:"Are you Tanner?"
Him:"Of course I am. I saw you downstairs earlier."
Girl to me:So, you are a **fireman**.
Me:"Let's not start over again."

We all got a laugh from this case of mistaken identity. The man's name was Tanner. He was a ventriloquist and in his act he always dressed in a fire lieutenant's uniform. (White hat and shirt including the emblems). It was obvious now how the girl mistook him for me. If I hadn't gotten such a dark tan in my yard we all would have missed out on a good laugh.

I didn't stay for his act because after him there was to be some sort of an animal act and already some guy backstage was looking at me in a strange way. Besides, I had other locations to visit.

STAGE FREIGHT

It's amazing how so many veteran performers can be so nervous backstage before the curtain goes up. Smoking behind the curtain is strictly taboo. There is a designated smoking area at each level for the actors to use. The performers know the rules, but some feel that their status exempts them from complying.

On one occasion Tallulah Bankhead was pacing backstage. She had her signature extra long cigarette holder and was merrily puffing away. She acknowledged my presence with a nod and continued pacing the length of the backstage area. She gave me a, "Hello Dahling", as she passed by, while holding that long cigarette holder with a flamboyant gesture by her ear as she blew a puff of smoke in my direction. (I gave her a look signifying she knew better). On her next pass, closer this

time, she gave me another, "Hello Dahling", as she took the holder
from her mouth with the usual gesture. I deftly plucked the cigarette
from the ridiculously long holder while she was still in motion. Then, as
she turned to me in mock amazement, I said, "no smoking dahling".
Forever the professional, she said, "you aren't such a dahling after all.".

LAPSED SECURITY

I had just arrived backstage at a Broadway theater when it became
evident that the fireman detailed was not doing his duty. Cigarette
smoke was evident throughout the most vulnerable backstage area. In
addition, cigarette butts were observed in proximity of highly
combustible stage scenery. I contacted the manager and had him
announce that all smoking be discontinued immediately while I tried to
locate the fireman assigned to the theater.

I finally found him in the alley separating the theater from the
adjacent building. He was so drunk that if not propped up by the brick
wall he would have fallen to the ground. I got his name and unit number.
I then had him remove his uniform jacket and cap and took him across
the street to a White Castle, an all night diner, and sat him at the rear
with a cup of black coffee with more to follow. He was not to return to
the theater or wear his uniform in this condition. I then notified his
company officer of the circumstances and asked him to send a
replacement. Not only was this fireman a disgrace to the fire
department, but he allowed a very dangerous condition to exist by the
widespread smoking backstage. It is common knowledge in the fire
service, that fires involving stage props and scenery are very fast
spreading flash fires that generally cause panic in crowded theaters. This
man had brought shame on the fire department. He had succumbed to
the glitter of mingling with celebrities and he partied with them to the
extent of going into a drunken stupor.

I remained until the arrival of his replacement. Fortunately
violations were corrected before a serious condition developed from the
lax atmosphere.

CAUGHT IN THE ACT

I was backstage during a television spectacular featuring many celebrities from stage and screen. In addition, there was to be a very popular animal act. Paul Winchell, the ventriloquist, had just completed his act and was backstage talking to a female singer. She was the lead chanteuse from the very popular Lucky Strike Hit Parade and was to go on after the animal act which was currently in progress. Suddenly, the tranquil atmosphere was broken by a series of screams from the audience. I rushed from behind the curtains prepared to take center stage to prevent a possible panic. I had no idea what the screaming was about until I got to the stage and was not prepared for the sight that greeted me.

The two bears in the act had revolted. The largest, a big brown bear, had jumped off his bicycle and rushed to attack his trainer which had prompted the screams. She was a slightly built woman and every time the bear lunged at her she would jab him flush on his nose. While this boxing spectacle was in progress the other bear, a smaller black bear, was running excitedly around the stage. The curtain separating the audience from all this activity was immediately dropped. While the confrontation between the trainer and the brown bear continued, the black bear had run down to the lower level. Soon you could hear screams from below and a procession of terrified singers and actors came running up the stairs. Not far behind came the bewildered black bear. At this point, I was left alone on the main stage together with the chanteuse who had frozen in place. The trainer was still fending off the charges of the brown bear.

As the black bear came charging across the stage seemingly in pursuit of the fleeing performers the singer screamed in fright. She then jumped behind me. The bear, attracted by the scream and our presence, stopped, looked at us and then at the big brown bear and the embattled trainer. He appeared to be confused as he looked back again at me and the terrified singer.

My impulse was to grab the singer, who was now sobbing uncontrollably, and run for cover which is usually not the wisest course of action. Instead, I looked the bear in the eye, pointed to the right wing of the stage and yelled out, "They went that-a-way". He gave me a dumb look and that was the direction he went. I then quickly got the chanteuse out the back of the theater.

Meanwhile, other trainers from the troupe arrived and were able to corral the big brown bear and the black bear that was running around backstage. That frail female trainer had shown outstanding courage in keeping the bear that had gone berserk at bay until help had arrived.

Without her timely action the bear may have jumped off the stage into the audience at the outset and started a panic. Later I learned that the big brown bear, was spooked and had revolted earlier before the show, and severely bitten the main trainer on the arm requiring hospitalization. This was one time that the tradition of "the show must go on" could have been dispensed with.

MANHATTAN OPERATIONS
ENGINE CO. 44
(PART III)

THE CHICKENSHIT DEPUTY CHIEF, ANTITHESIS TO THE CHICKENSHIT DC, POWER OF THE PRESS, FAMOUSBUFFS & VOL. FIREMEN, ENGINE CO. 44 RATING AT THE ROCK, TRANSFER TO DIV. OF TRAINING (INSTRUCTOR), M-38 - TWO TUGS, TELEPHONE BLDG EXPLOSION

Any normal person will, on occasion, drink a beer. After all, what good would a lunch of a corned beef sandwich be without a can of beer to wash it down with? As long as drinking on the job is not a problem in a company, I see no danger in having a glass of beer with lunch once in a while.

Well we had a chickenshit deputy chief in our division who was so obsessed with the prospect of hunting out a cache, or even a single can of beer, that he would visit each and every firehouse in the division, unannounced, and on staggered days (no pun intended). His routine never varied. He would proceed directly to the refrigerator open the door and check the contents for this dangerous contraband. He pursued this practice with the fervor of a german shepherd sniffing out a floor full of baggage for evidence of cocaine at an airport. He followed this routine so often that he was nicknamed Betty Furness who, at the time, was doing commercials on television for a leading refrigerator company. Her name has become synonymous with refrigerator door openings.

That was one of his endearing features. He had others. The most objectionable, to me at least, was that he had a burning hatred for Italians, especially for officers of Italian heritage who did not cringe in his presence nor share in his insecurity. This could partially be explained by his relationship with his immediate superior officer who happened to be an Italian who spoke with a heavy accent to boot! When Chief in Charge Muto came to visit this deputy in quarters the deputy would cower like some flea-bitten junkyard hound that had recently been castrated. It can be assumed that to counteract this humiliation he subsequently attempted to dehumanize persons of lesser rank.

My relationship with this chief further deteriorated on the occasion of a fire in our district where I was involved in a Class rated rescue. Upon arrival at the scene of the fire I was met at the front of the building by three policemen. They were holding handkerchiefs to their face and coughing. I was then advised that there was a person trapped on the second floor and that they had tried unsuccessfully to make it up the stairs due to the intense heat and smoke generated. I directed my men to stretch a hoseline to the front of the building and await further orders while I would attempt the rescue. At this time we were the only company at the scene as we received the alarm by radio dispatch when we were already out in the field on Apparatus Field Inspection Duty. The hook and ladder company had not yet arrived or an attempt at rescue would be their duty. In any event we couldn't put water on the fire until the trapped person was removed. I couldn't wait another minute so I ran towards the stairs but was grabbed by the three cops who were still by the front of the building. They kept saying, "Don't even try because you can't make it without a mask." I wasn't about to kill time explaining there were no masks on the rig as they were all expended at a third alarm on a previous day tour, so I told them to get away. This was my job, not theirs, and I made another attempt to get past them but I was again restrained. On my next try I got past them by elbowing the cop on my left and actually punched the one on my right in the chest which left me enough of an opening to shoot past them and made my way up the stairs. By this time the smoke was pushing out the front door clear to the other side of the street. I got to the second floor landing and kept my head close to the floor as there was only about 18 inches above the floor of visibility. I could see along the stair rail and into the railroad rooms and was met by a sickening sight. There was a man writhing in pain with part of his clothing on fire. The walls of the room and furnishings were also on fire. Blobs of burning paint were flopping down from the ceiling and the upper parts of the walls. There would be only one opportunity to reach him as the heat and smoke at this point were unbearable. I sucked in some air from about six inches off the floor and made a dash for him. As I approached him, in his crazed state of mind, he actually threw a punch at my face. I dodged this punch and as he was partially turned he attempted to grab at me. He must have felt that the devil himself had come to claim him!

Before he could make another grab at me I slammed him against the wall then grabbed him from behind and under his arms. The action of being slammed against the wall, and then my grabbing him, snuffed out some of the flames on his clothing. Who in hell needed this extra added preliminary bout? This was to be a mad dash and out. Now I was hoping I was going to be able to make it to the stairs and the street. When I got him down the flight of stairs the three cops were there and grabbed at him probably doing some damage to his skin. So intent were these intrepid cops in sharing in a rescue that the poor victim could have been dismembered by the frantic grabbing going on. I left him to them at the bottom of the stairs and rushed to the street for a breath of air. I thought my lungs would burst before I got the poor guy out. The hook and ladder company never got there in time. The man, his clothing still smoldering, was taken to the ground floor establishment which happened to be, appropriately, a funeral parlor. The whole rescue operation, which seemed like an eternity, took about twenty seconds. The hose line being stretched had not as yet made it to the front of the building.

When I got to the street, who should be there in front of the building, and now in charge of the fire, but our chickenshit deputy chief. I went to him, as required, and informed him that we had taken a severely burned man into the funeral parlor and that his driver should request an ambulance. His first words to me were, "Don't try to tell me my job and get back there with your men," as if I had abandoned them!

He seemed genuinely annoyed that I had performed a Class rescue. We couldn't have directed water into the room involved in fire or we would have steamed the man to death. Engine Company 44 then proceeded up the stairs and we extinguished the fire. After the fire was out I was approached by Battalion Chief Southoff who was in charge of the operation before the arrival of the chickenshit deputy chief, and was questioned about the details of the rescue and what part the police had in the rescue operation. Satisfied that I had acted alone in getting the man out and without the protection of a hose stream or a face mask, he took down all the information and said I would hear further on this operation. I never heard anything from anyone. The normal procedure in recommending a member for a commendation or medal is that the deputy chief in charge at the scene forwards a report detailing the circumstances. Battalion Chief Southoff had apprised him of the complete details. The next move was to be made by our chickenshit deputy chief.

When we returned to quarters I made the usual entry in the fire record journal of the operation at the fire. Address: 240 E.80th Street, hydrant, 229 E.80th Street, hose stretched, amount of water used to extinguish, etc., etc. I neglected to enter the details of the rescue where a man's life was saved by the lieutenant acting alone for two reasons: (1) I was taught early on that you never blow your own horn, and (2) the more important reason was that the deputy chief at the scene issues a follow-up report which is attached to the page in the fire record journal. My recounting of the rescue, besides being immodest, would be, in fact, redundant.

Scarcely an hour before this incident this chief had brought charges against me which are related elsewhere. The charges were so ridiculous that the battalion chief accompanying him as a witness was actually embarrassed. This turn of events, where he was duty bound to report on my rescue, presented him with a vexing and perplexing situation. On the one hand he was recommending punishment on a trumped up bullshit charge. On the same day on the same page in the journal he would be praising my performance. How would that play in Toledo, or in Peoria for that matter? He never made out the report. Never commented that a civilian had been saved from burning to death by anyone. It was as if it had never happened.

It was February 5, 1960, my brother Slim's birthday. I was wondering how I was going to tell him to reschedule the celebration dinner we always have. I kept being interrupted in making out the reports for the previous day's 3rd alarm. I was still feeling the effects of the blow to my head from the trapdoor and the sprained knee had swelled noticeably and painfully. We already had two runs and I was doing a pretty respectable impersonation of the Hunchback of Notre Dame, with my head hanging to the side from a stiffened neck, and dragging my sprained right leg. Why didn't I comply with the doctor's order to go on medical leave on the spot at the 3rd alarm fire? Okay, let's make it to 6 pm, and then I'll have 48 hours to shake off the injuries.

It was about 1:45 pm when we returned from operating at a building wall collapse. I went back up to my office and resumed typing out the fire reports that were accumulating faster than I could type them. Less than an hour later I get a call on my intercom from the house watchman who announces, "Chief in Quarters." I immediately slid the pole and was greeted with the glare of lots of gold braid from the chief's insignias. Who was it but the chickenshit deputy chief and the working chief of our battalion. I was a bit surprised and said to myself; "What do you know? It looks like my company is about to get a citation in recognition of our performance at yesterday's third alarm fire where the building had collapsed." The surprise was short lived when the Chickenshit Deputy Chief made his unexpected pronouncement, "Lieutenant, I am here with Chief Wade to inform you that you are being brought up on charges." I was so shocked that I couldn't help laughing. What else could you do? Here I thought we were to be commended for meritorious service and instead I was being brought up on charges. "Okay Chief," I said, "what are the charges brought against me?" When he told me what the charges were I couldn't believe my ears.

I was being "hooked up" because the padlock on the portable 55 gallon gasoline tank for the commissioner's department car was not snapped shut. During the third alarm fire of the day before, where it appeared that my entire working group had been trapped in the debris of the collapse, this chickenshit chief was checking out my quarters to see if he could find some violation that he could pin on me. When he could find nothing else, besides a match stick under a radiator, he fell upon the unlocked lock. This omission, he and his downtown cohort reasoned, was my responsibility even as my company was involved in a serious fire during the time that the Commissioner's driver, Fireman Louttit, was dispensing gasoline into the department car. The fact that the lock had not been snapped shut really did not matter as the quarters were protected by a 24 hour house watchman. Talk about first rate humongous chickenshit! Besides, the chief was about to screw up the charges. He misconstrued the orders from his downtown "deep throat" and was preparing to prefer charges for our own company gasoline supply for the pumper. I advised him that if he hooked me up for the company tank he would be in for an embarrassment downtown. He gave me a quizzical look, wondering why I would prevent him from making an ass of himself. He then dashed up to his office to confer with his "deep throat" cohort who was later revealed to be no less than a Deputy in Charge of the Borough. we were getting into some big stuff here. Could there be a budding "GasGate" scandal in the department? Now assured that I wasn't attempting to deceive him, charges were now brought against me and the captain who was on a 48 hour leave and had no idea of what was transpiring. He then tried to have me be a witness to the violation, which I refused. What crust! Shortly after, the commissioner's driver, who found out about the turmoil that had resulted from his dastardly act, called Engine Company 44 from his home and admitted that he had omitted snapping the lock shut in his haste to pick up the commissioner and rush to the scene of the 3rd alarm, 3-3-1095, that Engine Company 44 was operating at.

This admission should have completely resolved the issue since at no time was there any danger of gasoline being pilfered nor was any gasoline ever missing in our company. The charges went through however. To add to this travesty, when the trial date was announced I had to cut short my vacation and fly back to New York City from Florida as an essential witness to testify at the "trial". Can any sane person believe that a great institution like the New York FD could be reduced to such asinine action on the whim of one or two vengeful ignorant people such as the chickenshit deputy and whoever was his secret "deep throat" cohort?

Of course they went through a charade disguised as a "trial", and to soothe the deputy and his accomplice they had to do something to justify a trial so they found the captain of Engine Co. 44 guilty.

However, they let him off with a reprimand. What a joke! My nemesis was now after my butt with renewed purpose and resolve having failed to "nail me" this time. His next attempt to sock it to me came a month later. I came to work that morning in good spirits, wondering what the chickenshit...deputy would be cooking up this time. I came in earlier than usual as my company had building inspection duty scheduled. I had to prepare my papers for the buildings due for inspection and make out an itinerary for Battalion Chief Schulman of the 10th Batt. As I was leaving quarters with my working group on the apparatus at exactly 9 am, I noticed that our captain, who I had relieved, was still in the kitchen along with most of the outgoing crew. They were having coffee and breakfast, as is customary. Generally most firefighters don't leave immediately after a tour. Who knows, maybe there had to be another few gallons of water to be thrown on the fire they had last night!

At noon my company had completed our building inspections for the day and returned to quarters where we would prepare to have lunch. As the engine was being backed into quarters I noticed that the house watchman, Fireman Lotti, seemed to be extremely nervous as he came toward me. He was actually shaking when he informed me that our chickenshit deputy was in the kitchen and wanted me to report to him immediately as soon as we returned to quarters. He was in an extremely ugly mood, Lotti told me, as he was visited during my absence by Deputy Chief in charge of the Borough Muto, who had thoroughly blasted our heroic deputy on some administrative matters. In addition, he had made some unfavorable comments on the lack of neatness in the kitchen. Of course that was the responsibility of the outgoing platoon. However our "beloved" chief saw his opportunity to pin this on me. (Besides, the captain was not Italian and wasn't the captain involved in the gasoline incident.)

I went into the kitchen and respectfully saluted the deputy chief. I said, "I understand you wish to see me Chief." Well the barrage began. The fact that I was not present when this grievous violation took place didn't matter to him. He berated me unmercifully. I told the chief that I would find out who was responsible for not leaving the kitchen clean and he would be punished. This wasn't enough for our deputy chief. He continued with his blistering barrage although I showed him every respect and assured him that I would take full responsibility for the incident. Even that wasn't enough to pacify him and, sensing that he had me on the run, took the abuse to a more nasty and personal level. That's when the shit hit the fan. I must admit I really lost it. I really blew my cork! I started by taking off my uniform jacket, rolling it up, and threw it high up against the kitchen wall. My counter attack began with, "You Fat *%*$#@. Who the "bleep" do you think you are bullshitting?" At this point I noticed that the outgoing captain was at the housewatch desk with Lotti. As I started my tirade, instead of joining in my defense, as he was the real culprit, he ran out the door. No witnesses! I was just warming up and told him that although I had shown him every respect due his rank, and took responsibility without having anything to do with the condition the kitchen was left in, that if he was fit to be a deputy chief in the New York Fire Department, that should have been enough for him.

Now that he had taken the abuse to a personal level I was not going to stand still for it. He knew who was really responsible but didn't have the "guts" to follow through. He just felt that making me the "fall guy" better suited his purpose.

At this point, the kitchen became engulfed in smoke. The deputy chief had been frying onions to have for lunch with his steak. Furthermore, I told him to remove the frying pan before he also blames me for burning his onions. Now, he says, "I got you real good." Gross insubordination. It went something like this:

Deputy Chief: "Now I got you for something real serious. Insubordination. The house watchman heard it all, and will be a witness."

Lt. Chiarelli: "Don't bullshit about it. Go ahead and write me up in the journal, don't just talk about it. And don't forget to throw in the burned onions."

Deputy Chief: "I'm not blaming you for the onions." (Now wasn't that gracious!) "I got you for gross insubordination. I'll have your job for this."

Lt. Chiarelli: "Again, don't BS about it. Go ahead and write me up. And when you are finished I'm going to write you up. When I get done there will be plenty of red ink in the company journal."

As I was saying this, he stopped, and a bewildered look came across his face. He couldn't deal with this. No one had ever even suggested bringing a deputy chief up on charges, let alone actually do it! He came to a screeching halt. He could not think of his next move. He couldn't cope with this turn of events. How would this play out with his superiors? What was I going to write? Finally, in desperation and to my surprise, to save face he made this declaration:

"I'm letting this go for now but I'll get you for something worse."

With that I got my jacket from the floor where it had landed, and flew out the door and up to my office to make out my inspection report of the morning's activity. Meanwhile, the chief dumped his burned out onions, which were irredeemable, called for his aide and left quarters. He probably went to a diner or to plan a strategy for his next encounter with the crazy Dago Lieutenant.

I was so shaken and shocked by the abrupt outcome, which was totally unexpected, that I went down to the basement to relax while the designated cook of the day was to prepare some lunch. We had a regulation pool table which we had purchased from a local private club that had closed up. I then proceeded to run off 39 balls before missing. So much for being shaken!

I did not have to wait too long for the next encounter. I was very busy with reports all morning - monthly reports, fire reports, field inspection reports, etc. Typing is not one of my strong suits. In fact, this is the one facet of the job that I actually dislike. It was in the midst of my labors that I was greeted with the scream of "Lieuuuutenaaaaant" from directly outside my door. Who was it, but the chickenshit deputy chief, yelling for me to get out and explain to Battalion Chief Shulman, who he had brought along as a witness, why I make improper entries in the company journal." Chief Shulman, a fine gentleman and a good fireman, was obviously embarrassed by these proceedings and was trying to signal me to keep cool and not get excited. The whole fiasco played out like this:

Deputy Chief: "Now I got you good. I'm bringing you up on charges for making false entries in the company journal.

Lieutenant Chiarelli: "What entries are you talking about, Chief?"

Deputy Chief: "Look under that bed on the bunkroom floor. Don't you see the lint under the bed?"

Lieutenant Chiarelli: "Yes Chief, I see the lint. What has that got to do with making false entries?" (At this point Chief Shulman's jaw was starting to slacken in disbelief at what he was hearing.)

Since time immemorial, at exactly 1 pm the officer on duty makes an entry in the company journal that he examined quarters and found all satisfactory. Never in the history of the fire department did anyone ever make an entry that quarters were examined and found to be unsatisfactory. With that history, let us proceed:

Deputy Chief: "With that lint under the bed, do you say that the committee work was satisfactory in your 1 pm entry?" (Committee Work refers to cleaning quarters in the NYFD). "Isn't that a false entry?"

Lieutenant Chiarelli: "That would be a false entry if I made it. However, I did not make that 1 pm entry, as I was busy preparing papers for the afternoon pickup and have yet to examine committee work. Now that I see the lint I find that unsatisfactory. If you check the journal, you will see I did not make the 1 pm entry. Of course you may charge me for making a late entry." (Again that bewildered look. There is no provision in the regulations against a late entry of this nature.)

Deputy Chief: "Okay, I'll check the journal. I'll get you for something good yet. Chief Shulman has been notified to inform me of any infraction."

When I later saw Chief Shulman alone he advised me to humor him, even patronize him, as the chickenshit deputy chief was obsessed with the desire to bring me up on some kind of charge. I told Chief Shulman that the only way to satisfy the chief is to do something that he could hook me up for. I never mentioned the kitchen scene with the burned onions and my outburst. I'm sure the Chief didn't either out of embarrassment.

To make matters worse, there was no escaping this Chief's scrutiny. His office was directly over mine which was on the second floor of the firehouse. Another of his obsessions was the hydrant to the left of the firehouse in front of quarters. One summer night at about 8 pm, Fireman Monachelli stopped by to pick up his paycheck and left his car about 6 ft from the hydrant. It wasn't long before I heard the scream from above through the pole hole, "LIEUUUUUTENNAAAAAANT!"

Lieutenant Chiarelli: "Yes Chief."

Deputy Chief: "Look out your window. There's a car parked close to the fire hydrant."

I called down and was told Monachelli had stopped by to pick up his check and was leaving. Before I could tell this to the chief, he was again screaming down the porthole.

Deputy Chief: "Lieuuutenaaaant! Quick, get down there! He's getting away!"

Lieutenant Chiarelli: "Chief, that was Fireman Monachelli and he just stopped by to pick up his paycheck."

Deputy Chief: "I don't care who it is. Whoever parks near the hydrant gets a ticket. You let him get away on purpose."

Lieutenant Chiarelli: "I wouldn't have ticketed him anyway. He just came to pick up his check. You want to ticket him let your aide do it."

Deputy Chief: "Next time we'll see about that."

A few days later this chief's wife came to pick him up after his tour of duty. Naturally, she parked close to the hydrant in front quarters. I had one of the fireman go up to the chief's office to tell him his wife was waiting for him in the car in front of quarters. When he looked out the window he came down in just his pants and undershirt and had his wife move the car from the hydrant. With no other place to park he had her park in the fire zone across the street. A summons for parking in a fire zone is the same as for proximity to a fire hydrant. I'm trying very hard to look serious while all this was going on. I can just imagine what his wife had to say when they were driving home.

Not too long after this incident we had a particularly nasty cellar fire that my company was second due at. When I got there with my group I found Chief Shulman, the Battalion Chief in charge at the scene. He directed me to back up Engine Company 22 which was attacking the blaze in the basement. There was no ventilation and they were taking a beating. Lieutenant Vail was with the hook and ladder company trying to effect some ventilation from below to no avail (no pun intended). I went down with three men, Firemen DeGeorge, Rooney, and Weinberg. We had MSA masks which are no match for the Scott Air Packs. In very heavy conditions they were spent too soon, as shown by color indicators on the pack. When the color changed it was time to get out, and fast! Engine Co. 22 had had it at this point, their masks were expended, and they were still far from getting water on the fire. I couldn't see taking all this beating for nothing. Although masks were expended I asked each of my men if they were up to one last effort. Maybe another five minutes might make a difference. This was against FD procedure. Even if we made it to the seat of the fire and put it out we still had to go back out. Hell, this wasn't the first time rules were ignored. We made one last determined push. As we got close, the ladder company was breaking up the sidewalk above the fire. We hit the fire and as the smoke cleared there were the three Engine Co.44 men covered with soot with the fire put out. The opening was none too soon as breathing was becoming laborious.

Who should be standing over the hole broken in the pavement when the smoke cleared but the chicken shit deputy. He was still shaking, thinking the fire was getting away. I could see the look of relief vanish from his face when he recognized Engine co. 44 with his favorite "Lieuuuutenaaaant". While we were taking up our hose, out of the corner of my eye I spotted the chief coming in our direction. In a way, I was glad. He was going to say something nice and that would break the ice. In fact, I didn't hate him for what he was doing and was actually starting to feel sorry for him. As he came close I turned toward him. He went past me to the Engine Co.22 commanded by Lieutenant Farley, who we had relieved of the hoseline, shook his hand and told him he did a very good job then proceeded to walk past me and my men without a glance. Now that's class. Firemen DeGeorge and Weinberg turned to me with the look of "For this we risked our ass?". Lieutenant Farley looked at me with a "What could I say?" shrug of his shoulders.

We had other encounters but I had become inured and ignored him for the most part. Some time later, for some reason, the persecution lessened. I don't know if it was the real reason but ironically his favorite daughter married a fine Italian boy. Besides, my company with all its members had a fine reputation with good and sometimes daring firemen. As fate would have it, shortly after I suffered a broken bone in my neck. x-rays showed more than one injury. The first may have been the 200+ pound trap door to the head at the third alarm. Recurring dizzy spells finally prompted Deputy Chief Flynn, the Senior Deputy Chief of the 4th Division, also in our quarters, to send me to the Fire Department Medical Office for re-evaluation. I didn't want to lose my spot in Engine Co. 44. I loved my job and the men I worked with. I was already on record for two herniated discs in my back. The FD Medics would take no more chances on me. The job was dangerous enough even when 100% injury free. I was sent to see Battalion Chief Kehayes at the Division of Training. I did not want to be sent out of the job on disability although there were many who would give the proverbial "right arm" for a three quarter disability. BC Kehayes said he did not need anyone at the moment but would try me for a couple of weeks to see if he could use me at a future date. Well, we hit it off good. He soon enough recognized that I did not always follow the rules by the book. He also saw that I got good results. I was being closely watched although I wasn't aware of it. I think some unfavorable zings from the chicken shit deputy had preceded my arrival at the training school.

It had gotten back to Chief Kehayes at how I must have inspired the probationary firemen, because I seldom lacked for volunteers for any unpleasant duty. One day I had a group of twenty men, and I was given the task to perform an unusually dirty, filthy job on one of the abandoned buildings on Welfare Island. Actually, all I needed was ten men. After I had assembled the group and finished with knots and some calisthenics which we did every day, I announced that I needed ten men to do a very dirty job and since it was not part of the training I would only accept volunteers. When I asked them to step out eight stepped out immediately followed by one more to make it nine. I asked if anyone else wanted to make it ten - no takers. "Okay, you nine guys sit up on top of the stone wall and watch these non-volunteers tackle the job." After that I never wanted for volunteers. In fact, the men actually enjoyed being driven to their physical limits. After all, I never let them do what I myself was not doing. Somehow, nothing happened on the "rock", as the training school was called that Battalion Chief Kehayes didn't find out.

Thirty-one years later it seemed that fate decreed that an act of perfidy was destined to be uncovered. The 4th Division was phased out and all old reports were being removed and were to be discarded.

I had stopped by Engine Co. 44 on New Year's Eve, as was my custom for every year since my retirement, to extend greetings for the coming New Year, 1995. As if on cue, Jim Daly and Bob Reeb had deposited a stack of outdated reports from the division office onto a desk close to me. They were scheduled to be destroyed. From the large pile two sheets managed to partially make their way past the binding. Jack Paccione, in curiosity pulled the exposed sheets from the pile and noted the date 2/5/60. Knowing that I was on active duty in the company on that date he handed me the sheet which was for the fire in which I had fought off three patrolmen in order to rescue a man that was trapped on the fire floor.

It soon became apparent why the chickenshit deputy never sent a copy of this report for inclusion in the fire record journal of Engine Co.

44 as required although they were not at the scene until much later. He had *credited Hook & Ladder company 13 for the rescue.* Actually I never expected him to follow up on Battalion Chief Southoff's report on my action. The Brooklyn fire where Art O'Connor and I were involved, where he pulled out Mannino, and I the 350 pound woman, was more dangerous and punishing. And the ship fire where I carried out our intrepid lieutenant, from two decks below, including his thirty pound Scott Air Pak, was a heck of a lot more perilous and demanding. If those efforts didn't get recognition, why should this last action?

If every time that a firefighter, in the performance of his duty, is involved in a heroic act deserving of a medal, there wouldn't be enough medals to go around. What is shameful in this case is the extent this deputy chief went, even to falsifying a fire report, to avoid bestowing any credit on his favorite "lieutenant." Fortunately, this behavior is atypical in the New York Fire Department.

ANTITHESIS TO THE CSDC

From the afore-going, one might get the impression that all the top brass were chickenshit, timid or indecisive. That is far from the case. Most all the top brass that it had been my fortune to work under were good, decent, professional men. All that was required to gain their favor was to do your job and conduct yourself in a professional manner. Anyone that had been in the service of their country had experienced brown nosing and how it had curried favor in the military. Well, brownie points had no place in the fire department. Everyone is expected to carry his weight for the department to function efficiently. In no other job is it truer that leadership is set by example as in fire departments everywhere. One of the most important characteristics of leadership should be fairness in dealing with subordinates. Chiefs should be even-handed, tough, knowledgeable and predictable. To command respect, pettiness, as in the case of the chickenshit deputy chief, is definitely not tolerated.

When it was decided to place the deputy chiefs of the 4th Division in the third floor office of the quarters of Engine Company 44, the first chief to check out the new location was the senior deputy chief, John Flynn. He was a tough, decisive, and red-tape-hating individual. He was the complete opposite of the chickenshit deputy chief mentioned earlier. Well, talk about red tape, the office-to-be was presently occupied, though not manned, with equipment from the Civilian Defense Department of the U.S. Government. There was hardly any room left for the 4th Division to operate as practically every square foot of space was taken up by CD equipment. When Deputy Chief Flynn had reached the top (3rd) floor, I understand one could hear the bellow from the apparatus floor and beyond. The unfortunate lieutenant to be on duty at the time was my friend, John Cavanagh, The Red Head. Well, John was taking the brunt of Chief Flynn's assault as I was reporting in for duty. Word was left for me to report to the top floor to join the fray. Understandably, the chief was incensed that word had come in advance to the captain of our company and room for the division's occupancy had not been provided. I informed the chief that we totally agreed but word was left to John Cavanagh and myself, that under no circumstances was any of the U.S. Government CD equipment to be tampered with. With that Chief Flynn, being a fair minded gentleman, called the captain at his home for an explanation. The captain repeated the orders given to us and to him by higher authorities of the Civilian Defense and refused to take any responsibility in tampering with any of the equipment. After all, who is going to buck the U.S. Government - especially when this was close to the time of the Cuban Missile Crisis, and the possibility of a nuclear confrontation with the Russians was not to be ruled out. No one accepted responsibility. No bombs were falling at the time. Deputy Chief Flynn's action taken at the time earned him the nickname I immediately pinned on him, Buffalo Balls (With that, he also earned our respect. We knew we had a man that could act decisively in any situation). Well, Chief Flynn ripped out all equipment that interfered with the division's operation. The CD emergency rations were removed to the basement. John Cavanagh and I supervised the transformation of the office, with relish I must admit! Well, as I said earlier, Chief Flynn was predictable and you knew where he stood on any issue. He took a very stern position on drinking on the job, which is understandable. No one wants to see a drunken fireman, whether on or off duty. However, as long as a responsible officer is in full control of his company I see no objection to having a glass of beer, especially with a meal of corned beef and cabbage - one glass, that's all. I knew that BB (short for Buffalo Balls) would not stand for even that one glass. He was on duty in his office at the time and I did not want to surprise him, nor have him surprise me, if he came upon us with beer on the table. Also, I did not want to show any disrespect for his position on the subject. This was a very delicate position to take as I made my way up to the top floor.

I was thinking on the way that we had been at many fires and emergencies with Chief Flynn, with good results, and had earned each other's respect. He knew that we had kept to his standards and shown the respect due the rank. I got to his office and politely knocked:

Chief Flynn: "Come in. What can I do for you, Lieutenant?"

Lieutenant Chiarelli: "Chief, we are going to have corned beef and cabbage for lunch and would like to know if you plan to have lunch with us."

Chief Flynn: "I'm not sure. My driver will be right back. I will let you know then."

Lieutenant Chiarelli: "I want to be honest with you, Chief. I know you have a strong position on drinking on the job. However, I don't consider one glass of beer with a meal of corned beef and cabbage as drinking. On the other hand, if you don't agree, and decide to stay for lunch, we will forego the beer. I don't want to go against your wishes."

Chief Flynn: "You know my position on drinking."

That's all he said. So I went down to the apparatus floor. With that, the chief's driver got back. I told him of the invite to lunch and my talk with Chief Flynn. I was reminded he definitely was against any drinking, no matter the occasion. I had to respect his wishes. About a half hour before lunch time down came the chief and his driver. The chief thanked me for the invitation but they would be out on business in the division and wouldn't be back for a while. Without his saying anything further I could see that he wasn't going to spoil this meal for me and my men, but don't ever ask again, nor even suggest any deviation from his convictions. Funny how one look can tell you so much.

This question never came up again. One day my crew consisted of Firemen Andriuolo, Garone, Monachelli and Mazza - I called it my Italian Battalion. Anyway, a fine Italian meal was planned and while they were preparing the sauce one of the first steps was frying the garlic in olive oil. It wasn't long before I got a call to come up to the division office by Chief Flynn:

Chief Flynn: "Lieutenant, what in hell is that god awful odor coming up the pole hole?"

Lieutenant Chiarelli: "Chief, I was just about to come up and ask if you would have lunch with us. What you smell is the garlic frying in olive oil. We're having an Italian meal and you and your driver are invited."

Chief Flynn: "Thanks for asking, but the smell of garlic makes me nauseous. We will be going out. Don't let my problem interfere with your meals - now or any other time. Just let me know ahead of time anytime garlic is to be fried for a meal."

Lieutenant Chiarelli: "Sorry Chief. I'll keep that in mind."

On my way down to the apparatus floor I couldn't help being relieved and laughed all the way. Now, without asking, we could have a glass of red wine with the meal. If the Chief had stayed in quarters or joined us in the meal there would be no wine. Like a glass of beer goes with corned beef what would an Italian meal be without a glass of wine? I did not have to feel guilty that I was deceiving this chief that we all respected. After all, he seldom ate with us anyway. Now any time that we had a meal that called for a beer or wine we simply fried some garlic in oil and within fifteen minutes or less the chief was on his way out. I think Chief Flynn suspected this may be a ruse so I never abused this new found ploy. To this day I believe that maybe this was his way of allowing me this small favor without his having to compromise his position. Also, by this time he knew he could trust my judgment.

POWER OF THE PRESS

The famous reporter, Walter Winchell, would frequently be seen cruising late at night into early morning in search of some newsworthy tidbits. To his credit on the occasions that we crossed paths, either at the scene of a big fire or emergency that was to his interest, his unique nightly broadcast was very close to the facts as reported to him.

It is a well known fact that many newsmen have a propensity for coloring and bending the facts to make them more readable and interesting. In cases where the implicit reporting is of no consequence, that is all well and good, and makes for more entertaining reading.

However, there are times that someone may be damaged unless the newspaper account is to the letter.

A case in point is when several newsmen had called me at Engine Company 44 to verify that we had rescued a man that was drowning in cement. Some were trying to get me to say the cement was hardening rapidly around the victim. I told them it was not so - however, all the newspaper accounts had me racing against time to get him out "as the cement was hardening"! Now here it was okay because it was unimportant and no one was hurt.

On another occasion, a plain-clothes detective faced the possibility of being demoted because of how an article appeared in The New York Daily Mirror on May 18, 1961. The previous afternoon, a United Parcel driver was shot when he caught a thief rifling his truck. As the driver lay dying the thief and an accomplice got away in a car. The police were thoroughly combing the borough of Manhattan for the getaway car. It was a senseless killing and the cops were determined to find the car before the trail got cold.

That evening, at about 10:45 pm, we got an alarm for a fire in a vehicle on 81st Street on the East Side. We had just gotten the hose line charged when I was approached by a man identifying himself as a detective. He asked that every precaution be taken in extinguishing the fire as it was the car the thieves, now murderers, escaped in. Being an unusual circumstance I called a deputy chief to the scene and apprised him of the information that the detective had imparted to me. We used very little water and batted out most of the flames inside the cab of the car. Later, the car was left in custody of the police. When I returned to quarters I made out my fire report in minute detail. I gave the exact time, materials openly visible in the car, how extinguished, and most important of all (as it later turned out), was the name of the Detective, Valentine, who had approached and informed me of the hunt that was on for this car. Then, the usual model, make and license plate numbers. The next morning, on May 18th, on the front page of The Daily Mirror, "Stops Thief, Pays With Life". Then the bulletin, "When Engine Company 44 responded to an alarm, Lieutenant Chiarelli noted the registration of the burning 1960 Oldsmobile and license number. It was the tag of the car sought..." It appeared that while the whole army of police was searching for this car, a fireman was given credit for spotting it. That made more interesting reading especially if one took pleasure in embarrassing the police. I knew nothing about the car or plate number until told by the detective.

The next morning, I look out the window at Engine Co. 44 and see a familiar face looking up towards my office. I recognized him as the detective from last night. He seemed to be indecisive on whether to come in the firehouse. I called out to him and then went down to meet him. He then explained how he was in hot water at the precinct because a fire lieutenant had preempted him and the entire police force in identifying the escape vehicle. He had the newspaper account with him. I took him up to the office and showed him my fire report. I told him his superiors could request a copy which clearly gave him credit on the identification. He left smiling.

BUFFS

When I first came on the job I didn't know what a buff was. There were three regulars who spent many hours in Engine Co. 280: an elderly gent, Jack Mullen, Huey Martin, a local grocer, and Charlie Tyrell. A hard working gentleman known to me only as "Joe Cavallo the plumber" was a fourth.

Being that there were many days when the companies were running short of manpower, these buffs were welcome at fire operations. They sometimes helped in stretching out long hose lines, diverting traffic, and many other duties at a fire. They, of course, were not permitted to participate in fire extinguishment operations or to enter buildings involved in fire or other emergencies. My experience with these men was always good.

There were many famous persons that were fire buffs. Mayor LaGuardia was one. Another was Arthur Fiedler, who conducted the Boston Pops Orchestra. Mr. Fiedler believed that firemen were the only real heroes in our society. As a matter of fact, in an interview Mr. Fiedler was asked where he would want to be buried when he passed away. Being a worldwide famous personality, the interviewer went on, would he want to be buried amongst other famous people? Mr. Fiedler, without hesitation, declared he wished to be buried where most firefighters were laid to rest. Such is the fascination that many people have with the fire service. None other than the great Ted Williams of the Boston Red Sox, had many times considered leaving baseball to become a firefighter. Imagine this from one of the greatest ballplayers of all time!

On the other hand, there have been instances where buffs, and sometimes volunteer firemen, were involved in starting fires. In almost every case the fires were started so that they could help in the extinguishment or maybe even a rescue. It is very difficult to tell if a person is so disposed as they are normal in every other way. When I first came to Engine Company 44, we had a young chap that was a buff in our company. Everyone liked him. He seemed to be the type of boy we would all like as a son, a brother, or maybe just as a friend. Many of the members of our company, including myself, would give him chores to do, such as wash or wax our cars, so he could make some extra money especially during summer vacation. We would also send him to do our food shopping as the company was shorthanded most of the time. We really appreciated having this kid around. When he turned eighteen he went into the service during the Vietnam War. He was assigned to an aircraft carrier and would sometimes send us a card letting us know how he was doing and how proud he was to be serving his country. We all thought he was truly the All-American boy.

One day we were all shocked by a newspaper account of how this aircraft carrier had apprehended an arsonist aboard their ship. There had been many instances of small fires set in various areas of the carrier. After a while it had become suspicious and a thorough investigation had confirmed that arson was the cause. Later the arsonist was caught red handed. Who would it turn out to be but our own buff who we were all so proud of. Let's call him John Doe. We never found out what the final disposition was in his case. We never heard from him again and all of us felt a sense of loss. In retrospect, some curious incidents came to mind which we thought nothing of at the time. One time, while he was out shopping for our lunch, he had come upon a fire that was started in a hall by the cellar stairs. Smoke was visible from the street and the fire alarm box was pulled. Our John Doe assisted in stretching the hose line as we put out the fire. We never found out who pulled the alarm box although that was not unusual. As we all thought back, it seemed there were times when he had just came back from an errand, or had just come to visit, when we were on our way out to an alarm. This of course did not happen too often or we may have gotten suspicious. My experience with buffs on the job was mixed. Many would have made excellent firefighters had they taken and passed the test. Some could not qualify to take the test for physical or medical reasons. In past years the physical and medical requirements were very strict - more so than any other position, including the police dept.

BUFFS OF NOTE

One happy ending I can think of concerned a teenager who was a buff when I was a fireman in Engine Co. 280. His name was Jimmy Spillane. His main ambition was to become a fireman and he worked at it diligently by studying and keeping in shape physically until he passed the tests. Also in his favor was that he had never gotten into any trouble or been on any drugs, even marijuana. I had not seen Jimmy Spillane since I left Engine Company 280 in 1955, when I was promoted and assigned to Engine Co. 44. One day in 1989, 34 years later, while shopping in a large department store I hear this stranger call out to me. Well, he was no longer a teenager. He had made it to the Fire Department and had already risen to the rank of captain. I have no doubt that Jimmy will be a chief before he retires. It's a pleasure to see a man succeed in attaining a position that he was devoted to and well suited for. It's guys like Jimmy who have joined the department on their own merits and who demonstrate devotion to their duties who make up the vast majority of fire department personnel. Most have taken the job not just for the money but for the personal satisfaction of being in a position to help someone in need. Sounds corny but admit it or not, many of the members of the department feel that way. That's what makes this department what it still is today in sharp contrast to what the politicians and the "social engineers" are trying to do by compromising standards.

A case comes to mind that clearly demonstrates the distorted thinking of the New York City administration back in the 1960s. There was this young man I knew, from Freeport, L.I., who had taken the entrance examination for firefighter in the City of New York. I also knew his mother who worked in a local grocery. One day she told me how elated she and her son were that he had passed the written and physical parts of the examination. Not only was this young man a gung-ho volunteer firefighter on Long Island but on occasion, he buffed in some fire company in New York, such was this man's desire for the job. When he reported for the medical examination he was found to be one-half of an inch too short. The height requirement at the time I believe, had been lowered to 5 ft. 6 inches. No matter how he tried stretching he couldn't make the height and was rejected. As he was ready to leave, devastated by this rejection, he was called back and asked if he was Hispanic, a possibility as his name ended in an "O". He told them "no, his parents were of Italian descent." The matter was thus closed and this man's dream shattered. The distressing part of this story is that this man had been rejected for being about one-half inch too short and in the meantime the "social engineers" had forcefully, and probably illegally, injected into the department a minority applicant who had convictions for rape, robbery and assault with a deadly weapon. Which of these two would you have wanted to respond to your unprotected apartment or home during an emergency? It's a good bet that this practice has been repeated since then along with lowering the standards.

Despite the occasional unfavorable publicity where overzealous buffs or volunteers are involved in setting fires, this is only a tiny fraction of the men who give of themselves so selflessly. Without the volunteer fire departments, and the volunteers who also man the ambulances, many towns would be in chaos.

I know a volunteer fireman, Ralph Pomponio, who would be an asset to any fire company in the city. He has been a successful businessman for years and if he had his choice he would much rather be a fireman in New York City. But as his wife, Millie, put it, "We just couldn't survive on a fireman's salary." So my friend works full time and devotes the bulk of his spare time serving his community. There are many others like Ralph in communities without paid departments and their efforts are mostly taken for granted. I firmly believe that the towns that are the beneficiaries of these services should reward these men by excusing all, or at least a good part, of their property taxes.

Another prominent American and native New Yorker, who truly had much in common with firefighters, was the late Governor of New York, Al Smith. He not only supported firefighter's causes in rhetoric but in deed. In memory of his past accomplishments and unselfish service to his community, the New York Fire Department honored him by naming a fire boat after him. The following is an article excerpted from the summer edition in 1961 of the official magazine of the New York Fire Department, WNYF:

"The naming of our newest fire boat - the Governor Alfred E. Smith, was not only a tribute to a great American from our own "East Side, West Side, All around the Town", but a recognition of his lifelong love for the FDNY. This love had its beginning in his early boyhood when he was often taken to the quarters of Ladder 10 in Fulton Street where his uncle, Peter Mulvehill, was a fireman for 35 years.

"In Governor Smith's autobiography ,"Up To Now", he tells of his experiences as a "Buffalo". "The schools were closed (because of the great blizzard of 1888) and there was not much for the boys and girls to do, so I became a Volunteer Member of No. 32 Engine Company, located on John Street. Volunteer work of that nature was agreeable to me because I had always had a strong desire to be a fireman and perform my probationary duties under what was then called the Buffaloes. The Buffaloes were an order of young boys interested in fire fighting and in the glamour and excitement of the engine house."

"At every opportunity, in personal and official capacities, Alfred E. Smith showed his genuine affection for the FDNY and his interest in the welfare of the men for whom he had the closest fraternal feeling."

The naming of this boat was a fitting tribute to the "Happy Warrior", and a fine remembrance for all who knew of him. It was the latest of the 105-foot class boat and had an electrically operated bow pipe that could be controlled from the pilot house. It also carried a hydrojet. Rated at 600 gallons per minute at 120 psi, and a draft of only fourteen inches, this boat can go places that no other fireboat has ever gone before. (I'm sure that the Governor would have appreciated that exclusive distinction.)

Gordon Mullins, more familiarly known as "Moon Mullins", was one of the best known and most popular of buffs. He had been an Honorary Deputy Chief and ex-member of the Fire Patrol, and was employed as a dispatcher in the New York Fire Department at the time of his death in 1959. He is still fondly remembered by many on the job as the "Russian Dispatcher". He was given that nickname by the manner in which he used to "sign-off" his radio transmissions as "Dispatcher Leven Off".

He was an ardent fire buff who had been chasing fires since he was a little kid in Smithsburg, MD. His affections were transferred to the NYC Fire Department when his family moved to New York in 1910, just around the corner from Engine Co. 47. Fire Department work and firemen were his "first love", and led to his joining many organizations in the fire field. Among them were the 930 Post, the famous Bell Club, and the Cycle Club. His death occurred while he was attending the Eastern Fire Chief Association Convention.

As a tribute to the memory of "Moon Mullins", the P. Ballantine & Sons Company established the Gordon Mullins Memorial Trophy which was first donated in 1960. These beautiful trophies have become a much sought honor. They are awarded, in annual competitions, to volunteer fire companies in the Greater New York area. In a short period of time they have become as popular and significant as the Lambert Trophy is in Eastern Amateur Football circles.

BUFFS OF NOTE

The late Doctor Harry Archer was a true friend of firefighters and an ardent fire buff. He was to become an Honorary Medical Officer in the fire department and later a Deputy Fire Commissioner. In honor of his memory, the fire department named the Fireboat Marine Company 6 the HARRY M. ARCHER, M.D. after him.

His history with the department goes back a long way. In what was known as the "longest run on record", ten companies from the New York Fire Department responded to an awesome fire in Baltimore, Maryland at the urging of the mayor of that city. The frantic call for assistance came after the fire departments of Washington, Wilmington and Philadelphia had already sent 13 fire companies to the scene of the fast-spreading, devastating conflagration.

The fire had started on Feb. 7th, 1904 at 11 am By 2 am. on Feb. 8th, the call had come to New York City for help. The Mayor, George McClennan, Commissioner Nicholas Hayes and Acting Chief of Department immediately made plans to send nine Engine Companies: 5, 7, 12, 13, 16, 26, 27, 31 and 33 and one truck company., Hook & Ladder 5, in response to the request from the embattled Mayor Robert McLain. All the companies were manned by double crews.

To attest to the high esteem Dr. Archer was held by the administration, the chief of department asked him to make the trip with the men. Dr. Archer readily accepted and left hastily to meet the departing crews in Jersey City where nine flat cars were prepared to transport the companies by rail to Baltimore, almost two hundred miles away. In his haste Dr. Archer took all his available cash with him which amounted to $106 which was a sizable amount in those days. On responding the companies did not know they were going to Baltimore, so no one had any extra money. Dr. Archer became their beneficent angel.

The N.Y. companies operated with distinction, from early Monday afternoon when they arrived until the fire was finally brought under control. The companies returned to New York on Wednesday, Feb. 10.

The conflagration destroyed 2,500 structures built on 20 miles of streets in an area of 80 city blocks before being brought under control. Dr. Harry Archer's contribution to the "expedition" was greatly appreciated. It is a fitting contribution to his memory that Fireboat Marine 6 bears his name, " HARRY M. ARCHER, M.D." He was indeed a true friend of the firefighters.

TRAINING SCHOOL

After a period of rehabilitation being detailed temporarily at the Welfare Island Training School, I again reported to the Medical Office for fitness reevaluation to resume full duty at the firehouse. I had visited orthopedic doctors on my own before reporting to the Fire Dept. Medical Office. My neck still had a starboard list and one doctor applied a succession of hypodermic needles into my neck and shoulder. The starboard list was appreciably lessened and the knee was in pretty good shape. I felt that there wouldn't be any problem in returning to my original group at Engine Co. 44. I was checked out by Dr. Nayer, and he then asked about my activities since being on light duty. I was able to convince him to return me to full duty by recounting some of the physical feats I was currently engaged in such as four wall handball, softball, water skiing, and a few other pursuits. Some were true and some were exaggerated. I don't believe he bought it all but he decided to give me another crack at full duty.

When I got back to the company I was fortunate in that I wouldn't be working under the chicken shit deputy. The 4th Division deputies were Chief Flynn, who we had respectfully dubbed "Buffalo Balls," and Deputy Chief Edward P. McAniff, who later was to be the Chief of Department, the highest promotional position in the Department. Both men were tough and strict, but fair, and I was again enjoying coming to work without being nit-picked to death by my former nemesis. I managed not to get banged up for a while. However, like all the other line officers, I was not happy with the paperwork required in reporting fires, emergencies, MFAs (Malicious False Alarms), etc. Everyone agreed that "someone" should do something that would improve the antiquated ponderous system that should have gone out with the horses. I wasn't being continuously bugged anymore, who knows, maybe I missed it. So I decided to take up the challenge and streamline the Fire Report Writing System.

With about a week of research, I finally came up with a draft of a system which I aptly called "Running Log, Engine Co. #44." I made several copies and showed the system to lieutenants, captains and battalion chiefs. Without exception they were all enthusiastically supportive. I then made out a real fancy copy with a cover to match, designed by one of my firemen, John Ruffins, and sent it to the Fire Department Suggestion Panel. About a week later I got a response that came packed along with a ball point pen. They came up with some negative comments, all of which meant they did not think this would meet the requirements. They did however, thank me for the effort and told me to keep trying. Incidentally, the ball point pen did not work at all. That was going to be the subject of my next suggestion: give out pens that work. It also proves the axiom, "you can't teach old dogs new tricks". Also, from experience, the movers and stirrers do not like to be upstaged. Undaunted, I then went up to the chief's office and presented the new form I devised to Deputy Chief McAniff. I also told him that it had been shown around the division and in other divisions without one dissenter except for the Fire Department Suggestion Board.

Later on, when I had been transferred to the Probationary Fireman's Training School in Welfare Island, Ed. P. McAniff became the Chief of Department. The high Mucky Muck! One of the first things he did was to contact me at the training school and asked if I still kept a copy of the system. If so would I bring a copy to him and

Deputy Chief Constrastano for a feasibility study. I was only too glad to oblige. I was happy to see that it was finally adopted and put to use. The savings in bulk of the paper alone was in the ratio of about 20:1. The ratio was even greater in the cost, and in fact, made readily available more information than the old system. 1. I learned about the fire department adopting my system of reporting two years after my retirement.

LAND, SEA AND AIR (AIRCRAFT)

On Friday, December 16, 1960, an accident of major proportions struck the boroughs of Brooklyn and Staten Island, New York. The weather was miserable and visibility was poor as rain and snow fell over New York City.

At 10:34 am, the time that the first alarm was transmitted, two planes collided in mid-air over Staten Island. Later reports indicated that the two planes were supposedly "stacked" at different altitudes, awaiting landing clearances in approach of the New York airports. One was a DC-8 jet from Chicago headed for JFK Airport (known at the time as Idlewild Airport) with 84 persons aboard. The other plane was a TWA Super Constellation with 44 persons aboard from Dayton and Columbus, Ohio and bound for LaGuardia Airport.

The DC-8 jet landed in sections over the most densely populated sections in Brooklyn. Parts of the plane landed in rows of apartment buildings and various occupancies common to a residential area. The tail section was torn off in the collision and landed in the street at the intersection of 7th Avenue and Sterling Place. A close friend of my family, Tony Iengo, who operated a leasing company at the location, ran into the street suspecting a bombing incident. He later recounted his disbelief at the sight with which he was greeted.

The fuselage of the DC-8, which contained most of the ill-fated passengers, crashed into the Pillar of Fire Church (prophetically named), which was demolished in the resultant explosion and fire. Eighty-three of the eighty-four passengers were killed instantly. Miraculously, a young boy had been thrown clear of the plane onto a snowbank that had accumulated from an earlier big snow storm. He was rushed to a local hospital, but died the next day.

To the credit of the operating forces, the fire, which had the potential of a great conflagration and "fire storm," was held to a minimum from the time the first companies arrived. The first to arrive was Engine Company 269 which was located only four blocks from the scene. Engine Company 280, where I had spent my first seven years in the department, was also one of the first companies to arrive.

Alarms were transmitted in quick succession and within twenty minutes of the crash the fifth alarm was transmitted and special calls for additional units were sent out. Attesting to the spirit of cooperation of the fire services, Mayor Wagner and Fire Commissioner Cavanagh expressed their gratitude. More than 200 off-duty firemen of all ranks responded voluntarily and worked long hours without receiving, nor expecting, any compensation. More than 350 policemen were sent to the scene. For the next few days firemen were detailed to the scene from as far away as Manhattan. Beside the volunteers, Engine Company 44 had a man detailed to the scene for the full length of the operation.

The TWA Constellation fell in three sections at Miller Field, a little-used Army field in Staten Island. Such was the force of the mid-air collision that one of the DC-8's jet engines also landed in Staten Island. None of the 44 passengers on the plane survived the crash. The fire at this site went to a second alarm. However, no buildings were involved and fire operations were routine except for the grim job of removing the dead and the dying. It was the worst commercial air disaster on record.

In all there were 38 hose lines deployed and operated to contain the multitude of fires. The operation utilized 31 engine companies, six hook and ladder companies, three rescue companies and four special units. Given the population density at the Brooklyn site, it was a minor miracle that only six persons were killed and 15 injured on the ground. Seventeen firemen sustained injuries.

There were many acts of heroism and rescues by both firemen and civilians who helped evacuate the many burning buildings.

Another plane crash, dramatic at the time because it involved the famous Empire State Building, occurred on July 28, 1945 when a U.S. Army B-25 aircraft crashed into the 72nd floor of the building. Fires of this type, fortunately, are uncommon, but do, however, highlight the dangers of low-flying aircraft to the many skyscrapers in a big metropolis.

This disaster, although contained by the fire department and rescue units, was memorable to my wife, Natalie, as it involved a good friend and neighbor. On that day, Mary Kedzierska was working in her office which was directly struck by the B-25. She was killed instantly. As fate decreed, she wasn't normally at the office on a Saturday, but she was on a special assignment. Except for the unusual nature of the crash, the fire aspect was contained and damage was kept to a minimum. The impact of the crash gouged out a sizeable chunk of the building on the side in which the plane had plunged. The final death toll was 14. It was minimized by the fact that the plane's fuselage became imbedded in the building and because the crash was on a Saturday morning.

LAND, SEA & AIR (*GENERAL SLOCUM*)

Long ago sailors believe that a sea monster lived in New York Harbor and in the true tradition of the deep, swallowed up ships. Records of yore attest to the fact that more than 2,000 shipwrecks have taken place in the harbor. The most renowned of these tragedies took place on June 14, 1904, in the deadly currents of Hell's Gate.

In that year, the *General Slocum* steamboat was headed up the East River on a Sunday outing. They never made it to the picnic grounds. Along the way, 1030 persons lost their lives. It was the second largest disaster in the history of American inland passenger shipping. (the worst recorded was in April, 1965, when the Mississippi riverboat, *Sultana*, blew up and claimed the lives of 1,500 Union soldiers.)

The terrible tragedy that claimed the many lives on board the *General Slocum* was the result of a series of events that contributed to the disaster. It started innocently enough when a minor fire was discovered on the lower deck. When two seamen opened a door to the storeroom they were met by a burst of flames. The untrained crew went into action and pulled a hoseline from the reel on the wall. When the valve was opened there was no water, although the pumps were in operation. The hose was uncoupled and it was discovered that a solid washer had been inserted to keep water from dripping onto the deck! When the hose was recoupled and charged with water, it burst. Instead of being easily extinguished in it's incipient stage, the fire spread rapidly.

The First Mate, now in panic, reported to the Captain that a fire was in progress. Instead of taking charge, the Captain, curiously, took over the wheel as the steamer was headed for the strong currents running though Hell's Gate.

The Captain just steamed ahead, oblivious of the warning blasts from vessels tied up at the countless piers he passed. He simply could have pulled in and had the fire extinguished by the many engine companies available. As the ship churned onward, fire alarms were transmitted all along the shore. The responding companies sized up the situation and requested the response of the fire boat, *Zophar Mills*. Captain Van Schaick of the *Slocum* paid no attention to the firefighters, their horses and apparatus lined up along the shores. They were screaming, waving and yelling to deaf ears.

Meanwhile, down below, the crew was frantically trying to get water on the fire. Hoseline after hoseline continued to burst and they were helpless as the fire raged on. The fireboat, *Zophar Mills*, spotted the ship and gave chase, as did firemen who commandeered anything that floated and chased after the vessel, picking up victims as she steamed up the river. Before long she was being chased by a progression of tug boats, launches, the fireboat, a yacht from the Bronx Yacht Club, and anything else that could float that the firemen could lay their hands on.

As the fire raged, adult passengers began throwing children overboard to be picked up by pursuing rescuers. A female passenger lay on the deck and gave birth helped by a ship's mate and a passenger. The newborn was then wrapped in a blanket and as the fire was approaching, the crowd threw the mother and child over the side. They both perished. The last order given by the Captain was "Full speed ahead." To add to the confusion, the pilot sailed around to the far side of the island, thereby passing the sandy stretch of shoreline. To the very end passengers suffered untold horrors until they were consumed by the fire.

There was plenty of blame to go around, from the inspectors that overlooked serious deficiencies to the payment of bribes to ensure that minor violations went unrecorded. Major fines for serious violations had mysteriously been drastically reduced.

Ineptitude, greed, bribery and inadequate equipment were uncovered by the ensuing investigation. Belatedly, stricter enforcement was legislated so that future generations would have better protection on these cruise lines. However, bad judgment and panic cannot be legislated against. Unfortunately, it takes a major disaster to arouse public indignation and to see that laws already on the books regarding the protection of the citizenry are enforced.

The *General Slocum* disaster will long be remembered as the biggest calamity to hit New York City. It was a day that the "Red Devil" was an uninvited guest on the passenger list for this Sunday school boat ride.

The Captain of the *General Slocum* was tried on two counts of manslaughter. He was found guilty and sentenced to ten years at hard labor. He was later pardoned by President Taft after serving five years of "Hard Time."

When our company is engaged in "water drafting" drills at the East River pier, we can almost visualize that eerie procession of ships as that bizarre and deadly drama unfolded almost a century ago. It still evokes feelings of deep sorrow and futility.

SUBWAY FIRES

In addition to fires and emergencies that N.Y.C. Fire Departments are exposed to from land, sea and air, there are fires and emergencies to contend with below ground. The New York Subway System and the Long Island Railroad both present unique problems. They both have the potential to incite panic in passengers trapped between stations below ground. Another serious factor for the responding company to contend with is accessibility to the subway cars involved in order to effect extinguishment in the event of a fire, or evacuation of passengers in other emergencies. It is not unusual, as has often happened in fires where Engine Co 44 was involved, to start an operation, say on 77th Street, and complete the operation a couple of miles away on elevated tracks. In one case ladders were lowered from the street access points to the tracks below and later raised to the elevated tracks miles away. In fire conditions heat and smoke make underground operations almost unbearable, especially when trains are stopped between stations and power interrupted. As anyone who has noticed the rush of air from the above ground grates can attest, subway tunnels are ventilated mainly by the movement of the approaching trains pushing air before the train and out through the overhead grates. A good demonstration of this action is the famous photo popularized by Marilyn Monroe which was much to the consternation of husband Joe DiMaggio.

It is inevitable that we can expect to respond to fires and emergencies from the extensive underground systems of the LIRR and subway lines. The New York Subway System is the largest and most heavily traveled passenger railroad in the world. It accommodates almost 5,000,000 passengers daily in more than 8,000 scheduled trains. To give an example of the potential for panic, each train carries almost 2,500 passengers during rush hours. In case of fire or other emergency there are as many as 30 trains stalled, mostly below ground, when power is interrupted. Experience has shown that there have been more injuries caused by panic than by the actual fire or emergency condition. It is imperative that all company officers acquaint themselves with the access grates that are provided between stations of the subway system. Also, company officers are cautioned not to completely rely on Transit personnel when they are assured that the high voltage power has been shut down. On one occasion, after such assurance, four men and myself from Engine.Co 44 were running over the subway tracks toward a car surrounded by smoke from a fire in the undercarriage. Due to the urgency of the situation, and to hopefully avoid panic by the passengers, we didn't wait to verify by circuit test lamp if power had been shut down. If so, it had again been turned on as we had a train bearing down on us after about three blocks and had to take to the safety notches provided at the side walls.

At least the train slowed enough until all our group was safely off the tracks. We got to the train just in time, as the passengers were becoming anxious and frightened. Meanwhile, from the street the hook & ladder company had lowered a 35 foot ladder from the access grating to evacuate the most intrepid of the passengers. With the calming influence of the members of Engine.Co.44, everyone choosing to escape via the ladder was evacuated without incidence or injury. Others, after contemplating the climb of 25 to 30 feet to the top, opted to proceed to the next station escorted by a couple of firefighters. Given the heavy smoke condition in the still air below no one panicked. The important thing was that all were reassured by the presence of the firefighters and they had complete trust in us as we coaxed them along good-naturedly, whenever one faltered, especially on climbing the 35 foot ladder to the street. The people who chose to escape via the ladder were so fearful of the high-voltage third rail that they would have tried any other alternative. On the other hand the persons afflicted with acrophobia would have chosen to crawl on hands and knees to the next station, despite the smoke, to avoid the ladder.

On one occasion when I had visited Engine Co.44 after my retirement, the firehouse was occupied by a relocating company under the command of a Captain Bill Coleman. As I entered quarters a telephone alarm was received from the dispatcher for a fire in the subway system. Being unfamiliar with the access grates on Lexington Ave as it was not in his fire district, Captain Coleman invited me to respond, and act as a bird dog, which I accepted. The operation went along smoothly as it wasn't a serious fire but had resulted in a lot of smoke. When I later emerged from below from the cloud of smoke, I was captured on film by the TV crew of Channel 5. I was spitting and coughing and being asked countless questions. I had responded in my civilian clothes and was mistaken for a fleeing passenger from the stalled train.

This chance encounter was aired on the seven pm newscast.

3M ATTACK -- SUICIDE SQUAD

It was near quitting time after a fairly busy day tour of duty. Nothing big or stressful, but a lot of running. False alarms, food on the stove, a burning automobile fire, rubbish in yards, etc. -- mostly nuisance fires. On duty this day was what I referred to as my 3M attack team an overzealous bunch that operated more as a suicide squad than professional firefighters.

At 5:15 pm we got a special call from the Manhattan dispatcher for a complaint of smoke, called in by the superintendent of a five story tenement building. Besides Artie Walka, my MPO, there was my suicide squad, the 3M boys, John Magas, John Mazza and Larry Monachelli. In contrast to the occasional lump encountered on the job, they would attack a fire with a vengeance and in reckless abandon, with or without water in the hoseline. I was always in favor of an aggressive crew, but at a fire situation where the exact location is undetermined, it is best to exercise extreme caution until the seat of the fire is discovered.

I ordered enough 2-1/2 inch hose stretched to cover the full five floors if required. The firefighters were then to stand fast at the building's entrance until I had located the source of the smoke, which was now present on all five floors. At this time we were the only company at the scene, and when I could not locate the source of the fire, I had the MPO contact the dispatcher by radio to send a full first alarm assignment when available. I then checked, without success, each floor from the hall area for any visible indication of fire. On returning to street level I found that my enterprising crew, concerned that I hadn't returned immediately, had advanced the hoseline to the second floor. The reason for concern was understandable as the entire stairwell was completely enveloped in sulfur dioxide gas (SO_2) which can be deadly in small amounts when it is inhaled. We did not have any gas masks.

This operation was approaching dangerous proportions. There was no ladder company to provide ventilation to clear the stairwell, and the seat of the fire still had to be located. I had my men take the hoseline below the second floor landing, fearful that the fire might be below us in the concealed spaces of an apartment ceiling or wall. I again raced up the stairs to the fifth floor trying to locate the fire in vain. By now we were all being suffocated by the toxic fumes in the stairwell. Still the ladder company had not arrived. The longer it took to locate the fire the more dangerous our situation became.

There was a window located between the second and third floors facing an air shaft. John Mazza tried to pry it open to afford us some relief from the poisonous gas. The window was stuck tight and John proceeded to force it open by banging upward on the sash of the window frame. I noticed that he was not wearing his protective gloves and called out for him to stop, but it was too late. The glass shattered an cut Mazza's wrists. He began to bleed profusely. Instead of having pity on him, John Magas and Larry Monachelli felt that we should slit his throat as well for such a foolish move. I felt like hanging him from his heels in the stairwell for the position he had put us in by not heeding my command to stop his attack on the sash without his gloves. We could ill afford to lose a man as we were already undermanned.

Luckily by this time the first alarm assignment had arrived along with a Battalion Chief. The stairwell was vented, and on the next sortie after we broke into an apartment on the fourth floor, a section of the tin ceiling was discovered to be scorched. We notified the Battalion Chief, had the hoseline charged with water and advanced to the third floor. We were prepared to get at the fire after the ceiling was opened. The scorching of the tin ceiling was much more noticeable and had spread. When a truckman from the ladder company dug his hook into the corner of the ceiling and pulled downward we all got an unpleasant surprise. Almost half of the tin ceiling was blown down when the trapped gasses ignited explosively as soon as air was sucked into the concealed ceiling space. The entire room became fully enveloped in flames. Fortunately, the room had been ventilated and the truckman that had pierced the ceiling was positioned partly into the stairwell. He fell flat on his gut with the first puff of smoke, thereby escaping possible serious burns. My company quickly advanced the 2-1/2 inch hoseline to the fire floor and commenced to extinguish the flames emanating from between the bays of the open ceiling. Finally the entire ceiling was removed and all of the flames extinguished.

We were indeed lucky to have found the source of the fire before it had progressed further into the concealed spaces of the walls and ceilings of the other floors, in which case the initial blast by the backdraft would have been more violent and widespread and may well have resulted in burn casualties. Even with the stairwell ventilated, the strong odor of the sulfur dioxide was still present. The source of the gas leak was an old fashioned refrigerator on the fifth floor. The unit had overheated and the SO_2 refrigerant escaped and enveloped the entire building since the gas is much heavier than air. The only factor in our favor was that the SO_2, although very high in toxicity, is not explosive.

Our dauntless suicidal firefighter was taken to Lenox Hill Hospital for treatment and then placed on sick leave. He returned weeks later and the ribbing he received from the troops followed him throughout his career on the job. These over-aggressive firemen all went on to become bosses on the job. Mazza was promoted to Lieutenant. Monachelli retired as a Captain and John Magas went on to become a Battalion Chief. One thing they all had in common, which I consider to be the ultimate attribute, "they were good firemen."

RATING AT THE ROCK

Things were going along really smooth. The chicken shit chief was off my back and the problem "phantom fireman" had transferred out and was replaced by one that didn't shirk his duty. In our company drills we concentrated on the evolutions in the "fireman's manual" with special attention to knots and the use of "fittings" as the "Rock" was in full operation. The so-called "Rock" was on Welfare Island and was run by a group of training officers. The object was to keep companies on alert. No one knew in advance when they were going to be called. Right after the 9:00 am, 11-11 signal is transmitted, the company chosen for "slaughter" that day was immediately special called on the alarm bells. What wasn't known at that time was that a shoofly from the Rock was stationed at the corner from the fire company. He noted the time from receipt of the special call signal to the actual time the company left quarters. The time the company took to arrive at the destination, taking into account traffic conditions was also noted. Many companies feared being called to the Rock because of the heavy-handed methods that some of the training officers employed. You were tested and rated on every aspect of the job. Even the officers were rated on leadership and command qualities.

The one day that I was late reporting for duty was the day Engine Co. 44 was called to the "Rock". As I pulled up to the firehouse, and searched for a parking spot, 11-11, the 9 am time signal was sounding. The next thing I heard was the pumper starting up and pulling out of the fire station with Lieut. John Cavanagh in command. He had worked the night tour. He was evidently in deep shock as he didn't realize I was already there. Engine Co. 44 proceeded at full speed to the "Rock". With my car still in the fire zone I was advised by the outgoing members that the company had been special called to the Training School at Welfare Island. I ran in, got my turnout gear, returned to my car and raced after the rig hoping to catch it before they got to the "Rock". I was flashing my lights and blowing my horn to get their attention. My men on the back step (the day tour,) recognizing the situation, yelled for Fr. Rogers over the roar of the exhaust pipe, to stop. He must also have been in shock as they sped onward oblivious to my frantic pursuit. They didn't stop, or slow up enough, until after shooting through Queens County. It was only when they slowed up to cross the bridge leading to Welfare Island that I chased John out of the rig, much to his relief, and he returned to our quarters with my car. I was confident, because my working group had been going over what we expected to be tested on during our regular company drills. We were the first group in our company to be called to the "Rock" and I was determined to make a good impression.

I was met at the entrance to the training grounds by an assemblage of officers with the demeanor reminiscent of pall bearers. They broke up my working group and they were tested individually in separate areas of the training ground. I was asked some pertinent questions by the captain of the headhunters. It wasn't long before an emissary came to us with a declaration that my company was deficient in the subject of knots. I ran to the area where the knot test were conducted and was met by none other than Deputy Chief Ward who was in charge of the whole training school. He was there as an "observer" as these testing procedures were in their infancy. He met me with a scowl and in no uncertain terms, told me my company was to be failed in knots. His tone and actions had my Fireman, Jim Logan, distracted to the point that he initially failed the simplest of knots. I knew Jim was one of the most proficient in the subject of knots. For one, he was a Navy man, and two, he was unerring at company drill. Now the chief and the other training officers, by their arrogant and intimidating actions, changed my attitude on the testing procedures from one of apprehension to righteous anger. I was ready for a battle.

I started my attack right at the top. I asked Chief Ward how he could prejudge a company on just one knot. I walked over to Jimmy and reminded him that he knew all the knots and not to be shaken by all these vultures breathing down his neck. He then made the knot with ease.

The chief then chose the knots to raise a 35-foot ladder to the roof. I just told Jim to show his stuff. I then turned to Chief Ward who was in kissing distance of Jim's neck and said; "And you, Chief, stand back away from him with me." I don't think that statement earned me any "brownie points". Jim then came through by expertly negotiating the knot. A good thing, too, because Fr. Rogers was next and he was so nervous he had trouble operating the hydraulic jack where the only motion is "up" and "down".

Next, I get an emissary telling me the "hatchet men" were giving one of my best firemen, Bob Andriuola, a hard time on a drafting and pumper operation at the end of the grounds. I could see where the agility part of the entry examination came in handy as I ran to the location. When I was shown the hookup and fittings used by Bob, I sized up the situation and it went something like this:

Lt. C. "So what's the problem?"

Training Officer: -- "It's not the way we teach it at the school."

Lt. C. "That's the way I teach it at company drill."

Training Officer: "But it's not a solid to solid connection on the fittings that we want."

Lieut.C. "Not from your perspective. We still maintain your solid to solid. The sequence we use here is a quicker method. I was an MPO for six years, used both, and this here is superior. If you insist, we can do it either way, but you will see this is much better." Another round won by the good guys (E.44)!

The biggest farce was yet to come in the dreaded "Fittings Room". There is a full complement of all the fittings in use in the department, about 20 in all. A training officer then designates one of the firemen to come forward and he is given a problem which usually involves connecting from two to four or more brass fittings to accomplish a given "hook up". In this instance Fr. Tom Rogers was given the problem with everyone looking on. Tom got the first piece O.K., and was on his knees surveying the field of "gold" with his face getting redder by the minute. It was getting embarrassing. I myself was mentally working out the problem. That's when I directed an outburst at the captain and lieutenant conducting the test. First I told Tom: "That's enough Tom. Get up." I then turned to the officers: "Are you guys trying to play games or are you conducting a legitimate test?"

Captain: "What do you mean Lieutenant?"

Lt. C. "There's no way you can complete the hook up you described with what's laid out."

Captain: "Everything is laid out from the previous test."

Lt. C. "Let me see how you and the Lieutenant do it. It appears there is a 3 inch to 2 1/2 inch reducer missing."

The captain then stepped up for a closer look and the fitting was, indeed, missing. He apologized, saying it was unintentional, and got the fitting from the storeroom. By this time Tom had been clued in by the banter and completed the hook up. I'm not too sure if the incident was unintentional. It may have been a test of the whole company, or maybe even the officer of the company.

As we gained confidence, we went through every evolution, stretching of hose, and every other problem without a hitch. We were the first group in our company to be rated. We had done a good job. That should set a good tone for the groups to follow as we could clue them in on the operations at the "Rock".

When we got back to the company quarters after being dismissed, Lieutenant John Cavanagh came in for a visit to see how we made out. I asked him why he raced off from the firehouse when I was calling out for his attention. He claimed my chauffeur, Tom, was so shocked by the unexpected call to the training center that John's attempts at slowing him down went unheeded. It was like he was in a "twilight zone" type trance. Knowing Tom that was quite possible. However, that "French Connection" type car chase through the streets of Manhattan and Queens was enough to give a normal person a heart attack.

Last Days at Engine Co. 44 then to Div. of Training

Things were going quite well at the firehouse. The usual runs and workers, nothing spectacular but enough to keep us from getting stale. The dead wood had transferred out and I had a real gung ho bunch in my working group. The only problem now was that I couldn't get rid of the starboard list in my neck and the recurring dizzy spells which were getting progressively more frequent. I was reluctant to again visit the medical office but Deputy Chief Flynn kept insisting that I do. It was only a few months since I had convinced Dr. Nayer that I would have no problem in resuming full duty. I had to give up my "moonlighting" job in the construction and paving business, the proceeds of which were needed to pay off the $4,000 down payment loan to procure a home mortgage.

My string finally ran out on one of my day tours of duty. I was in my office typing out the month's field inspection duty results when suddenly I had absolutely no control of my neck or my left arm. My neck just went limp. I was almost convinced that I had a stroke but didn't want to think in those terms. It was all I could do to make it to the bunk. I laid down flat on my back and waited for the feeling to return but it never did. It was near the end of my 9 am. to 6:00 pm. tour and luckily my relief, Lieutenant Tim Barrett, came in about an hour early and made some remarks about laying down on the job. When he saw it was no joke, he notified the medical office and the medical officer on duty gave orders I not be moved and he would leave immediately to examine me at the firehouse. After he came and made his examination he was ready to call the department ambulance to take me home as I refused to be taken to the hospital. That presented another problem as I lived outside of the five boroughs, but had a "legal address" in Queens, N.Y. Finally it was determined that they would send for my younger brother Peter, who would drive me home. Dr. Nayer also prescribed some pills and advised that if the condition did not improve by the next day, I was to be admitted to a hospital for further tests. As soon as I was ambulatory I was to report to the Medical Office for further evaluation.

When I was able to get around again, and before going to the medical office, I went to an orthopedist and a roentgenologist in Long Island for a complete examination of the neck and back. I hoped that the findings would be useful in my request to return to full duty. The opposite was the result. Evidently that blow to the head by the 200-pound trap door had broken off the tip of one of the spurs in my neck. The dislodged bone chip was now "calcifying" much like a bit of sand in an oyster. After consultation, the doctors concurred that I only perform sedentary duties. When I told them I was currently an active firefighter, they emphatically advised me not to return to full duty. The dizzy spells persisted although not as frequent. I was very disappointed with their findings and I admit I did not share the results with the fire department doctors. They of course had already determined that I be placed on limited service. For a while I was placed on "theater detail duty", a much coveted assignment supervising the firefighters detailed to the Broadway theaters and TV studios. It was interesting for a while, but there was no challenge or satisfaction and I begged to be reassigned. Meanwhile Chief Kehayes, who was the head of the Probationary Fireman's School at Welfare Island, learned that I was available and asked if I would be interested in returning to the Division of Training as an Instructor. I immediately accepted. There would at least be the satisfaction in applying the years of experience and knowledge in molding young men into first class fire fighters. The work was mostly outdoors and the simulated fire drills and operations conducted were very close to the real thing. In fact, during one of the graduation exercises we started a fire in one of the abandoned buildings that almost got away from us. The upper echelon chiefs at the ceremony, attended by hundreds of graduates and their parents, were having many anxious moments.

The probationary firefighters who were initially putting out the fire as part of the exercise, were removed as they weren't permitted to take so much of a "feed" of smoke. For realism, the training officers in charge of assembling the materials to be set on fire in the building thought it would be a good idea to include some old automobile tires as they gave off lots and lots of dense black smoke. In their enthusiasm they had put too many tires in the mix. They made a fast burning foundation that was very hot, smoky and difficult to extinguish fire.

After the probationary firefighters were removed, a full attack on the blaze was ruled out because it might disrupt the graduation exercises. Instead I and one other training officer were left in the building with two inadequate hose lines. The deep-seated fire in the tires flared up the instant it appeared we were making headway in extinguishing the pile. As the chief had reassured the top brass that there was "no problem", we didn't even have face masks on. We took quite a "feed" from this operation and were very happy when exercises in that vicinity were concluded and moved to another area. We then, with extra help, flooded the pile with additional heavy streams. I later told Chief Kehayes, "If being smoked to "well done" constitutes limited service, please send me back to full duty."

As the Civil Service Commission kept on lowering the standards for the entrance examinations, the effect on the quality of the personnel soon became obvious.

The men were instructed on each and every facet of the job, even the seemingly simple matter of sliding the pole safely. I would position myself on the very narrow landing around the brass pole in the pole hole. I would then have each probie, in turn, face me at the opposite side of the pole hole. I would show him how to place his leg against the pole and then wrap his arm around the pole. With the next motion the other leg comes into play as the pole is slid. The pole is thus grasped between the two legs and the crook of the elbow as you slide down. I purposely go over this routine slowly and deliberately and do a few slides myself with everyone looking on before I take on the first probie. The first few were able to negotiate this simple exercise without mishap. Then came M-38. I took special precaution with this fellow because I had noticed some lack of coordination on his part in other activities. He got the first leg in position, as demonstrated. Then in quick succession he wrapped the crook of his arm around his neck, instead of the pole, and started to jump into the pole hole. I immediately grabbed him and the pole and stepped on his foot which was still on the narrow landing. It wasn't enough that I had yelled to stop. He was bent on smashing his head in the pole hole. Before having him try again I had a few others slide without mishap. Of the twelve I took on at one time only one other probie made the same dangerous mistake as M-38. I believe I could have taken in a dozen teens from the street and they would have slid the pole without any instruction! I made the two do several slides before we secured that operation. M-38 gave me cause for concern in a few other activities. Occasionally I would observe him give a half-step-stumble for no apparent reason. On the other hand he was as strong as an ox and tenacious as an Italian Bulldog. He endured any punishment in the "smoke room" without complaint. On stretching hose up a stairwell he appeared able to pull up the hose and any firefighters hanging on. If strength and tenacity were the only criteria, he would have been at the top of the class. Unfortunately, there was that subtle defect that could make him vulnerable to injury or worse, in an emergency situation. On one occasion when I had a group stretch hose to an area around the corner from my position he was a long time in returning as the hose was being taken up. I sent a couple of men around the corner to check on him. I didn't have the heart to berate him as he was caught in a tangle of three lengths of hose that he was attempting to return single-handedly. I think he knew of his shortcomings and wanted to impress me with his strength.

One story regarding M-38 that became legend unfolded during an evolution where we simulate a condition where a multi-versal nozzle is to be raised to the roof of the building at night. The firefighters located on the roof drop down one end of a roof rope to the firefighter located at the street level who then ties the prescribed knot on the nozzle. Since the operation is supposedly taking place at night, the signal to the men on the roof to raise the nozzle is given by the man in the street by two tugs on the rope.

Lieutenant John Kearns was supervising this operation, which employed one of the most difficult knots, when he came across M-38 proudly standing by the multi-versal nozzle. Lt. Kearns examined the knot and was surprised that it was expertly done.

Lieut. Kearns: "O.K. M-38, that's a nice knot."

M-38: - "Thank you Sir."

Lieut. Kearns: "Well, aren't you ready to have it raised to the roof?"

M-38: "Yes Sir." (Still standing proudly)

Lieut. Kearns: "Well go ahead and send it to the roof. Do you know the signal?

M-38: "Yes Sir." (Still admiring his knot.)

Lieut. Kearns: "Well, what is the signal?"

M-38: "Two tugs!"

Lieut. Kearns: (Getting a bit annoyed at the delay) "Well go ahead and give it."

M-38: (Looks up to the roof, cups his hands around his mouth and as loud as he can, yells out:) "two tugs!"

It was all John could do to keep from doubling up as this unexpected signal echoed through the yard. When he recovered, he explained to M-38 that the proper procedure was to apply two sharp tugs on the roof rope which he finally executed. The poor fellow was embarrassed and we never chided him. He showed so much honest determination that you had to like him. Still, there was that lack of coordination that occasionally showed up. I had to bring that to the attention of Chief Kehayes with my recommendation that he be held over until the next class. Sadly, I recommended to the chief that M-38 be neurologically tested and reevaluated. I feared that he would be a danger to himself and to others. I hoped it was a temporary condition that could be controlled. Except for this flaw he would have made an excellent firefighter. His father was so proud of him as he dropped his son off at the training school in the morning and picked him up at the end of the classes. You could almost feel the love and affection between the little "old guy" and this big lovable, clumsy ox of a probie. The "old guy" was always early and waited at the far end of the parking area for our M-38.

Another case that I believe deserved closer attention by the investigative arm of the Civil Service Commission concerned a young black boy. Let's call him Prob. Fr. Scott.

On the day before I was to give an examination on all the tools and equipment used during the week, I reviewed each and every piece of equipment in detail with the class. The object was not to pass or fail anyone, but to familiarize them with the tools of the job. The next day the test was given in multiple choice form. Not surprisingly the average mark achieved by all except Prob. Fireman Scott was close to 90% with the lowest 85%. Prob. Fr. Scott scored 15%. I did not announce the scores openly so as not to embarrass him. However, I took him aside later and went over the entire subject matter again and informed him that I would give him the same test the next day. When I rated the next day's effort, on the same test, Prob. Fireman Scott scored 17%. This demonstrated a serious learning disability and there was no way this kid could have passed the written entrance examination on his own. Another example to bear out this conclusion was that when Prob. Fr. Scott was given two fittings to connect together. He was able to do it. Whenever a third brass fitting was introduced, however, he was not able to connect them. I spent countless hours on my own, going over the fittings, until he was able to connect them together. The next day he was again at a loss. The same trend was evident in other simple problems. He and M-38 were only two of the few that I recommended for reevaluation and possible release from the department. The Civil Service Commission in their infinite wisdom simply stated: they passed the written tests. It's your job to make them firefighters. Both were eventually assigned to companies.

TELEPHONE BUILDING EXPLOSION

On October 3, 1962, we were just breaking for lunch when we received an urgent call from department headquarters at the training school. There was a report of an explosion at the New York Telephone Building located in uptown Manhattan. The need was for manpower which we had in abundance, as the probationary fireman's school was in session.

Chief Kehayes quickly dispatched a bus load of probies to the location. The chief and a contingent of fire officers followed in a department car. As we made our way through the Harlem streets, we came upon a truck which was blocking our passage with a driver and a passenger sitting in the cab. At first I thought that the vehicle was disabled. Instead the two clowns in the truck cab seemed to be enjoying the fact that they were disregarding our siren. It was a time where disobedience and disruption of the establishment was in vogue along with the protests and riots of that era. The attitude of the administrations at the time was and still is, patience and tolerance as there was always the threat of violence and riot in the "black community" at the slightest provocation. I became so incensed at this flagrant disregard of the law and their obstruction of an emergency vehicle, for no other reason but to demonstrate contempt for authority, that against the cautions of the others in the car I rushed out of the car and ran to the truck. Realizing that every minute here could mean a life squandered at our destination, I must have appeared like a madman as I yanked open the door of the truck. I can't repeat here what language I used, nor do I remember, but by the time my tirade was completed the truck was immediately moved, accompanied by a weak excuse and an attempt at a watery apology. Without further mishap we arrived at the telephone building where we were greeted with scenes of horror and devastation. In property damage it appeared to be a miniature of the Twin Tower explosion. But loss of life was extensive.

We immediately set about removing debris from the collapsed main floor in order to search for victims. However, practically all the dead and injured had already been removed to a hospital. All that was left in the rubble was body parts. One of the victims was the sister-in-law of one of the veteran firemen from the training school. We sent him off to the hospital to check on her condition.

The explosion itself was a freak occurrence and it couldn't have happened at a more inopportune time. Almost all of the deaths were in a cafeteria located in the basement area of the building. Besides having lunch, it was also a meeting place for employees in the building., It was also open to employees from adjacent company buildings.

The morning had started innocently enough with a tradesman performing repairs on the building's steam boiler in the basement. He was working on the electronic combustion safeguard controls when it was time to break for lunch. Fortunately, for him he decided to go off premises for lunch probably because the lunchroom may have been full to capacity at the time. During his absence, according to the official version, there was an enormous build up of steam in the boiler due to an electronic malfunction. The result was that the upper rear plate of the boiler blew open with a violent escape of high pressure steam resulting in the boiler becoming jet propelled. A very large boiler of this size is like having a runaway locomotive on the loose in the basement, tearing from its cradle and fuel attachments, and careening through walls and ceiling on its way to wreak devastation and death to the occupants of the cafeteria. Initially, the boiler thrust upward breaking through the concrete ceiling and causing a receptionist and her desk from the main floor to fall into the basement. The damage from the initial explosion was insignificant compared to the physical damage from the runaway boiler itself. Ironically, a building superintendent having a noontime siesta on a bench in an adjacent cubicle, felt only a "whoomph," as he described it, as he felt himself being lifted from the bench. He was unhurt. The final count was twenty-three dead, many others wounded.

ROAD TO RETIREMENT

FIRE PROTECTION ENGINEERING, INSURANCE FIELD SCAMS, UNUSUAL RECOMMENDATION COMPLIANCE, VITAS GERULITIS (CO POISONING), TRUMP MANSION INSPECTION, CREATIVE, FIELDMAN ACTIVITIES

In the spring of 1964, I was again summoned to the Fire Department Medical Office for reevaluation. This time I had to face a five-member board who decided, against my protestations, that I submit my request for retirement papers. To me that was tantamount to quitting and throwing in the towel in a boxing match. The Medical Examiners had determined that, based on the nature of the neck and back injuries revealed by the x-ray records, I had become a liability to the department in the event that some serious consequence, such as injury or death, could be traceable to my being allowed to continue on duty with reduced physical capacity.

I was adamantly against putting in my retirement papers until I at least had a full twenty years of service in the Fire Department. Falling short of the 20 years of service meant that the prior nine years of service with the City, which included my 2 1/2 years of military service, would be wasted and not reflected in my pension.

In my 26 years of service in the New York Civil Service Retirement System, there is no credit for my time in military Service. In addition to other unacknowledged activities, I now also became the "stealth serviceman".

I was very grateful when I learned that Battalion Chief Kehayes (Yogi Bear) and Deputy Chief Ward, who were in charge of the training school on Welfare Island, submitted unsolicited letters requesting that I be permitted to remain as an instructor. They had stressed that I had been very effective in that position and had in fact initiated some training procedures that had benefited the training program. To read their letters of commendation you would think that the fire department couldn't survive if I left.

The medical office responded politely but restated their position of liability. I then offered to sign a waiver where my family would hold the City of New York unaccountable in the event of any accident attributable to any preexisting condition. This, of course, wasn't even given any consideration. In June of 1964, I retired from the New York Fire Department. We had a small gathering at Welfare Island with a farewell luncheon for myself and Captain Timothy Barrett. Before being assigned to the Welfare Island Training School, Timothy and I were both active lieutenants in Engine Co. 44 for many years.

Yogi (Chief Kehayes) and the training staff gave Timothy and myself parting gifts and expressions of appreciation which I sadly accepted. Timothy was more upbeat. He had more than twenty years of service and had requested retirement. I later learned there were ways that I would have been able to remain on duty until ready to retire on my own. None of the available options were "kosher" and required unethical, if not illegitimate actions, so I did not even attempt to pursue that course. Unfortunately, working honestly within the established system of politics is unrewarding at best. In retrospect I could see the position of the Medical Board. I also reasoned that my retirement would open a position for a full duty officer for some deserving fireman on the list.

For the first year or two, after retiring, I went bananas. The conditions that led to my retirement precluded my doing any of the work that I had done in the past to supplement my income. I had to find some activity that could earn some income before I went stark raving mad. It was then that a friend I had kept in touch with from our days aboard the CG. Cutter "Hibiscus", Nick Jeannette, who had a successful agency in Huntington, New York, suggested that I go to school and become an insurance broker. After attending an accredited school I took the next broker's examination and began a new career as an insurance broker. From the start I could see that I wasn't going to be happy in this endeavor. There was no challenge. No spiritual satisfaction. The sometimes outrageous demands of the insurance underwriters and the contacts with an uninformed public were hard for me to deal with. I decided to go into fire protection engineering.

FIRE PROTECTION ENGINEERING

There were considerable jobs open working for insurance brokerage firms which involved simple inspections and filling out forms that were no-brainers. I decided to go after the giants of the industry, the companies that were a conglomerate. I started by making phone calls to some of the top companies in the industry. That was a mistake. For one, they almost always required a graduate from a university that specialized in fire protection engineering. The next obstacle was the age factor. As soon as the over 40, in my case 46 years of age, was revealed, it seemed they were ready to throw shovels of dirt in my face. You may just as well be deceased. Next I tried writing to each of the top companies giving my experience in the building industry and the fire department in lieu of the college graduate requirement. That was mistake number two.

I next decided to go in person to one of the top rated and most respected companies. They had a main office in White Plains and I was at the door when they opened for business at 8:00 am. I was not alone looking for a position. There were ten applicants seated in the lobby. One by one we were escorted into an office to be interviewed. The examiner listened to my qualifications courteously although he flinched when he heard my age. He then told me that when the company needed someone with my experience I would be notified. That was it. I was at the door, ready to leave, when I was notified that they were conducting a five-part test on that very day and being I was already there, would I like to take it. I was delighted at the opportunity. I had already struck out as far as the interview was concerned. When my turn came I was placed in a glass surrounded cubicle and given the first of the exams which mostly dealt with reading comprehension. Once that was done in the allotted time it was collected and another test given. By the time the third was completed it was time for lunch. The Asst. Chief Engineer, George Stafford, advised me of the break and would I have lunch with him. We went to a nice restaurant and when the waitress asked if we would like a drink before lunch, George immediately told her we would skip the drink. That's when I made mistake number (3). I told Mr. Stafford that I would appreciate a drink after all the tests.

I also told Mr.Stafford that if the drink was not in his company lunch allowance it would be my pleasure to buy him a drink. He declined. Years later I learned that the lunch was part of the test. The one drink that I had cost me some points on the final test scores. If I had ordered two drinks it could have been disqualification, although you wouldn't be told. During the lunch George also garnered additional information on my background, education and experience. After lunch, we went back to the test cubicle. This test was mostly on physics, math and chemistry. I polished that off pretty quickly, and had lots left on my allotted time, so I kept busy by doing the crossword puzzle in the old Herald Tribune newspaper which had been left in the room. Soon the man came to collect the test. When he saw I was writing he asked if I required additional time. I told him I had finished test #4 a half hour ago and I was putting the finishing answers to the crossword puzzle. When I finished the last of the tests, I was brought into the examiner's office again. He said he was impressed with the results of the tests I had taken. He then said that there was another test that was given only to the graduate engineers, provided they had completed and passed the basic five tests that I had already taken. It was now 4:00 pm. and I asked if I could call home before I took the last examination. I later learned that being a considerate family man also weighed in the final determination. I completed the last test in half the allotted time. I again was escorted into the examiner's office as the test was being scored by the Chief Engineer.

Almost seven hours earlier it appeared I was being dismissed with a "don't call me, I'll call you" routine. Now, to my complete surprise, he was offering me a job on the spot. After all the disappointments by mail and phone interviews I couldn't believe it. There was still hope for a life after retirement.

I gave notice that I couldn't accept the offer until I had divested myself of my insurance brokerage portfolio, which may have been a conflict of interest with the offered position. I accepted the offer, in principal, and promised to return in about two weeks. I arranged for Nick Jeannette, of the Jeanette Agency, to take over my entire portfolio. When I returned I attended a school for fire protection engineering. A four year accelerated course was condensed into thirteen weeks. It seemed that every other day a written test was given and homework was assigned for each and every night. There wasn't any time for anything except schooling, homework and tests. We didn't take much time off for suppers as each night we were to prepare for testing the following morning. Travel home was out of the question so the candidates established residence close to the IRM building in White Plains. With two other students, Ron Costello and Jack Jones, we rented out the upper floor of a private home in the area, owned by a Mr. & Mrs. Zobel. They had some strict rules! No noise, no women, no late nights, etc. Drunkenness wouldn't be tolerated. With our very hectic schedule there wouldn't be time for any of that nonsense anyway. At the end of the course some of the candidates were eliminated or, in some cases, required additional training.

When we came to the part of the course that dealt with firemanics, sprinklers, extinguishing systems and related subjects, I assumed the position more as an instructor than a pupil, which to some degree, was appreciated by the lecturer. When the duties, job description, responsibilities and assignments (which included some traveling) were explained, I could see that it presented a challenge that I welcomed. In addition, the skills learned and utilized in the conduct of building and industrial occupancy inspections during my years of service in the NYFD would be put to good use. A very important facet of the duties assigned to the engineering department was to make recommendations to reduce the hazards for fire and other perils.

IRM Years - Arson Insps. Etc.

It didn't take long to realize that the no nonsense, candid, approach that was used in the fire department was not the modus operandi of choice in large corporations. One example to illustrate this point was where one of our field men, Nick Senyszyn, also a retired fireman, sent in a down to earth factual report on conditions he found on inspecting a factory in another state. After filling in the routine questions on the inspection forms, Nick flatly stated in the remarks section that the unexplained nature of the storage materials and location suggested that the risk location was preparing "to set the place on fire." These were his exact words or some other like phrase, designed to get the attention of the underwriters and examiners in the main office.. Instead of taking the alert seriously the report was greeted with derision. A week later the occupancy was burned down to the ground. No one was laughing then when the last inspection report was reviewed.

On another occasion I was sent to inspect some problem areas in and around Baltimore, Md. One of the occupancies, a decrepit building in a high crime, "inner city" area (a buzz word I picked up on the job,) didn't seem to me to measure up to the good reports submitted by various inspectors for the past five years. Not only was the building substandard, especially for the amount of insurance, but the nature of the stock storage for the amount of insurance was also suspect. Further investigation revealed that much of the storage included obsolete and therefore worthless parts used in the aircraft industry. Then in checking with the local volunteer fire department, other serious deficiencies and the history only added to the conclusion that this occupancy presented a "moral hazard". Further investigation of the property and perimeter revealed the presence of highly flammable materials, not in keeping with the occupancy. Parts of the outer section of the plant had been involved in suspicious fires that had not been reported to the insurance company. There was more cause than stated here to convince me that this place was ripe to be torched, and soon. I was certain that if I just sent in a report on conditions that it would be too late. Also, there was the reception to Nick's alert a year earlier. That's when I called the chief engineer and had a 3-way conversation with the underwriters and advised that they immediately cancel this risk. I was amazed to find it was listed as a highly protected risk (HPR), classed as very desirable, with the lowest premium rate!

I then returned to the location and met with principals of the company and recommended the removal of all violations. The sprinkler system and central station alarms must be restored to operable condition. They also feigned surprise at the alien "fire loading" of orange crates and other highly flammable materials. The immediate and forceful action, I'm certain, forestalled an arson in the making. This was the worst scenario I encountered. Later there were other instances where thorough investigation of fire losses resulted in more equitable settlements. It was good to learn that I was working with a very reputable company that stood behind their employees when in the right. They were very fair and helpful whenever any of their insureds suffered a fire loss, all of which earned them respect in the insurance industry. Unfortunately, being aggressive and not faking reports earns one respect in some quarters but enmity in others. The work ethic which is common in the fire department is not shared by all in the outside job market. The irresponsible, easy way out mentality by some employees is not unusual. All too often the integrity, commitment and industry of leadership doesn't trickle down to all the underlings.

As in the fire department, there are big men in big jobs which works out fine. Then there are small men in big jobs which doesn't work out so good. However, the institution survives despite the failings of the underlings because of tradition and leadership from the top. Unlike the fire department where ineptitude is revealed by action at the first punishing and stressful situation the misfits and fakers in big corporations can go undetected, and even gain promotions, their stupidity covered by a paper trail.

From the start I appreciated the challenges encountered as a fieldman in this new position. The experience I had gathered as an active firefighter and the schooling provided by the fire department training schools could now be put to good use. It seems however that I had never ceased being a firefighter. Whenever I encountered a situation during my fire insurance inspections, I shared that information with the local fire companies. In the event of a fire at that occupancy, they would be aware of the extra hazard and be able to plan ahead. In every state that I had been assigned to this procedure was very much appreciated. Indirectly, I felt that some big fire loss or loss of life might be avoided by the reduction of hazards that the fire companies would be exposed to. There was a mutual respect earned especially when the local fire companies learned that recommendations to remove fire hazard violations at a high risk plant were complied with more readily when made by an insurance company than by the local authorities. The reason being that if the hazards were not reduced or removed, the company would be faced with paying a much higher premium, or even with cancellation of their insurance. This last remedy was feared more than having to pay local nominal penalties for a noncompliance of violations.

On the subject of compliance on fire and safety recommendations, they are not always met with benevolence. Some enlightened CEOs and plant managers are very receptive and anxious to comply with any recommendation that would improve the safety of an operation or procedure in manufacture. Especially, when it is a successful company wishing to guard against a fire or other mishap that may cause a shut down which could result in economic loss, loss of jobs for an extended period, or worse, in the event of a total loss of the building.

On the other hand, there are some insureds that are violently opposed to any suggestions concerning their business. Some consider recommendations as intrusions on the conduct of their operations. In keeping with our company's reputation to "improve a risk", special efforts are made to effect compliance, especially on essential recommendations. Some of these efforts have been met with determined resistance by some of the insureds and in some cases, fieldmen have actually been physically assaulted. At the same time, there are various considerations that must be weighed by the underwriters and dispatchers in the parent company not to alienate the brokers, agents and member companies by canceling a problem insured outright. It was against this background that I got a special request from underwriters Ed Cook and Sam Salvo to make a last ditch effort to retain a rebellious insured in another fieldman's district. This was to be the last chance on compliance or the company's insurance was to be canceled. The regular fieldman adamantly refused to make another visit himself as he had been physically abused and bodily thrown out of the plant on his previous visit. That is when John DeGiso the investigations and inspections coordinator, got the bright idea to offer me up as the sacrificial goat.

My iconoclastic tendencies were already known in our company. I never hesitated to employ unorthodox methods to effect compliance on recommendations. When all else failed in accomplishing an objective by using the standard conservative and unimaginative methods, John DeGiso heroically volunteered my services. During the floods in Pennsylvania one year where even bridges were being washed out and entire towns were being evacuated, John fearlessly dispatched me to the center of the flood area to arrange for loss control procedures for any of our insureds exposed or in imminent danger. When record heat conditions were wreaking havoc on our insured interests in Florida, John immediately and without hesitation sent me down there for most of the summer.

This unenviable reputation for effecting compliance by creative means might have gone undiscovered by top management had not an insurance broker of one of our clients called to complain. He claimed his insured's company was pressured to build an extension to his plant when it wasn't necessary and it was not even required to comply with recommendations made by us. He complained that I had drawn his client into a gambling scam and insisted that I be censured or maybe even fired. I was called into the Chief Engineers office, presented with the brokers complaint and asked to explain the charges, especially the gambling. I went on to explain that this insured location was a metalworking plant that had some serious violations outstanding on the storage of flammable liquids.

After years of non-compliance with recommendations to remove the hazards involved in the storage the underwriters were considering canceling the account. As I had established a good record on getting results with difficult clients, John DeGiso contacted me and asked that I make an informal visit to the plant in an effort to convince the principals of the company to at least comply with the basic essentials for storage of flammable liquids.

When I got to the plant the odor of paint thinners and other flammable liquids was intense. There were violations everywhere throughout. It was a veritable firetrap. Had this been a fire department inspection the place would have been shut down until all the violations were removed. I took the two partners on a tour of the entire plant pointing out the dangers involved in the many deficiencies and suggested methods on compliance with the least amount of expenditure. Also, there would be a minimum disruption on the normal operation of the plant. As a further incentive, with the essential recommendations completed, there would be a reduction in the premium. Unlike many who refuse to cooperate, the two partners were very polite and courteous but were adamantly opposed to complying with **any** suggestions at all. They politely informed me that to try persuasion was a waste of my time and theirs, and further, if we persisted in demanding compliance they had instructed their broker to place their insurance with another carrier. They thanked me for my time and candor as I was being escorted out of the building.

On the way out we passed a room which was used for leisure. It had a soda machine, some chairs, a table and a dart board with what appeared to be three personalized darts in a tight grouping and in close proximity to the bull's eye.

In the late 1960s and early 1970s pitching darts were quite popular. Many local pubs held tournaments. There were prizes for individuals and teams that competed. Those competing had their own personalized darts and took great pride in their accomplishments in the tournaments. I asked if the darts were placed so close to impress someone or was that an actual score. With that one of the partners proudly exclaimed that was his last pitch that had cost his partner five dollars. He asked if I played darts in any tournaments to which I replied I only played at home with either my son or my brothers. Suddenly I was more of interest to him and he invited me to play a couple of rounds just for fun. I immediately smelled the **hustle**. However, I preempted him with a suggestion that we make the rounds a bit interesting. I told him there were about ten outstanding recommendations on the plant. Suppose I take one practice round and then I will wager two dollars against one of the recommendations. It was immediately agreed on. I lost the first three rounds. The guy was pretty good. I figured if I got to lose the next two tosses, I would realize it was a bad match, cut my losses and get out. However, now that we were on a more personal level, I was going to give getting some violations removed another shot.

However, I got sharper and he started to lose confidence. After an hour of this "fire protection engineering" activity, none of which was taught in our accelerated course, I had cleared all of the recommendations on the sheet. Plus, he was going to have to build a separate, cut-off concrete block room, adjacent to the plant, as a flammable liquids storage room. I had to fight my way out. This guy didn't want to quit and I had other plants to visit. He really didn't have to do some of the additional recommendations I had "won". I told him as much, but he was a serious sort and impressed on me that when he loses, "he pays up". I told him I was more than satisfied just to have him comply with the original recommendations, but he would have none of it. That is what brought his personal broker to complain to my company when he found out the details. I then had to contact the insured pleading with him that he didn't have to add a separate room. You guessed it. Again: "When I lose, I pay." "Besides," he tells me, "if it makes you feel any better, I often thought about adding another room." This from the same guy who wouldn't comply with even one of the many safety and fire recommendations for over eight years! That's a dedicated gambler for you!

I had just gotten home on a hot summer day, prepared to type out a rush report on a chemical plant that I just surveyed, when I got an urgent call from our White Plains office. I was informed that there was a "disturbance" in Wyandanch, a predominantly black populated township in Western Suffolk County. This was not my regularly assigned district. I was already falling behind on report writing as it appeared that all inspections and reports were on a "rush" basis in this highly competitive market. I was given a location where our company had a row of stores in a shopping center at risk. John DeGiso, ever ready to dispatch me on a suicide mission, got on the phone and begged me to immediately rush out to the scene to check if any of our insured risks were involved in the reported fires and vandalism. He claimed that the regularly assigned fieldman for the location couldn't be reached. Mind you, John was a good friend but he seemed to enjoy sending me to the fore-front whenever a dangerous problem presented itself. As he put it, he "was utilizing my years of experience," which is not the way I saw it.

When I got to the location I learned that the "disturbance" was the early stages of a full blown riot. Fires had been set in stores. Cars had been stopped in the streets and occupants dragged out of their cars and beaten for no reason other than being in the area. Cars had been overturned and some set on fire. With this backdrop, I went to the row of stores insured by us. There were fires already started at opposite ends of the row. I climbed through a broken store window of one of our risks which was a wholesale food emporium specializing in custom-cut meats, packaged and frozen for delivery. The place was ransacked and there was hardly anything left of value. The concrete block wall to the next occupancy had been broken through and that also had been cleaned out. I went to the end store that had a fire going in its early stages and found a trap neatly laid out for the responding volunteer firefighters, when it was deemed safe to respond. This occupancy was next to an auto supply store and the concrete block wall between stores was broken through. From the fire in that store, which was getting larger by the minute, a trail of gasoline and oil soaked rags led directly to some gasoline-filled gallon cans placed in a pool of oil and gasoline contained by a dike formed by rags and plastic sheets. I quickly broke the "rag trail" and got the hell out before the place blew prematurely.

It didn't take much to imagine what would have been in store for the responding firefighters if they had entered either of these stores in an effort to extinguish the blaze. The broken trail, at least, temporarily foiled that plot. I advised the responding company of the dangerous condition at the auto supply store. My office was waiting for me to report on conditions ASAP (as soon as possible). That's when I made a stupid blunder and went into a laundromat on the main street to use the pay phone while tense confrontations were still in progress. I was only in the phone booth a short time and gave our vice president Warren Bennett a preliminary report when I saw that I was the only white person in the laundromat and that everyone in the place was looking at me menacingly. Most of the occupants were women who were pointing to the booth when a couple of young men entered and I was pointed out to them. I relayed the scenario to Warren, hung up, and made my way to the front door where these two men had placed themselves. I dared not show any fear or I was sure I would have met the same fate as others in the street that weren't residents.

To say that I wasn't apprehensive due to the position I had placed myself in would be putting it mildly. However, I kept up my outer demeanor as I approached the goon closest to the door, pushed him aside and strode out the door to my car parked directly in front. Thinking back, what saved my hide was that they must have taken me for one of the detectives that responded to the riot. Who else would be stupid enough to thrust himself into the midst of an ongoing riot, where whites were targeted, unless they were from the Police Department? To add to the illusion, I was neatly dressed in a suit, tie and hat and the big dark sedan at the front of the store certainly resembled an "unmarked" police car. I later learned that on one of the streets a woman had been pulled from her car and smashed in the face with a two by four hunk of lumber.

Since the riot had not reached the proportions of the full blown incidents of the late 1960s, it got scant news coverage. I love the buzz words that emanate from these encounters where riots are downgraded to "civil disobedience". Tell that to the innocent passer-by whose face was rearranged by a 2" x 4" piece of wood.

Probably disappointed that I had survived the mini-riot in Wyandanch, John DeGiso and Sam Salvo were conspiring to inject me into the midst of an ongoing problem with two insureds in Brooklyn. Their policies were coming up for renewal and were probably going to be canceled due to non-compliance with essential recommendations. One was a commercial laundry and the other a catering house. Both were out of my jurisdiction in Brooklyn, N.Y. In both cases, the CEOs steadfastly and violently resisted complying with fire and safety recommendations. As alluded to earlier, the CEO of the laundry had actually assaulted the last fieldman to inspect his business.

I sensed that I was being set up when John, Sam and I were having dinner after working hours on a day when I had been detailed to the home office in White Plains. We had a nice friendly dinner with a cocktail or two, maybe three, and I knew that a plot was brewing when they refused to have me pay my share of the bill. With a little convincing, I promised to work these into my schedule. By some "strange coincidence" they presented me with the folders, that just happened to be in Sam's briefcase, containing results of all previous inspections. I didn't get to read through them until they were included in my itinerary. The last inspector was thrown out before he got past the outer foyer when he was announced. The previous inspector was actually assaulted inside the plant when he made some counter-threats to the CEO. I could see that I was in for a "fun" day.

When I got to the plant I was met by the receptionist. I kept my clip board and folder in my leather briefcase so she assumed I was either a salesman or client. When she asked what I was there for, I just replied that I was to meet with the CEO (who I mentioned by name). She pointed to his office and told me to just go in. As I opened his door he was on the phone having a heated discourse when he looked up at me:

CEO (angrily):"What do you want? Are you from the insurance company? "

Me:The only answer I could think of was, "No."

CEO:"Then come in and sit down," (motioning to a chair next to his desk.)

He then continued his violent dialogue on the phone including outright threats, curse words that were wilting the live plant by the desk and other unpleasantries. This went on for at least another twenty minutes which gave me time to reflect on how do I extricate myself from this corner I had painted myself in by deception.

Finally, he got off the phone. He was extremely agitated and began telling me about the four-flushing, thieving son-of-a-bitch he just hung-up on. Of course, I was agreeing with all he said and was commiserating with him. This went on for about ten minutes and I gave him my support on actions he was contemplating on his antagonist, who also was delinquent on payments past due to the laundry. He was so angry and red faced I feared he was headed for a stroke. He finally calmed down a bit, with my help, then turned to me:

CEO:"O.K. now, what are you, a salesman?"

ME:"No."

CEO:"You're a jobber." (whatever that was).

ME:"No."

CEO:"Alright, you're not a salesman and not a jobber, what the hell are you?"

ME:"To start with, I'm a liar. Actually I'm from the insurance Co."

CEO:"Then, why the $%#@ did you lie to me when I let you in?"

ME:"I read the report on how you handled the last inspectors. If I said insurance you never would have let me in and heard what I have to say. To begin with, I can see where you got angry on some of the recommendations. Maybe we can reach an agreement. Suppose we go over your laundry and see what all of these are about. After, if you still don't agree, you can take a poke at me and throw me out like the last two guys, with my compliments."

I took him around and told him to disregard the first recommendation on the sheet, which wasn't at all important, compared to the others. This gained his confidence and before long he promised compliance on all of the recommendations, especially when convinced it would improve conditions in the plant. He then related that he had come to resist any inspections after some Fieldmen exhibited a "Wyatt Earp Syndrome". It was obvious that by his nature, this CEO violently opposed being forced into doing anything. Before leaving, he offered me a drink of whiskey from the bar in his office. I told him I had to refuse as I had another visit to make. He then took a bottle of Canadian Club rye whiskey from his rack and insisted I accept. As I tried to pull away the bottle fell to the floor. Luckily, It didn't break. With that he said if I didn't accept, as a good will gesture, he was prepared to throw me out and not comply with my recommendations. Of course, the latter was said in jest.

The one hurdle now left was the catering house in Brooklyn, which had a full scale cooking facility in the kitchen. The insurance industry was experiencing a rash of fire losses in restaurants and catering establishments, especially where deep fat frying was conducted without automatic fire extinguishing systems. The management here was violently opposed to complying with the existing recommendations for installation of the required system. As with the previous inspection, this was to be a last ditch effort on getting compliance or the insurance was to be canceled.

On arrival at the location I was met by the manager. It was immediately obvious that my presence was not welcomed. We got to the kitchen which was neat and orderly but it lacked the required automatic fire protection. We then went into his office to discuss what action was to be taken to comply with the outstanding recommendations. As the discussion progressed he became more and more agitated and belligerent. I was trying to present the insurance company's position in a courteous manner when he arose. He stood over where I was seated in an intimidating posture and proceeded to lambaste me with a tirade of vulgar epithets and profanity that took me by surprise. I had not threatened cancellation, as others had done, in an effort to avoid getting him excited. Instead, I was trying some gentle persuasion and reasoning which was a waste of time in this situation. There was no stopping him and he became increasingly intimidating and vulgar. I just remained seated, without comment, waiting for the storm to blow over. Which it didn't. He then progressed to the next plateau and began attacking me personally.

Manager:"What makes you think some guinea %$#@ like you can come in and order me on how to run my business?" He then went on with outright threats of assault coupled with additional ethnic slurs and denunciations. By now I had heard enough.

Me:"If you don't mind I would like to use your telephone."

Manager:"Why, are you going to report me to the company, as if I give a %$#@."

Me:"No,I'm going to call my company and resign my job."

Manager:"What the %$# are you resigning for?"

Me:"Because I represent a respectable and honorable company. As such, I have taken all your abuse and personal humiliation without a word. After I resign, and no longer represent my company, I'm going to knock you on your ass."

Manager:"I'm over six feet and 240 pounds."

Me:"That makes for a louder crash when I send you flying over your desk." He now is looking at me quizzically. I certainly didn't scare him. This was one tough hombre.

Manager:"You're really serious, aren't you? You're really ready to quit to get even for what I've been calling you?"

Me:"That's right. I don't believe in bluffing."

Manager:Steps back and says, "I admire your guts. I like a man that has principles. Now let's go over what you want done. Not for my broker or the insurance company, but because of the way you stood up to me. Let's go into the kitchen again."

We went into the kitchen and he took out a large aluminum tray. He then proceeded to stock the tray with stuffed cabbage that had just been cooked in the oven.

Manager:"Here, take this home to your wife, I hope you like stuffed cabbage?"

Me:(I still hadn't cooled down completely.) "That's not what I want done. What about the automatic cooking protection?"

Manager:"Everything on the recommendation sheet will be done by your next visit."

Me:"In that case I'll take the stuffed cabbage. By the way, I did not mind the dagos, Wops and other things you called me, but the accompanying vulgarity."

Manager:"I'm sorry, but I get carried away when I'm really mad."

We parted as friends of a sort. I was glad to have averted the near physical confrontation. Not only would I then be out of a job, but I might have had my head handed to me on a platter in the process. This is not a classical example on how to make friends and influence people. He did comply with all the recommendations as promised. I then advised my benefactors in the home office, John and Sam, that this last close encounter had convinced me not to take any more of their "Problem Risks".

One of the first full surveys that I was involved with was for a country club in Glen Head, Long Island, under the tutelage of Charley Zook, Asst. Chief Engineer. The manager of the club was a Mr. Bill Ellis, a capable administrator who was receptive to any recommendations that would result in improvement of the club's operation and fire and safety protection. After a couple of days working under Mr. Zooks direction, I was left to complete the survey and make any recommendations that I deemed pertinent. Being my first survey, I went over the premises and came up with several routine deficiencies to be corrected, most of them having to do with the fire protection of the kitchen operation.

From a fire fighting standpoint however, I was concerned with the fact that this country club was located **about one and a quarter miles** from the nearest public hydrant and for that reason was classified as an "unprotected" risk." The private hydrants located inside the property were flow tested by myself and Mr. Zook and found to be totally inadequate to supply even one feeble hose stream. After a couple of days Charley called and asked if my survey report was ready. He was getting impatient. Although an "unprotected risk", with all other considerations in order, it was insurable. I was "nagged" however by the distance to the public hydrant and visited the local fire station. As I suspected, to get a usable hose stream to the country club, the firemen had to employ a relay operation, using two pumpers, and sometimes three, and the stretching of many hose lengths. This would be a tedious and time-consuming operation, and the fire company at times held drills in the event this operation was ever needed to put water on a fire at the club. They were not happy with the situation, and neither was I, especially when I had learned that a few years earlier a country club (The Plandome) had burned to the ground because of a glaring deficiency in "public fire protection". Before concluding my report I was determined to see if anything could be done to improve the public protection aspect. I met with the manager Mr. Ellis, and requested a plan for the piping of the sprinklers that were used to water the fairways. The water had to come from public water somewhere, unless it was all from underground aquifers.

After studying the plan, and noting that there was a connection to a city main one hundred and fifty feet from the nearest public hydrant,(which was a mile and a quarter from the club), I made an unusual recommendation that I considered too logical and basic to ever be implemented. As expected the solution was met with derision by the unimaginative detractors of the office. Charley overrode them.

He admitted the solution was "not a bad idea" and probably would never be done, but in deference to me, as I had expended time and energy on the research, he included the recommendation.

About a month later, after we had accepted the risk "as is", I got a call from Charley at my home.

Mr. Zook: "Carl, about that recommendation on the water supply at the Glen Head Country Club."

Me:(I broke in) "I know, they think it's ridiculous..."

Mr. Zook: "No. I got a call from their Chief Resident Engineer who designed the system and wants a meeting for further information that may lead to implementation. Give me a date and I'll set up an appointment."

The Engineer, a Mr. Kaye, set up an "extended lunch" meeting at the exclusive Swan Club. After a couple of cocktails Mr. Kaye asked if there was another such system that he may investigate. Negative. He then asked me to explain, leaving out all the negative aspects of the complicated system currently in effect, of which he was painfully aware.

In brief, I described to him how a stand pipe with a Siamese connection, or another hydrant, be provided at the junction of the six inch private main connection to the underground public ten-inch main. The connection would be downstream of the check valves isolating the private water from the public potable supply. For greater efficacy, Charley added a double check valve.

After this connection was made, the fire department would simply hook up a pumper to the public hydrant in the street, and then simply pump into the newly installed private hydrant located 150 feet away. The fire department would then be able to operate hose streams directly from the private hydrants located around the main clubhouse. The fire department was extremely happy with the prospect of not having to deploy extra pumpers and hose for one and a quarter miles. This arrangement also made for an efficient supply to the sprinklers and provided protection for the kitchen and clubhouse areas. Mr. Kaye, a very knowledgeable and unpretentious gentleman, showed some class when he allowed that. "I should be a bit embarrassed as I designed the entire system. How come I didn't think of that solution?" I replied, "That's because you weren't trained to think like a fireman."

FIRE SAFETY INSPECTION GERULITIS-TRUMP

There is no disputing that a fire safety inspection of any occupancy, conducted by alert and competent inspectors, can be a life saver. The operative words here are **alert** and **competent**. Next, the recommendations to correct deficiencies should be taken very seriously and immediately acted on. A seemingly innocuous hazard, potentially dangerous and life threatening, is present in every household and occupancy provided with heating equipment whether it be a boiler room, portable heating appliance or just a simple hot water heating unit.

Just recently, an easily preventable tragedy claimed the life of a prominent former champion tennis player, Vitas Gerulitis. Mr. Gerulitis was attending the world championship tennis matches in 1994 when he had accepted an offer to spend the night at a friend's summer home. From all reports, it appears he had become an unsuspecting victim of carbon monoxide poisoning occasioned by an improperly vented hot water heating unit in proximity to the area where Mr. Gerulitis spent the night. Unfortunately, carbon monoxide is an odorless, colorless and tasteless gas which makes it such an efficient silent killer. A thorough and competent Fire Safety inspection of the premises, although not required, may have saved a life in this case.

Unfortunately, this sad tragedy occurs time and again throughout the country, often wiping out complete families in their sleep. During Fire Prevention Month every October, New York fire companies go out into the field distributing literature on fire safety and answer pertinent questions from civilians during these activities. Not surprisingly, unless fire safety concerns are initiated by a fire department, it is rare that an individual or company engages a fire protection engineer on their own to conduct such an inspection.

Sometime after my retirement from the fire department, and after I was engaged as a fieldman for a group of leading insurance companies, I continued as a freelance consultant in fire protection engineering.

During this period I met Mr. Donald Trump on several occasions through a mutual friend I had come to know from my association with the New York Fire Department branch of the Steuben Society, a German organization.

At the time that the Trumps were moving into the mansion in Greenwich Village, Connecticut, our mutual friend, who was also an employee of the Trumps, suggested that I be engaged to perform a fire safety and protection inspection of the premises, especially since young children were to be occupants in the new environment. Safety was a primary concern. To the Trumps' credit they enthusiastically agreed to the inspection. On the day I arrived I was greeted by Mrs. Ivana Trump, a stately and attractive lady. She introduced me to their caretaker, Mr. Patrick, who provided me with a plot plan of the mansion. Then, at my suggestion, I was left on my own until ready to report on the results of the survey. The inspection included reporting on the construction, occupancy features, ordinary hazards (heat, light power, etc.) and any special hazards that may have been built into the mansion - such as concealed spaces. Ordinarily special hazards are not expected to be found in this type of occupancy. Nothing however was taken for granted and every square foot was inspected from the basement to the attic. On completion I reported my findings directly to Mr. Trump along with recommendations which were mostly routine and of a safety nature. However, the attic was protected by a most unusual and antiquated automatic fire extinguishing system which involved carbon tetrachloride (CCL4) as the extinguishing medium. Although CCL4 was at one time approved - mainly in hand type and portable extinguishers - it was extremely toxic especially in fire conditions and was later outlawed even in hand type extinguishers. This action was taken only after a history of serious health problems, some resulting in death due to exposure to the fumes of carbon tetrachloride.

About a week after the inspection I kept thinking about that antiquated system and its potential for disaster. In my twenty six years in the fire protection field I had never encountered such an arrangement. The engineer that designed it certainly had no idea of the deadly nature of the extinguishing medium. Nor did it appear that this system would have been effective in extinguishing a fire of any consequence.

Although alien in nature, it was an impressive looking arrangement, with many five gallon canisters of carbon tetrachloride suspended from the ceiling in the attic and concealed spaces. In the event of a fire the heat generated was to melt a fusible link which controlled the restraining mechanism thus releasing the contents of the canisters. With the history connected with the use of CCL4 before being outlawed, it was obvious that if the fire didn't get you, the fumes from the extinguishing agent would. In addition, the mechanism containing the liquid was showing signs of corrosion and it was only a matter of time before it would no longer provide a tight seal.

From experience, I know people were reluctant to comply with recommendations when it involved dismantling an existing system, especially if they didn't realize the true nature of the hazard involved. In this case it was very serious even without any fire involved. In the event that the carbon tetrachloride corroded its way past the seals, the fumes created, which are over five (5) times heavier than air, would filter down into the sleeping and living quarters below and either anesthetize or asphyxiate the occupants in their sleep. There have been instances of such dire consequence on record.

I was continually nagged by the possibility that the caretaker of the Trumps' mansion had not complied with this, the most important of my fire safety recommendations. I decided to check it out myself, immediately.

I called the caretaker directly and as I suspected, all recommendations were completed, except for the dismantling and removal of the carbon tetrachloride system. It was partly my fault for not being forceful and explicit enough on the dangers involved. Knowing that the canisters already showed early signs of corrosion, I called Donald and Ivana Trump at their home in Manhattan. This time I laid out the whole scenario and followed up with a written report emphasizing the toxicity and danger involved from inhaling the CCL4 fumes - especially in contact with fire. To drive home the message I included copies from the NFPA handbook indicating that as little as two percent (2%) by volume of the vapor in air was sufficient to cause serious injury and even death in one hour - without fire involved. It was more lethal in fire conditions. As I imagined, Mr. Trump had left orders with the caretaker to comply with all the recommendations I submitted and assumed that they were all completed. After discussing the matter with the Trumps, and in keeping with their reputation for impatience in resolving matters, the caretaker was busily dismantling the system within the hour. From this experience who knows? Nothing may ever have happened, but why live with a potential for disaster directly overhead?. To add to the insidious effects of this liquid, in the initial release of the fumes it has a sweet and pleasant odor, promoting drowsiness and a feeling of well being before being rendered unconscious.

The reason I couldn't get that system and its deadly potential out of my mind , stemmed from an experience that almost wiped out my own family during my early teens when we lived in a cold water flat in Manhattan. It was a five room railroad apartment and the only heat was from a small pot belly stove in the kitchen. On cold winter nights the heat generated was not sufficient to warm the entire apartment so the heat from the stove was supplemented with a kerosene fired, portable space heater, which was normally located at the opposite end of the apartment from the coal stove. (With the advent of central space heating these dangerous units are seldom used today and have, in fact, been declared unlawful for use in many municipalities.)

At about two o'clock in the morning, during a particularly cold spell, I awakened with a severe headache. I never was a sound sleeper anyway and I looked over at my brother Angelo as we shared a double bed in the bedroom adjacent to the living room which housed the kerosene space heater. When he turned towards me, in the dim light of a candle that was kept burning on our dresser, I was amused to see that he was sporting a dark, black mustache of the type later made famous (or infamous) by Hitler. I looked into the mirror over the dresser and saw that I, too, had the same Mustache. For a while I forgot the headache and went into the living room and saw that the kerosene heater flame was flickering and giving off an odor and light smoke which permeated the apartment. I turned on the lights and went into my parent's bedroom and saw that they too had the dark, black soot extending from their nostrils down to their upper lip. I had a hard time waking them up. By this time we all had king-sized headaches.

My father then completely retracted the wick in the kerosene heater and moved the heater onto the fire escape and closed the window to that room. He then opened the windows at the opposite end of the apartment. We didn't realize it then, but we were all experiencing the early stages of carbon monoxide poisoning. Had we not awakened in time before the full effects of the gas took hold, my entire family may very well have perished in their sleep. Communications weren't as extensive as today, with radio and television accounts warning on the dangers of space heaters. My father simply had the wick replaced and we continued to use it for supplemental heat never realizing the close call we had.

Years later when all of the dangers associated with portable space heaters became known, they were justifiably outlawed in many jurisdictions. Later on when there was a fuel shortage in the 1970s, occasioned by the cutback on deliveries by the OPEC nations to the United States, the kerosene space heaters made a remarkable comeback. Although vastly improved and less dangerous, if not properly maintained, they are still a danger and remain a health and life hazard. When the fuel crisis was over, kerosene heaters almost completely disappeared much to the relief of fire departments throughout the country.

EPILOGUE

Since my retirement I have been in close touch with members of Engine Company 44. At times I also visit the quarters of Engine Company 280 in Brooklyn where I spent the first seven years on the job. I also visit the Division of Training which was my last assignment.

A close relationship extends to the present. The tradition handed down through the years continues to be followed by the current officers and members. They never fail to invite the retirees to their various annual functions. The annual Christmas parties held at the quarters of Engine Company 44 are rarely missed by any of the past or present members. Santa Claus never fails to slide down the pole on schedule to the excited cheers and screams of the many children and adults assembled on the apparatus floor. It is the one affair attended by the entire family that is never a disappointment.

We have now entered into the new year of 1996. For the fire department is has been an ominous and depressing beginning. Two firefighters within one week have paid the ultimate sacrifice. In both instances they ventured into exceedingly dangerous buildings involved in fire in search of persons that might have possibly been trapped inside.

Ironically, on New Year's Eve the first firefighter fell victim to the conflagration that had been purposely started by the very person that the fire officer thought might have been trapped inside the decrepit building. In an act of revenge the arsonist set a fire in the building's basement and departed. He was later apprehended and will pay for his crime, which is no solace for the family left behind. Within a week tragedy struck again when another brave and productive life was sacrificed in the performance of duty at a fire. As one of the fire officers that was present at the scene of both of these tragedies into known dangerous conditions, "That's your job. That's what we do. Some of us die."

As long as the fire department continues to be an aggressive, determined and dedicated force there will inevitably be casualties. In my years of experience on the job, I was involved in, and witness to, situations where even the thought of a rescue appeared to be hopeless. There were always some daring firefighters ready to challenge the Grim Reaper in an all-out attempt to accomplish the impossible. These heroic acts often resulted in lasting personal injury and sometimes in death.

To attempt to name the hundreds of firefighters that have paid the supreme sacrifice and the circumstances causing their deaths would be the subject of a complete novel.

At the time of this writing, 764 firefighters in the New York Fire Department have given their lives in the performance of duty.